SHORTCUTS TO ELEGANCE

THE ART OF SEWING
THE OLD WEST
THE EMERGENCE OF MAN
THE AMERICAN WILDERNESS
THE TIME-LIFE ENCYCLOPEDIA OF GARDENING
LIFE LIBRARY OF PHOTOGRAPHY
THIS FABULOUS CENTURY
FOODS OF THE WORLD
TIME-LIFE LIBRARY OF AMERICA
TIME-LIFE LIBRARY OF ART
GREAT AGES OF MAN
LIFE SCIENCE LIBRARY
THE LIFE HISTORY OF THE UNITED STATES
TIME READING PROGRAM
LIFE NATURE LIBRARY
LIFE WORLD LIBRARY
FAMILY LIBRARY:
    THE TIME-LIFE BOOK OF THE FAMILY CAR
    THE TIME-LIFE FAMILY LEGAL GUIDE
    THE TIME-LIFE BOOK OF FAMILY FINANCE

TIME
LIFE
BOOKS
®

THE ART OF SEWING

SHORTCUTS TO ELEGANCE

BY THE EDITORS OF TIME-LIFE BOOKS

TIME-LIFE BOOKS, NEW YORK

TIME-LIFE BOOKS

FOUNDER: Henry R. Luce 1898-1967

Editor-in-Chief: Hedley Donovan
Chairman of the Board: Andrew Heiskell
President: James R. Shepley
Chairman, Executive Committee:
James A. Linen
Group Vice President: Rhett Austell

Vice Chairman: Roy E. Larsen

MANAGING EDITOR: Jerry Korn
Assistant Managing Editors: David Maness,
Martin Mann, A. B. C. Whipple
Planning Director: Oliver E. Allen
Art Director: Sheldon Cotler
Chief of Research: Beatrice T. Dobie
Director of Photography: Melvin L. Scott
Senior Text Editors: Diana Hirsh, Ogden Tanner
Assistant Art Director: Arnold C. Holeywell

PUBLISHER: *Joan D. Manley*
General Manager: John D. McSweeney
Business Manager: John Steven Maxwell
Sales Director: Carl G. Jaeger
Promotion Director: Paul R. Stewart
Public Relations Director: Nicholas Benton

THE ART OF SEWING
SERIES EDITOR: Carlotta Kerwin
EDITORIAL STAFF FOR
SHORTCUTS TO ELEGANCE:
Assistant Editors: David L. Harrison,
David Lawton
Designer: Virginia Gianakos
Text Editors: Kathleen Brandes,
Gerry Schremp
Chief Researchers: Helen M. Hinkle,
Wendy Rieder
Design Assistant: Sanae Colton
Staff Writers: Sondra Albert, Angela Dews,
Marian G. Goldman, Joan Reiter,
Michèle Wood
Picture Staff: Carole Kismaric,
Kathleen Shortall, Gabrielle Smith
Research Staff: Rhea Finkelstein,
Nancy Jacobsen, Ginger Seippel,
Cinda Siler, Vivian Stephens, Reiko Uyeshima
Art Staff: Patricia Byrne,
Catherine Caufield, Robert McKee
Editorial Assistant: Kathleen Beakley

EDITORIAL PRODUCTION
Production Editor: Douglas B. Graham
Assistant: Gennaro C. Esposito
Quality Director: Robert L. Young
Assistant: James J. Cox
Copy Staff: Rosalind Stubenberg (chief),
Susan B. Galloway, Mary Orlando,
Florence Keith
Picture Department: Dolores A. Littles,
Jessy S. Faubert

Portions of this book were written by Michael
Durham, Margaret Elliott, Katie Kelly and Henry
Moscow. Valuable assistance was provided by
these departments and individuals of Time Inc.:
Editorial Production, Norman Airey; Library,
Benjamin Lightman; Picture Collection, Doris
O'Neil; Photographic Laboratory, George Karas;
TIME-LIFE News Service, Murray J. Gart.

THE CONSULTANTS:
Gretel Courtney is a member of the staff of the
French Fashion Academy in New York. She has
studied pattern making and design at the Fashion Institute of Technology and haute couture at
the French Fashion Academy in New York.

Annette Feldman is a knitting and crocheting de-
signer, both for clothing and interior decorating.
She is the author of *Knit, Purl and Design* and
Crochet and Creative Design.

Tracy Kendall has worked in many capacities for
various fashion firms in New York. She is pres-
ently a freelance costumer and set designer for
television commercials and print advertising.

Belle Conway Rivers, a graduate of Pratt Institute,
has been a designer for McCall's Pattern Company and is currently the director of the Talon
consumer education department. She is also
hostess of *The Joy of Sewing,* a nationally syndi-
cated television series.

Julian Tomchin is a textile designer who has been
awarded the Vogue Fabric Award and a Coty
Award of the American Fashion Critics. A graduate of Syracuse University's Fine Arts College,
he has been chairman of the Textile Design Department at the Shenkar College of Fashion and
Textile Technology in Tel Aviv and now teaches
at the Parsons School of Design in New York.

CONTENTS

1 ELEGANCE WITH LITTLE EFFORT   6

2 TOOLS TO SAVE TIME   20

3 FABRIC WITH AN EXTRA ELEMENT   38

4 BETTER RESULTS FROM SIMPLE TECHNIQUES   54

5 A SYMPHONY OF SHAPES AND FORMS   120

6 GIANT STRIDES WITH YARN AND NEEDLE   156

APPENDIX   184
CREDITS, ACKNOWLEDGMENTS   189
INDEX   190

1
ELEGANCE WITH LITTLE EFFORT

legance, like perfection, may sometimes seem impossible to attain. Yet there is satisfaction, even magic, in the search for it; and in the case of contemporary fashions the goal of elegance is within relatively easy reach even of the busy home sewer.

By nature it is a shifting goal. As fashions change, the quest is pursued in different ways; the wasp-waisted *élégante* of the New Look era, with her tapering ruffled

A FRESH NEW STYLE FOR HOME SEWING

parasol and touches of crisp piqué, is today little more than a memory and often a subject of parody.

The key to elegance was once thought to lie more in ornament than silhouette. The crinoline, the bustle and the lampshade skirt were the height of refinement for decades. Fashion interest lay in the disposition of a swarm of ruching, embroidery, lace, flounces, tassels, paillettes, feathers and beads that might now strike the eye as the very opposite of elegant. This preference for details rather than essentials was already beginning to fade in the 1870s when the French diarist Edmond de Goncourt, who gave minute, lifetime attention to all matters of taste and style, saw fit to bemoan what he considered the passing of an era. Goncourt commended "the Parisienne of old," who insisted "on having pretty shoes, pretty gloves, and pretty ribbons: the dress in those days was just an accessory."

Historically, this old order of priorities in elegance is associated closely with France, a land of rarefied courts that were graced by fashion-loving royal favorites and empresses. The governments of France gave official encouragement to the silk weavers who provided the glorious stuffs for court gowns. French style springs from the traditional dressmaker's skills applied to such luxurious fabrics, expressed more in folds and gathers than in seams, and excelling in delicate trimmings applied with fine needlework. It was a fundamentally feminine branch of elegance.

A second approach to elegance, and one more familiar to our own time, gives precedence to the shape of clothes and emphasizes their cut. This ideal of wrinkle-free fit, often achieved with the help of intricate seamings and ingeniously concealed facings, linings and paddings, is the elegance associated with the couturier and the custom tailor. Traditionally it originates in Great Britain, a nation with a Puritan influence that discouraged any kind of ostentation and a wool industry that was the greatest in the world. This kind of tailored elegance is

essentially masculine in character and reached its acme with Beau Brummell in the early 19th Century. Though a dandy, Brummell placed immense value on restraint; he once put down a young buck who ventured a compliment at Ascot with the searing remark, "I cannot be elegant, since you have noticed me."

In the last few years we have seen the emergence of a third variety of elegance. This new style, breaking completely with past conventions, is founded on genuine simplicity; and its stature is only now being widely recognized. It is thoroughly modern —often called the "unconstructed" style, because it employs no complicated custom design techniques. And its inspiration is particularly American. Of all varieties of elegance, it is the one that may be most successfully re-created by the home sewer, and it is the subject of this book.

Readily approached by way of shortcuts, the new style is intrinsically simple. And the shortcuts themselves are elegant as well as simple—not contrived imitations and artificial embellishments but fundamental materials and methods: bold patterns, durable fabrics and timesaving sewing techniques that enhance the character of a freewheeling, unencumbered style. A classic example of such built-in elegant simplicity is the striking cape seen on pages 6-7.

Like tailored elegance, the new style has little in common with the penchant for trims and folderols; unlike tailored elegance, however, it dispenses with the hidden tricks and secret aids of the bespoke tailor. It rejects the implication that elegance is the exclusive property of a social elite, and it reflects the erosion of both class-consciousness and the idea that clothes should always reflect the age of the wearer. (The proprietor of a famous dress shop with a wealthy and "established" clientele once observed haughtily that no one under the age of 45 could ever aspire to elegance.)

But the new elegance stands on its own feet (even if the feet are sometimes bare). It has evolved from unpretentious, comfortable styles of popular origin, such as blue jeans, T-shirts and leotards, once worn primarily by young people. High fashion has elaborated on the functional shapes and fabrics of these once-modest earthbound uniforms. The new elegance reflects its beginnings on the slim and youthful-looking figures where it originated. And in the metamorphosis it has retained a certain svelte character. The style is neither exclusively masculine nor feminine, but it combines aspects of both.

The new elegance looks more to the future than to the past, and it anticipates the seemingly inevitable time when clothes will be molded to fit the body without a single seam. In fact it might be said that Balenciaga, one of the most forward-looking couturiers, introduced the new elegance with so simple a design as the one-seam coat (page 11). In this brave new fashion world, linings —if such are needed—will be bonded directly to the fabric of the garment and hand labor will be eliminated unless it is undertaken merely as a hobby. The time may not be far off when something that resembles a bodysuit will form the basis of rational dress for both sexes, and when all vestigial clothing traditions—the ties that men still string round their necks, the buttons that trim the sleeves of men's coats and women's dresses—will have finally succumbed once and for all to progress.

This progress has made itself felt more in women's dress than in men's. It may be seen in the almost daily changes in technology and social attitudes that sweep away the traditional trappings and pare down what we wear: girdles and garters have nearly vanished; and, for the most part, so have hats, white gloves, and seams in stockings and brassieres—not to mention brassieres themselves.

Practicality and ease of movement are of paramount importance in this new style. Trousers and sweaters in all their variations are a natural part of it, like anything that pulls on in a second. Halters that free the back and variations of the dolman sleeve, which liberates the arms, inspire many of the modern designs. Knitted fabrics play an important part in expressing the new mood because they are supple and fit closely to the body without the need for complicated darts and seams.

The development of a new style in design closely parallels developments in the manufacture of synthetic fabrics. The haute couture has traditionally worked with the natural fabrics—silk, cotton, linen and wool —and uses them to perfection. But the contemporary school of clothing designers, for whom the mystique of custom tailoring and Paris is remote, has grown up surrounded by man-made fibers. These designers understand synthetics well enough not to waste their time trying to make them behave in ways that only natural fibers are likely to behave, and to concentrate instead on the unique advantages that the synthetic fabrics offer. And it is that same spark of imaginative design that endows today's clothes with their own elegance.

Everything that technology can bring to the assistance of suppleness and simplicity, and anything that eases chores—tubular knits to minimize seamings, for example, or preelasticized or preshirred fabrics to simplify both sewing and fitting—is cheerfully pressed into the service of the new style. This new school of design has rejected, along with the idea that only natural fabrics can be considered elegant, the long-held belief that elegance must be complicated, expensive and exclusive.

These changes affect clothes of all prices, from the couture of Halston and Giorgio di Sant' Angelo to the bargains of mass production. And, above all, the new designs are within reach of the home sewer.

Equally important, the new fashions and fabrics simplify all manner of sewing procedures. Many handsome contemporary designs—like those displayed on pages 128, 136 and 146—are no more than sets of triangles, circles or rectangles that have been seamed together. Bared and collarless square or V-shaped necklines eliminate the jigsaw assembly of traditional collars; and

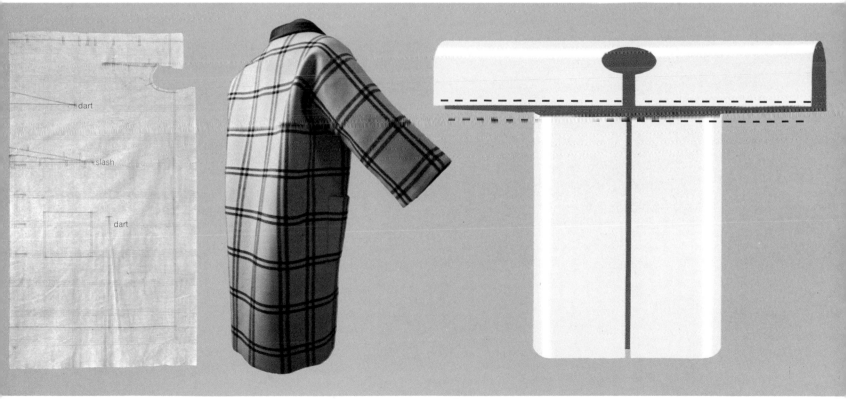

Simplicity combined with craftsmanship is the hallmark of the Balenciaga coat seen above (center). The coat requires a single seam, which runs from the front opening to the armholes. Using the basic pattern (left)

Balenciaga cut the coat from one piece of folded fabric. After making the darts and cutting the slashes shown in the pattern, he folded the fabric over to form the top, and in at the sides to make the sleeves and front (right).

waists that can be drawn in to fit just by tying a belt permit the home dressmaker to bypass the several steps involved in meticulously adjusting a fitted waistband.

In addition to the ease of current designs, synthetic fibers, used alone or in blends with one another or with natural fibers, provide eminently sewable materials that resist both needle marks and wrinkles and lend themselves to professional pleating. Many of them are machine washable and dryable, a boon in the do-it-yourself age.

It is no coincidence that, in a period that saw great developments in textiles as well as the birth of a new style, the industry that supplies the home dressmaker was also undergoing revolutionary changes. The people whose support caused the recent boom in the home-sewing industry—the young, the well educated and the adventurous —were completely receptive to innovations in style. Unlike many of the home sewers from earlier generations—who had to sew all the clothes for the entire family merely to make ends meet—this group is just as interested in fashion and in the satisfaction of sewing as in economy.

Two decades ago it was hard to find the latest fashions in pattern catalogues. Today the new fashions show up in pattern books as soon as they do in ready-to-wear garments because many books are revised monthly. And textile makers and distributors have come to value a purchase of three yards each by a thousand home sewers as much as an order of several thousand yards from a large manufacturer. In fact, now there is such coordination between designers, pattern makers and textile manufacturers that the home sewer can have the satisfaction of buying the fabric she sees in a photograph.

Dressmaking differs from other modern crafts in that it involves not merely the individual seamstress, her manual skills and the joys of "creativity," but also the complicated economic teamwork that exists between the consumer and the suppliers of cloth, paper patterns, braiding, seam tape, zippers, thread, buttons and other paraphernalia. Today's home dressmaker can expect solid support from an increasingly sophisticated industry. Special tape that makes it possible to iron a hem in place without any stitching or double-faced fabric that makes a garment reversible provide shortcuts that are too useful to ignore. Even hand knitting and hand crocheting, long the epitome of painstaking craftsmanship, have become less demanding with the advent of larger knitting needles and crochet hooks that use bulkier yarns to produce fashionably oversized stitches.

The new designing talents have, in a certain sense, joined the team on the home sewer's side. The sewing machine has become an integral part of modern dress design and construction. So instead of pretending that unseen seams are actually hand-sewn ones, innovative designers now openly advocate machine stitching as a part of their design. Over the past several years machine stitching has come to be accepted simultaneously as construction, decoration and signature—setting a comfortable precedent that the amateur dressmaker can happily and easily follow.

John Kloss hemmed the dresses in one

of his collections with machine-made blanket stitches; Clovis Ruffin uses his own version of the union stitch, which was invented originally in order to machine-bind the edges of undergarments; and Stephen Burrows' knit and chiffon creations may always be immediately recognized by their lettuce hems and their machine-stitched zigzag seams. Burrows' brilliantly designed clothes, lacking the buttons, zippers or other paraphernalia that might distract from the grace and freedom of his striking effects, are probably the clearest and most original examples of the new style.

Thus today's elegance keeps tending toward greater economy of style and effort and concentrates on the few details of design that it chooses to invest with significance. A splendid evening coat from a collection presented by the designer Zandra Rhodes is a perfect illustration of the principles that are characteristic of the new philosophy of style. The color is a vibrant pink, and the material is felt. No effort is squandered on finely turned or buttoned cuffs; instead the wrists are elasticized. The time that has been saved from not having to finish the seams and hem on the felt is lavished, rather, on the circular collar that is ringed with rows of black machine stitching and satin-stitched velvet ribbon. Sets of snaps sewn around the neck edge are then paired together so that the collar has a pleasing pleated effect and ripples up around the wearer's ears, framing the face with a dramatic, flower-like ruff.

Elegance, in short, is much more than just good form: it must also have the electricity of boldness and romance. When the Chanel suit first appeared in the 1920s it was practically a manifesto, a symbol of revolt against all the fussiness of the dressmaker school of style. Yet even this classic "understated" style—which appears to brush aside the high cost of fine tweed, jeweled buttons, silk for linings and blouses and handmade braid trim—is suspect and under a certain amount of scrutiny. For the youthful new elegance insists above all on an air of complete honesty. It is not in the least interested in pretending to be poor when it is actually rich, or rich when it is poor, or simple when it is complex.

Honesty is implicit, also, in the relationship between the home sewer and the industry that provides her with the raw materials for all of her projects; it is far more profitable to educate the customer and win her lifetime allegiance than to fool her into making a single ill-chosen purchase that probably would discourage her from persevering. And the irony is that because of these current ground rules of the partnership, it is the once-dowdy sewing periodical or pattern book that now indulges in the photographs of ideal, elegant creatures in exotic settings that the fashion magazines no longer dare to feature.

It seems entirely appropriate that elegance should be so well promoted by an industry whose job is to pass the message to a newly fashionable consumer—who proceeds to run up her own interpretation of it. Like the contemporary home sewer, the new style is quite level-headed. And that is simply because while home sewing is not so humble as it once was, elegance, though often dazzling, is no longer so aloof.

Today's mode: simple and dramatic

Beauty without the baste, a once-impossible dream, is fast approaching reality. Even sinuous, clinging fashions no longer demand time-consuming sewing. At right, the regal, figure-defining gown is a column of tubular knit that requires only a minimal amount of seaming. Springy Lycra fiber makes the bathing suit fit snugly without darts. On the poppy print at left, preshirred, elasticized fabric creates a molded bodice. Today's textile wizards are eliminating the hours of needlework once required to set off an attractive figure.

Flair with bulky fabrics

One of the most exciting ways in which the fabric maker has aided the home dressmaker is in producing bold and bulky materials that provide drama without drudgery. These fabrics must be treated simply, if only because of their bulk. But the designers have cut the materials into stark geometric shapes that have the presence and authority of modern abstract art—and require little sewing. The thick-textured fabric of the dress at left, for instance, has an innate stiffness that keeps its triangular shape naturally. The brilliant striped dress of upholstery fabric is nothing more than a large square (skirt) attached to three identical rectangles (sleeves and yoke). And the double-faced wool of the cape and skirt comes in an outsized width that eliminates piecing, leaving the long, bold line unbroken.

The built-in
beauty of detail

These handsome evening costumes save a step by making their decorative finishing touches a functional part of the initial design. The lettuce hem *(page 115)* of Stephen Burrows' toga at left does its basic job of finishing a raw edge and also adds a festive grace note. "Tunneling" *(pages 99-100)* at the shoulders, wrists and waist of the center gown lends distinction while assuring a trim fit. At right, the process called cording *(pages 102-103)* transforms the essential halter strap into a beautiful accent in Burrows' diamond-pointed design.

2
TOOLS TO SAVE TIME

Sewer's helpers, shown here in action, include buttonhole attachment (*above*), seam gauge (*top*), knit-fabric scissors and zipper tape (*right*).

With no more male chauvinism than befitted the tenor of his 18th Century times, Voltaire observed in his *Dictionnaire Philosophique:* "Very learned women are to be found in the same manner as female warriors, but they are seldom or ever inventors." That could be. But few women would want to claim credit for some of the devices that have been conceived and constructed through the years for the

WORK-SAVING EQUIPMENT THEN AND NOW

express purpose of making sewing easier.

Scores of useful sewing inventions survive from early incarnations in streamlined form today. A representative sampling of these timesaving devices appears on pages 26-37. Yet for every successful contrivance, historians can count dozens that are more appropriate to Rube Goldberg than to the efficient sewing room.

Among the wackier devices was one that actually was used in 19th Century England

—that is until the Royal Society for the Prevention of Cruelty to Animals stepped in. It was a sewing machine powered by small leashed dogs on a kind of treadmill. Thomas Edison supposedly invented another sewing machine—though his biography discreetly makes no mention of it—that worked on voice power: a membrane mounted level with the operator's mouth transformed sound waves into energy. The principle itself was valid, but Edison—who was deaf—overestimated women's ability to keep talking.

Still another sewing machine was pocket-sized and looked like an eggbeater; a turn of the handle operated the device. Sailors who found themselves far from their dexterous wives considered it a boon for those long off-duty hours at sea.

Sewing machine accessories, like the machines themselves, had their successes and failures. One gadget that never quite caught on was a musical sewing machine cover, patented in 1882, that held a player-piano roll and was run by treadle power. The treadle also activated a sewing machine fan patented in the 1870s and marketed for a dollar. It must have constituted the greatest advance toward summer sewing comfort since the invention of lemonade.

Accessories of all kinds were available. The market was so lucrative that it inspired not only inventors but also poets of a kind. The Wood Sewing Machine Co., in an 1867 advertisement, thus versified:

No longer is wrought the gusset and band
With ceaseless stitch and wearied hand
For sewing is pleasure by magic art
Since curious machines well play their part.

One such curious invention was the Weiss Junior Pinking Machine, which resembled a meat grinder and fitted onto the edge of a table just as the familiar kitchen apparatus does. Sold for five dollars, it satisfied the Edwardian amateur seamstress' apparent passion for pinking. If pinking scissors existed, they were not advertised, but of others there was a plethora.

One pair of scissors, invented in France, boasted 18 different uses: it supposedly served, among other things, as a straight edge and ruler, a nail file, a screw driver, a pen knife, a glass cutter, a wire cutter, an ink eraser, a pattern perforator and a cigar clipper—presumably for the rare seamstress who enjoyed a cigar while she sewed. At the end of its long day this device could be employed as a stereopticon viewer. Somehow, despite its incredible versatility, the scissors did not become a popular item. Neither did the fish-shaped silver brooch that had a hidden container on its back to hold a knitting needle.

Thread winders were carved like small pepper mills and sometimes they were made of ivory. There were tape measures that emerged from miniature barrels, and some that responded to the turning of the tails of little metal donkeys. One novel metal thimble, devised by a rather ingenious Victorian, offered a glimpse of the city of Ipswich, England, through a peephole in the top. Its sewing value, however, might well be open to question.

There was a whole separate machine —which has now been replaced by a sewing machine attachment—for making buttonholes. Yet another machine—now also replaced by a sewing machine attachment —was used just for sewing on buttons. And for amateur seamstresses who were far too busy to bother with sewing on buttons, there were the automatic bachelor buttons locked onto sharp steel shanks that were pushed through the cloth. To facilitate this process, there was the Heaton Button Fastening Machine, which was actually little more than a pair of pliers. A variation on the bachelor button, the Padlock Pants Button, was especially designed for use in those prezipper days "in cases of emergency." A box of a dozen buttons sold for 45 cents, and presumably no foresighted male ever ventured out of his house without a couple of spares in his pocket.

Fly buttons, of course, are a memory, though many a man has longed for a device that would perform a like service with fly zippers. Someone is probably working on such a gadget, but one thing is sure: with the steady flow of new, streamlined attachments reaching today's market, the store of ingenuity that was brought to bear on early sewing equipment shows no sign of abating in modern times.

Like the Model T Ford, home sewing aids in the early 20th Century lacked streamlined elegance; some seemed styled for garages rather than households. But the ads *(right)* from contemporary trade papers show that there was a gadget for speeding everything from sewing on buttons to measuring and marking a skirt. The skirt marker's curved ruler *(immediate right)* for example, facilitated the measurement of the full garments then in vogue. World War I was exploited by advertisers *(top right)* who said their devices would help "win the war."

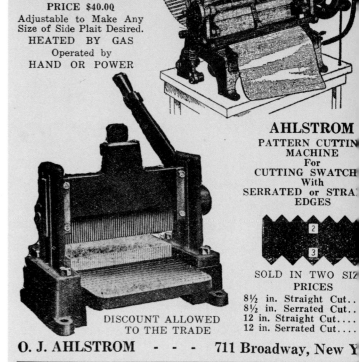

AHLSTROM
No. "0" SIDE PLAITING
MACHINE
Width of Knife 9 Inches.
PRICE $40.00
Adjustable to Make Any
Size of Side Plait Desired.
HEATED BY GAS
Operated by
HAND OR POWER

AHLSTROM
PATTERN CUTTIN
MACHINE
For
CUTTING SWATCH
With
SERRATED or STRA
EDGES

SOLD IN TWO SIZ
PRICES
8½ in. Straight Cut..
8½ in. Serrated Cut..
12 in. Straight Cut....
12 in. Serrated Cut....

DISCOUNT ALLOWED
TO THE TRADE

O. J. AHLSTROM - - - 711 Broadway, New Y

WEISS' WORK ROOM QUARTET
A SEWING MACHINE SIDE LINE

WEISS UP-TO-DATE SKIRT
MARKER

A perfect measure without experience.

Pin Stops Skirt Slipping.

Projecting rim gives marking edge.

CHILD'S WORK!

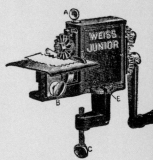

WEISS JUNIOR PINKIN
MACHINE.

Lowest Priced Practical Pi
on the market.

Write for circular.

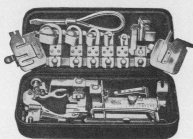

25

Devices for faster cutting and marking

Even before you insert the fabric into your sewing machine there are some aids that will make it easier and quicker to prepare your material. Two specialized types of scissors can ease the cutting chores. Electric scissors *(right)* save time if you have a lot of straight cutting to do on layers of heavy or bulky fabric. Finely serrated scissors *(right, below)*, designed for knits, cut cleanly through stubborn or slippery synthetics without snagging the fabric.

While a tracing wheel will transfer pattern markings for many fabrics, there are others too fine for this usual method—or too coarse-textured for the tracings to show. In such cases tailor's chalk *(opposite, above)* or a metal marker *(page 29)* will transfer markings just as well.

Many special-purpose measuring devices—really variations on rulers—can help you perform some marking tasks more quickly and accurately: for example, the six-inch sewing gauge *(opposite, below)*, and the skirt marker and hem gauge *(page 28)*. All of these sewer's helpers are shown, with instructions for using them, on these four pages.

TO CUT HEAVY FABRIC

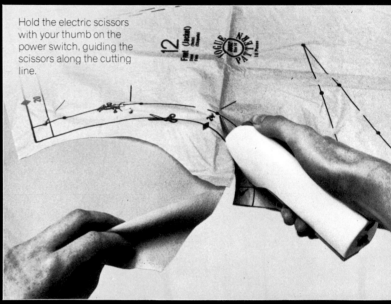

Hold the electric scissors with your thumb on the power switch, guiding the scissors along the cutting line.

TO CUT WITHOUT SNAGGING

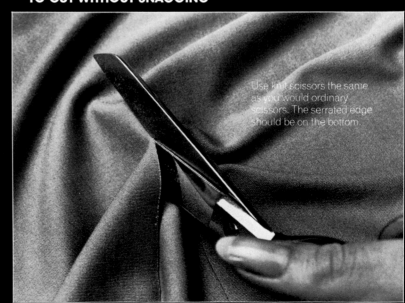

Use knit scissors the same as you would ordinary scissors. The serrated edge should be on the bottom.

TO MARK WITH CHALK

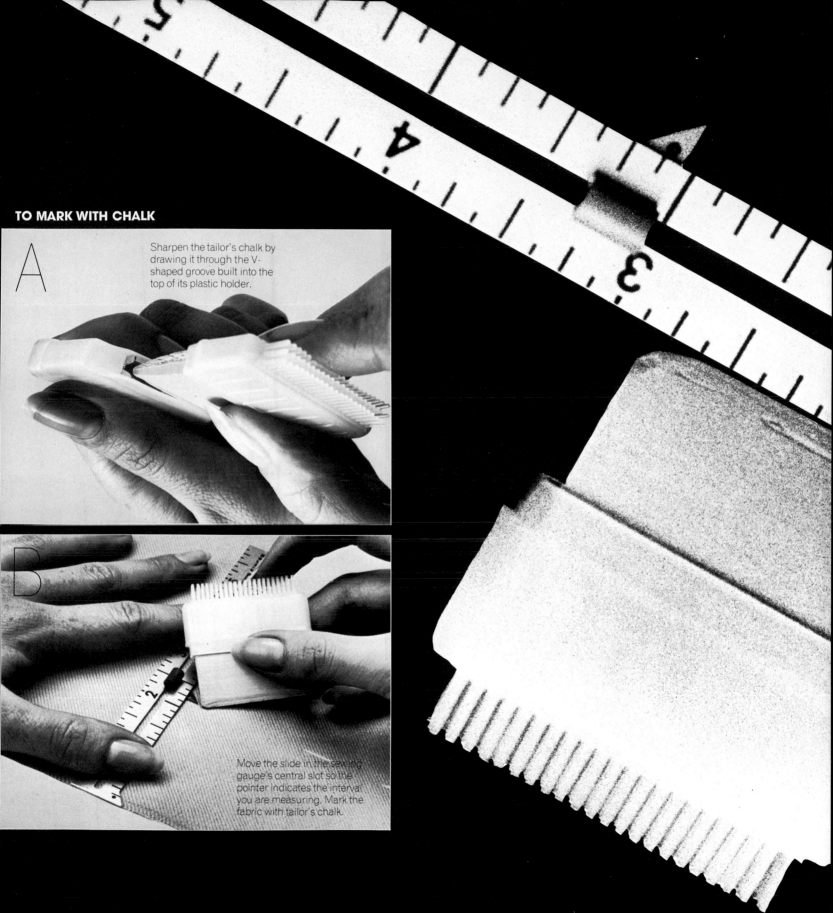

A Sharpen the tailor's chalk by drawing it through the V-shaped groove built into the top of its plastic holder.

B Move the slide in the sewing gauge's central slot so the pointer indicates the interval you are measuring. Mark the fabric with tailor's chalk.

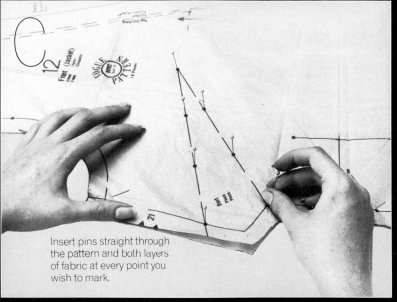

C 12

Insert pins straight through the pattern and both layers of fabric at every point you wish to mark.

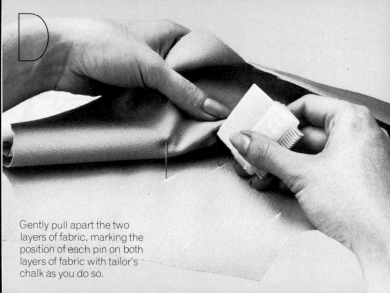

D

Gently pull apart the two layers of fabric, marking the position of each pin on both layers of fabric with tailor's chalk as you do so.

TO MARK THE HEM

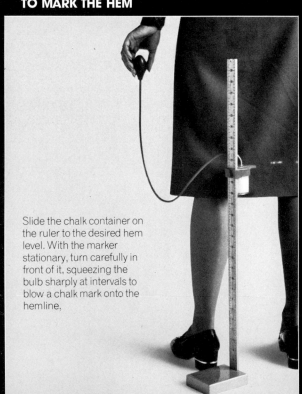

Slide the chalk container on the ruler to the desired hem level. With the marker stationary, turn carefully in front of it, squeezing the bulb sharply at intervals to blow a chalk mark onto the hemline.

TO MEASURE THE HEM DEPTH

With the hem folded up over this hem gauge, use the lines on the gauge to measure the desired hem depth. You can then trim the hem evenly.

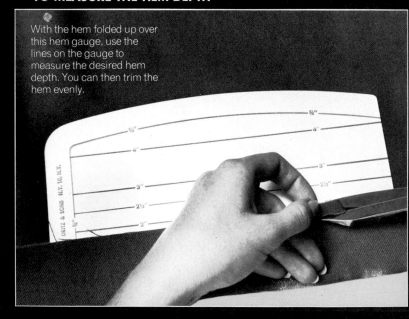

TO TRANSFER PATTERN MARKINGS

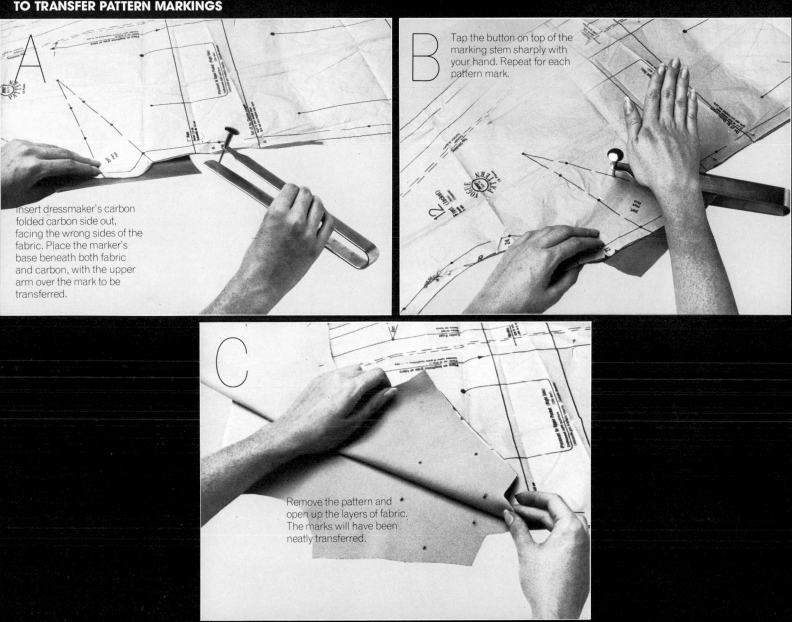

A Insert dressmaker's carbon folded carbon side out, facing the wrong sides of the fabric. Place the marker's base beneath both fabric and carbon, with the upper arm over the mark to be transferred.

B Tap the button on top of the marking stem sharply with your hand. Repeat for each pattern mark.

C Remove the pattern and open up the layers of fabric. The marks will have been neatly transferred.

Ingenious additions to your machine

Your sewing machine can do many more jobs than just stitching forward or backward. Sophisticated models can do all sorts of things with the flick of a dial, but even basic machines can be adapted to perform many tasks. Whether the device is built in or an attachment designed for your model, the manner in which it works is essentially the same. One attachment makes perfect buttonholes *(right)*. Others are adapted to the newer techniques and textiles. The invisible-zipper foot *(page 32)* ensures accurate stitching close to the fine coils of the modern invisible-zipper closure. The even-feed foot, for use with machines that do zigzag stitching *(page 33)*, is especially useful with fuzzy, bulky or slippery fabrics; it makes sure that both the top and bottom layers of these fabrics move through the sewing machine at the same speed.

The handiest sewing machine attachment of all is the simplest: the seam guide. If the throat-plate of your machine is not ruled with numbered guide lines, you can buy a seam guide *(page 33)*, which can be adjusted for—and will hold—whatever seam width you desire.

Fasten the buttonholer firmly to the presser bar in place of the regular presser foot.

Place the garment under the ruled cloth clamp, and line up the rulings on the edges of the clamp with the chalk marks on the garment indicating the position of the buttonhole. Lower the clamp to press against and hold the fabric.

Holding the needle thread, take one stitch to pull up the bobbin thread to the upper side of the garment.

D

Holding both the needle and bobbin threads, take several more stitches to secure these threads. Clip them to 1/2 inch.

E

Press the foot pedal or knee lever of your machine. The buttonholer does the rest.

F

Pull the threads to the underside, tie and clip. For greater strength, stitch around the buttonhole again. Using buttonhole scissors, cut open the buttonhole.

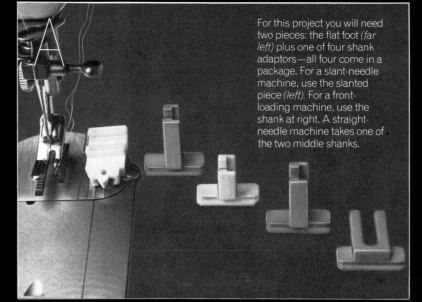

For this project you will need two pieces: the flat foot (far left) plus one of four shank adaptors—all four come in a package. For a slant-needle machine, use the slanted piece (left). For a front-loading machine, use the shank at right. A straight-needle machine takes one of the two middle shanks.

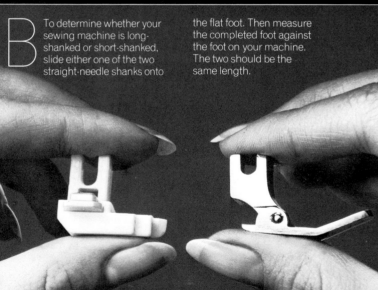

To determine whether your sewing machine is long-shanked or short-shanked, slide either one of the two straight-needle shanks onto the flat foot. Then measure the completed foot against the foot on your machine. The two should be the same length.

With the special foot attached, draw the needle thread down through the hole in the foot. Position the garment so the zipper coil feeds smoothly through the groove. See page 108 for full directions on inserting an invisible zipper.

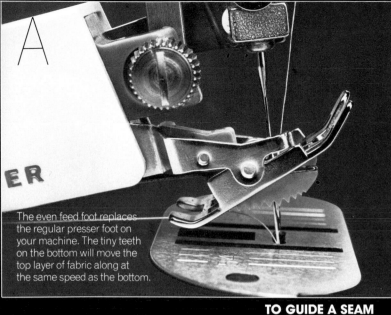

A

The even feed foot replaces the regular presser foot on your machine. The tiny teeth on the bottom will move the top layer of fabric along at the same speed as the bottom.

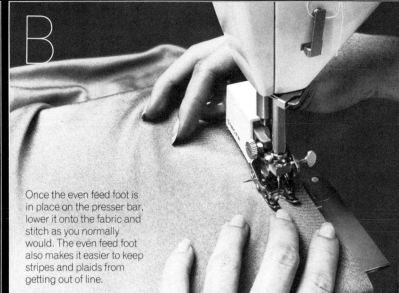

B

Once the even feed foot is in place on the presser bar, lower it onto the fabric and stitch as you normally would. The even feed foot also makes it easier to keep stripes and plaids from getting out of line.

TO GUIDE A SEAM

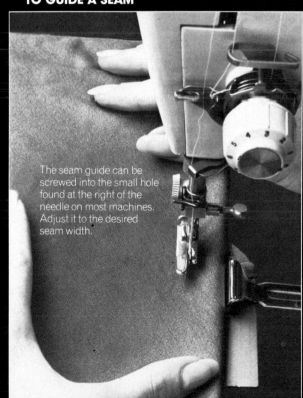

The seam guide can be screwed into the small hole found at the right of the needle on most machines. Adjust it to the desired seam width.

Gadgets that eliminate extra steps

Besides the many aids to marking, cutting and making a versatile tool out of your sewing machine, there are some gadgets that will save steps by doing everything from holding your fabric in place to pulling it inside out; and there are some aids that even eliminate the sewing itself.

The tape shown at near right, for example, is adhesive on both sides and eliminates the need to baste by holding the zipper to the cloth as you stitch. Another tape, sticky on one side *(opposite)*, holds unruly fabrics in place while you sew and can be easily ripped away. Both tapes can also be used to hold patterns onto fabric for cutting, to attach pockets temporarily and to hold up hems while you try on the garment.

For making fine fabric tubing for buttonhole loops *(page 112)*, there is a device called a tubing turner *(page 36)*. And the gadget that helps you avoid sewing altogether is iron-on bonding material *(page 37)*, which comes in several widths. It can be used to form interfacings, reinforce areas, tack down facings or turn up hems. The heat of the iron fuses the fabrics together without the need of a single slip stitch.

TO TAPE A ZIPPER

A

Apply tape on the front side of the zipper, pressing it in place along both outside edges. Remove the protective paper strip from the tape.

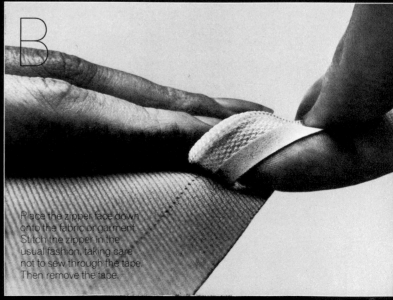

B

Place the zipper face down onto the fabric or garment. Stitch the zipper in the usual fashion, taking care not to sew through the tape. Then remove the tape.

A

Press the stitching tape along the seam edge of a stretchy or slippery fabric.

B

Stitch through the tape, using its lines as a guide. Then peel off the tape.

35

TO TURN A TUBE

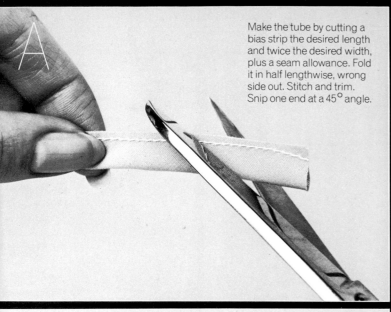

A Make the tube by cutting a bias strip the desired length and twice the desired width, plus a seam allowance. Fold it in half lengthwise, wrong side out. Stitch and trim. Snip one end at a 45° angle.

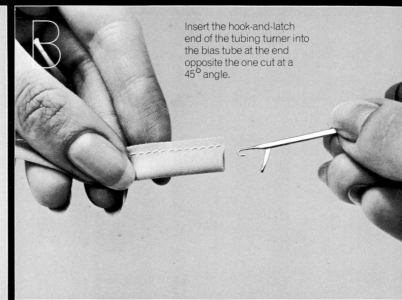

B Insert the hook-and-latch end of the tubing turner into the bias tube at the end opposite the one cut at a 45° angle.

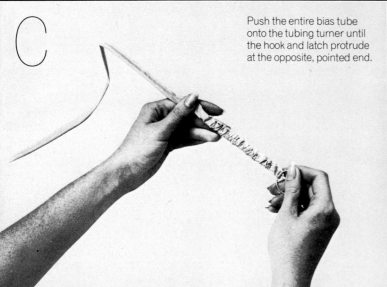

C Push the entire bias tube onto the tubing turner until the hook and latch protrude at the opposite, pointed end.

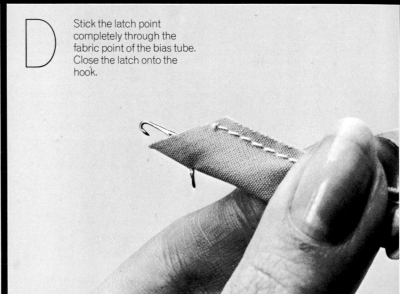

D Stick the latch point completely through the fabric point of the bias tube. Close the latch onto the hook.

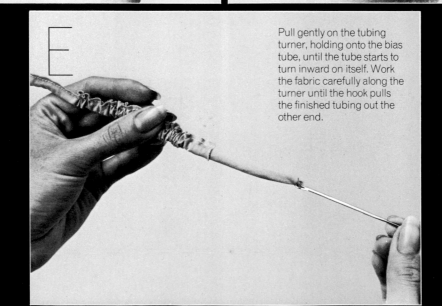

E Pull gently on the tubing turner, holding onto the bias tube, until the tube starts to turn inward on itself. Work the fabric carefully along the turner until the hook pulls the finished tubing out the other end.

TO HEM WITHOUT STITCHING

A

Insert the bonding strip within a pressed hem, taking care to cover the bonding material completely.

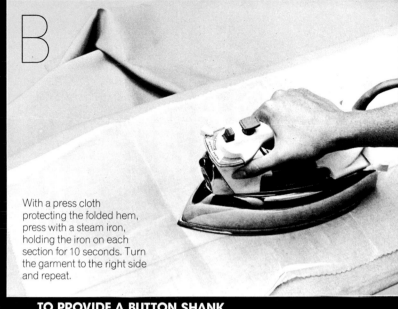

B

With a press cloth protecting the folded hem, press with a steam iron, holding the iron on each section for 10 seconds. Turn the garment to the right side and repeat.

C

When the garment has cooled, lift the edge of the hem to make sure the bonding strip has dissolved into the fabric. If not, repeat the above pressing procedure.

TO PROVIDE A BUTTON SHANK

So that a button will be loose enough to allow for the thickness of the buttonhole, slip the shank gauge between the button and the garment while sewing on the button. Use one or more shank gauges, depending on the thickness of the fabric with the buttonhole.

3
FABRIC WITH AN EXTRA ELEMENT

Scarlett O'Hara, in one of the more memorable episodes of *Gone With the Wind,* exemplified the amateur seamstress who knew where she was going and how to get there in a hurry. Destitute and desperate for $300 to save the family mansion from the tax man, she determined to find Rhett Butler in Atlanta and wheedle the money from him. But she would need a bewitching dress and there was none in her tattered wardrobe. So

A VARIETY OF VERSATILE MATERIALS

she yanked down the moss-green velvet curtains in the parlor, cut and stitched late into the night—with a pattern from the attic and set out for Atlanta in style, a rooster's tail feathers in her bonnet.

Except perhaps for the feathers, Scarlett in her velvet curtains would be considered fashionable today. Upholstery fabrics are frequently used for elegant dress design. So are handsomely printed drip-dry bedsheets, brilliantly dyed felts and a host of other products of modern textile technology and design. "These are the fabrics that will give you a maximum of drama with a minimum of sewing," says one designer. "These are the fabrics that will produce a knockout with two seams and a button."

With only a little of Scarlett O'Hara's ingenuity, you can seek out powerful colors and eye-catching prints in unconventional fabrics; and many may suggest their own shapes. There are also fabrics into which the manufacturer has built some shortcuts. Such fabrics come preshirred, prepleated, prequilted or preembroidered. With a head start like that, it takes only a seam and some elastic around the waist to produce what the fashion trade calls "a really exciting" evening skirt.

To achieve elegance with ease, you do not have to be a Pucci, but you do have to know how to choose the right—though possibly surprising—fabric for your purpose. Upholstery materials, for example, become graceful, unique dresses (pages 16-17). But for results that are spectacular despite simplicity, the fabric should be dramatic in color, texture and design. A soft, clinging cloth in a solid color, chosen for the same ends, might prove less easy to work with and less striking in appearance.

Bedsheets, which come in bright colors and designs and in the greatest widths of any fabric available to the home sewer, lend themselves easily to garments that require extra-wide fabrics, such as the blouse and pants outfit made from large circles as shown on pages 136-145. (There should be enough fabric left over from this project to make the matching beret.) Besides being wide, bedsheets come hemmed; with those advantages, you eliminate the piecing that requires seams, and you can start making the garment from the 4-inch hem up.

Felt too has diverse possibilities: brilliantly colorful sportswear, loose-fitting jumpers and evening coats, capes, overblouses, envelope purses. It has the advantages that it is reversible and needs no hemming. But you would not choose it for an all-weather coat because felt becomes mush in the rain, and it cannot be washed.

So besides knowing how to choose the esthetically correct fabric for your particular project—with the help of the charts on pages 50-53—you should know how the material will behave under the needle, how it will behave when you wear it and how it will behave when it needs freshening.

Clinging fabrics such as jerseys and other knits stretch to fit—and thus simplify tailoring—but they slip when being sewn if not pinned or basted. Tubular knits are stretchy and require only a few steps and no side seams for an instant dress; but they do not tailor or pleat well. Double-faced wool requires its own technique for seams.

Let none of this discourage you. You can learn to avoid the pitfalls, as the illustrations and text on pages 63-67 and 118-119 demonstrate. The essential goal here is to match the characteristics of the fabrics, as well as their looks, to your own purpose.

Any fabric derives its characteristics —warmth, weight, durability, stretchability, appearance—from its origins, which may go back to a prehistoric chance discovery in a desert, or be as recent as a 1970s experiment in a chemist's laboratory. Felt, for example, first came into use—legend has it —when camel drivers of antiquity put camel hair inside their sandals as a buffer against the heat of the sands. The pressure of their weight, the moisture of their sweat and the high temperature matted the hair into felt. A French version of the legend credits St. Feutre of Caen—the patron saint of the felt industry—with the discovery, citing similar circumstances, except that St. Feutre naturally had to use wool rather than camel hair. Whatever the truth, felt still is made in basically the same way, with heat, moisture and pressure applied to a natural or synthetic fiber. The very name sums up the process—the word felt comes from the German *Filz,* which means a fabric that is matted and pressed.

It was many centuries ago that man tried to manufacture fabric to replace natural materials. The ancient Polynesians beat the bark of mulberry trees, converting it into cellulose cloth called *tapa* and adorning the result with geometric designs.

Centuries later, in 1664, the British scientist Robert Hooke wrote: "I have often thought, that probably there might be a way found out, to make an artificial glutinous composition, much resembling, if not fully as good, nay better, than that Excrement, or whatever other substance it be, out of which, the silk-worm wire-draws his clew. If such a composition were found, it were certainly an easie matter to find very quick ways of drawing it out into small wires for use."

But it was no "easie matter." Not until 1855 did George Audemars, a Swiss, find a way to produce rayon out of nitric acid and the same cellulose from the mulberry tree that the Polynesians had used. And it was 1889 before the Count Hilaire de Chardonnet was able to devise a commercially feasible way of manufacturing Audemars' fiber, imitating the silkworm in forcing a syrupy liquid through tiny apertures in a device called a spinneret—which resembles a shower head. Now rid of the rather sleazy look and feel that cost it its popularity for a long time, rayon has a deep luster and performs like fine cotton.

After World War II a newly mobile and leisure-oriented society began demanding man-made fibers for fabrics that resist wear and wrinkling and require minimal care. Besides, the technological advances made during the war enabled industry to provide them. Acetate, a cousin of rayon that was soft to the touch, draped gracefully and dyed vividly—but did not wash well—has taken on new life as Arnel triacetate, which preserves the luxurious look, but shrinks less, holds pleats and can be washed and dried in a machine. Nylon, introduced just before World War II for toothbrush bristles and stockings, was first distinguished for its enormous strength. Now it thrives as Antron, Nomex, Cantrece and the luxurious, silklike Qiana. Polyester, a 1941 British invention, was introduced to the United States by Du Pont in 1951 and given the American name Dacron. Also called Fortrel, Kodel and Trevira, polyester blends well with cotton and rayon, has resilience and takes a permanent press.

Since no single fiber—either man-made or natural—can claim every virtue, research continues. Wool and cotton will always retain their importance in the marketplace, but ever since 1968 synthetics have been the principal fibers used by the clothing industry. Acrylic—known by the trade names Orlon, Acrilan, Creslan and Zefran II—resulted from Du Pont's search for light, fluffy fibers that can substitute for wool and resist sunlight and chemicals. Acrylics lack nylon's durability and will tend to pill (the synthetic equivalent of fuzz), but they are enormously versatile; they serve in blankets, draperies, carpets, paint rollers and insulation as well as in knit dresses and sweaters.

Modern stretch yarns came into being in 1947, when the Swiss firm of Heberlein and Co. tried twisting nylon yarn, setting the twist with heat and then twisting in the opposite direction. The result, called Helanca, showed up in the first stretch ski clothes. But they stretched only one way. Then spandex—which Du Pont calls Lycra—was developed; it can stretch 500 per cent without breaking, and then snap back into shape. It not only makes excellent sportswear, but better-fitting knits.

With the variety of fabrics that 20th Century science has developed, and with the techniques described on the following pages, you can now produce more elegance with less effort than at any other time in the history of dressmaking.

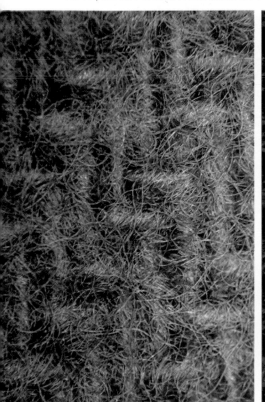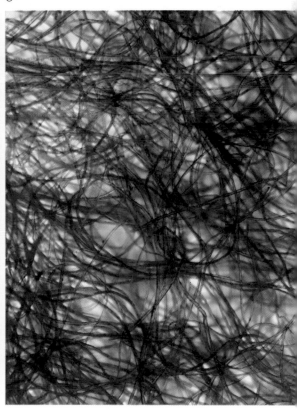

When magnified, these three woolen fabrics show how they differ in sewing quality and use because of their construction. At the left, the familiar warp-over-weft weave produces the strong, versatile cloth used in most wardrobes. The loops of the tubular knit in the center contribute stretch, which facilitates fitting. Felt, at the right, is made from random, compressed fibers; it has no grain and thus needs no hem to keep it from raveling.

Fibers that are fashioned for easy sewing

Eye-catching as they are, the fabrics shown here and on the following pages do much more than just look beautiful—they also work beautifully to save time and sewing steps. Stretch fabrics, for example *(opposite and below)*, minimize the need for darts and gussets and allow your clothes to move with you. Both the ribbed, washable natural wool on the cube and the synthetic blend on the pyramid are tubular knits that seek out the contours of the body so well that they may need only top and bottom seams to become elegant garments. Some stretch fabrics, like the spandex on the ball at center, owe their resilience to elastic fibers. The stretch terry covering the cylinder is another timesaving fabric. It is a blend of cotton and textured nylon fibers that give the knit an extra degree of elasticity.

Upholstery to drape the body

A handy source of easily worked material is upholstery fabric. It drapes in rich folds under its own weight, making fussy fitting and interlining unnecessary. Its width—usually 48 to 54 inches—simplifies cutting. And those with large designs minimize problems of matching. Best of all, many upholstery fabrics are ready-made substitutes for handwork: the tapestry-like weave on the cylinder at right, for example, or the parqueted stripes on the pyramid above it. The cube at right is covered with a vivid version of flame-stitching; and a crewel design encloses the ball.

Decorative touches that are ready-made

One of the best timesavers is felt, like the vivid cover on the cylinder. Made from fibers that are matted without a warp or woof to come unraveled, it needs no hem. There are already-pleated fabrics like the polyester crepe on the cube. Preshirred material, such as the cotton on the sphere, permits you to concentrate on the dress rather than its decoration. And the double-faced wool on the pyramid—with two layers of material joined by invisible threads—is reversible: you can make two costumes from it in the time you would normally spend on one.

Selecting and sewing the fabrics

The special fabrics discussed in this volume have unique virtues—as well as unique characteristics that must be respected in order to get the best results. Before working with knits, upholstery or slipcover fabrics, or special step-savers like felt, you should study the accompanying charts for hints on how to select and use these fabrics most effectively.

It is most important to know what you are buying. Look on the hangtag or bolt end of the fabric for a description of its fiber content; the law requires that this information be provided, plus the country of origin if the fabric is imported. In addition, ask for directions on the care of the fabric —washing or dry cleaning, storing. The store must supply a care label that can be sewn into the finished garment. Knowledge of fiber content is essential not only to help in the sewing procedure but also because the success of a special-fabric garment often depends on its components being compatible. So be sure to use these chart guidelines to select the zipper and thread recommended for the particular fabric and fiber type you select.

KNIT FABRICS

	CHARACTERISTICS AND USES
PLAIN OR JERSEY KNITS	These knits are probably the most versatile. They are smooth and have no pronounced pattern. Jersey knits, for example, are particularly suitable for a fluid dress with a floating lettuce hem.
RIB KNITS	These knits have vertical ridges, great stretchability and considerable warmth. They are most appropriate for sweaters, close-fitting dresses, cuffs or collars. (Double knits are a less stretchable variation of rib knits.)
PURL KNITS	These knits have pronounced horizontal ridges and, like rib knits, are ideal for sweaters or dresses.
	Since all knits have a wide range of weight and fiber content, they offer a great many possibilities. Elasticized waists, gathered bodices, and simple square, bateau and V-necklines can all be used with a variety of knits. Cap, dolman and T-shaped kimono sleeves likewise can be made from all three kinds of knits.

HOUSEHOLD FABRICS

FABRIC TYPE	USES
UPHOLSTERY AND SLIPCOVER FABRICS **cotton** **linen** **silk** **wool** **synthetics** **blends**	Upholstery and slipcover fabrics tend to fall in full folds, so garments with loose lines are most suitable for these materials. Standing, square, bateau and V-necklines (with alternate facing fabric) and the T-shaped kimono sleeve can all be made with these fabrics. Avoid pleats, gathers and styles with close body lines.

SHOPPING SUGGESTIONS	SEWING ACCESSORIES	PRACTICAL TIPS	CARE
Choose your pattern carefully. Select one with simple, easy lines and little detail. Because knit fabrics vary in stretchability, you must distinguish between the two basic pattern types that are available for use with knits. Patterns marked "For stretchable or unbonded knits only" are sculpted closer to the body than standard patterns, and they must be used with knits that recover easily when stretched. Check the fabric's stretchability on the stretch gauge printed on the pattern envelope. Patterns labeled "Recommended for knits" or "Suitable for knits" are simply standard patterns whose easy styling and uncomplicated detail make them especially appropriate for use with knitted fabrics. They are a good choice for low-stretch knits. For knits with directional shading, purchase the yardage specified on the envelope for "with nap" fabric. Buy all the necessary sewing accessories at the same time as the fabric, to ensure that the color, fiber and stretch are compatible.	*Thread:* polyester *Zipper:* conventional nylon or polyester for all knits; invisible nylon or polyester for heavy knits only *Hem binding:* stretch lace *Equipment:* straight-edged shears with one serrated edge ("knit scissors"); ballpoint pins; ballpoint needles.	Make all pattern adjustments before cutting. Preshrink washable fabrics and fabric sewing accessories. If the knit is not straight, pull it diagonally to straighten it. If you are using a tubular knit, avoid incorporating the original foldline (which may not press out) into any pattern piece. Reposition the fabric so the original foldline is in an area of the fabric that will not be used. Pin and cut on a large, flat surface. Never allow fabric to hang over the edge. Mark pattern symbols on the wrong side of the fabric with tailor tacks or pins and chalk. Check your sewing machine for nicks and burrs that might snag the fabric. A small-hole throat plate is extremely helpful when working with lightweight, slippery knits. An even-feed foot attachment *(page 33)* is especially useful for heavy or slippery knits. Test a double-thickness fabric swatch for tension and stitch length. In general, the heavier the fabric the fewer stitches will be required per inch. Machine stitch curves and other off-grain edges to stabilize them during assembly. Use seam tape to reinforce the shoulder seams of stretchy knits. If the seam allowances curl, finish them with two rows of stitching. Reinforce buttonhole areas with lightweight facing. Hang the garment for 24 hours before hemming. Double-hem very stretchy and heavy knits.	Care is largely dictated by fiber content. Many knits can be hand or machine washed, but some must be dry cleaned. Note that garment trimmings also affect care: unless every component of a garment is washable, it must be dry cleaned. Use a pressing cloth when pressing the right side of a garment. Between wearings, heavy and very stretchy knit garments should be folded (with tissue paper to prevent foldlines) and stored flat. Prolonged storage on hangers can cause them to stretch out of shape.

SHOPPING SUGGESTIONS	SEWING ACCESSORIES	PRACTICAL TIPS	CARE
Avoid very heavy or very closely woven fabrics that are excessively stiff. Before choosing a water-repellent, stain-resistant, mothproof or flame-resistant fabric, be sure it is suitable for your purpose; the special finish may add stiffness, reduce comfort and hinder easy cleaning. Select patterned fabrics that do not require matching. Note that some upholstery and slipcover fabrics can be used on either side. Buy all the necessary sewing accessories at the same time as the fabric to ensure that the color and fiber are compatible.	*Thread:* mercerized cotton (No. 50 or heavy-duty) or polyester *Zipper:* conventional or invisible cotton, nylon or polyester *Equipment:* dressmaker shears; glass-head pins; Size 14 or Size 16 machine needles; long-eyed needles ("sharps"), Sizes 5 to 10, for hand sewing.	Unless fabric is labeled preshrunk, preshrink it by washing or dry cleaning, depending on care instructions. Some upholstery fabrics come folded with the right side out. Be sure to refold the fabric with the wrong side out before pinning pattern parts in place. If the fabric is heavy, cut out the pattern pieces one layer at a time. Use lightweight fabrics for facings. Test a double-thickness swatch of the fabric for machine tension and stitch length. Heavy fabrics usually require fewer stitches to the inch. Increase the seam allowances on lengthwise seams of heavy fabrics from 5/8 inch to 1 inch. Finish seam allowances with a zigzag stitch or bind with bias tape to arrest raveling.	Dry clean unless the fabric label specifically suggests washing. Follow the cleaning instructions carefully. Always test a swatch of fabric marked "washable."

STEP-SAVER FABRICS

FABRIC TYPE	USES
DOUBLE-FACED FABRICS **natural fibers** **man-made fibers** **blends**	Double-faced fabric is rather firm and sometimes bulky, making it most appropriate for loose styles. Wraparound designs, a poncho or a reversible cape are ideal for this fabric. Use patch pockets only. To make a reversible garment, choose a pattern with details that can be worked on both sides. Square, bateau or V-necklines and dolman and T-shaped kimono sleeves can be made with this fabric. Avoid intricate collars, complicated closures, pleats and gathers.
CREPE **100% polyester** **100% triacetate**	Crepe is a soft, fluid, drapable fabric suitable for almost any style that features graceful lines, such as the dolman and T-shaped kimono sleeves, elasticized waists and yokes on a gathered bodice. Polyester and triacetate have an added advantage: they are receptive to permanent pleats. (Pleating should be done to your specifications by a commercial pleater. Check your dry cleaner or the yellow pages.)
FELT **100% wool** **rayon and wool blends**	Felt should be used for simple, loose-fitting garments. Its width and absence of grain make it appropriate for such styles as circular skirts and capes. Because felt is comparatively inexpensive yet rather fragile, it is excellent for novel, special-occasion garments that receive little wear. Unfaced square, standing, bateau and V-necklines, plus the T-shaped kimono sleeve, are suitable. Avoid fitted styles, gathers and pleats.
PRESHIRRED FABRICS **natural fibers** **man-made fibers** **blends**	Because of the preparatory work done to shirred fabric, it does not require a pattern or any special techniques. With a single seam, a simple skirt or strapless dress may be made from preshirred fabric. It is also useful for making instant cuffs and cummerbunds.

SHOPPING SUGGESTIONS	SEWING ACCESSORIES	PRACTICAL TIPS	CARE
Select simple patterns with tailored lines and few details. (Do not confuse double-faced fabrics with bonded fabrics.)	Choose novelty closures such as frogs, toggles, clips and punched eyelet holes that can be closed with lacing.	Facings and linings are unnecessary. Make reversible hems and seams. Use a 3/4-inch seam allowance. Use tailor tacks or chalk for marking.	Carefully follow the label instructions for the fabric.
Crepe will not remain permanently pleated unless the fabric is at least 75% polyester or 75% triacetate. If possible, buy 100% polyester or 100% triacetate for this purpose. Buy all sewing accessories at the same time to ensure that they are compatible with the fabric.	*Thread:* polyester *Zipper:* conventional nylon or polyester *Equipment:* dressmaker pins; knife-edged dressmaker shears; Size 9 machine needle; long-eyed needles ("sharps") for hand sewing.	Preshrink the fabric. Unless you are sure your crepe is non-directional *(i.e.,* it will look the same from all angles), use the pattern layout marked "with nap." Pin carefully on the grain without stretching. Test a double-thickness swatch of the fabric for machine tension and stitch length. Lightweight fabrics usually require more stitches per inch. Machine stitch curves and other stress points to stabilize them during assembly. Use lightweight facing. To prevent shine, use a steam iron at the low setting to press open seams on the wrong side. If pressing on the right side is necessary, use a pressing cloth.	Permanent-pleated garments should be hand laundered in warm water and drip-dried. For garments without pleats, follow the fabric care label. If pressing is necessary, use a steam iron at low temperature. If possible, work on the wrong side of the fabric. When pressing on the right side, use a pressing cloth to prevent shine.
Both light- and medium-weight felts are available in fabric departments. Some felts have been specially treated for increased durability; check the bolt end or care label. Choose a pattern with simple lines and a minimum of seams and details.	*Thread:* mercerized cotton; polyester; silk buttonhole twist for topstitching only *Zipper:* invisible nylon or polyester *Equipment:* pinking shears for decorative edges.	No facing, linings, seam finishes or hems are needed. Felt has no grain, so pattern pieces can be laid out in any direction. Use either chalk or pin-and-chalk markings. To finish necklines, armholes and other openings, trim the seam allowances and stitch close to the edge with either straight or zigzag decorative topstitching. Make machine-worked buttonholes or stitch a rectangle around the buttonhole location on the wrong side and slash through the center. Test a double-thickness swatch of fabric for machine tension and stitch length.	Felt should never get wet. Dry clean only. Press with a dry iron.
Preshirred fabric is shirred (or elasticized) at only one end of the bolt; it is measured and sold by the inch at the shirred end. The depth of the shirring can vary from bolt to bolt.	Facings and linings are unnecessary.	*Thread:* polyester *Equipment:* even-feed foot (optional).	If the instructions call for washing, do not use bleach.

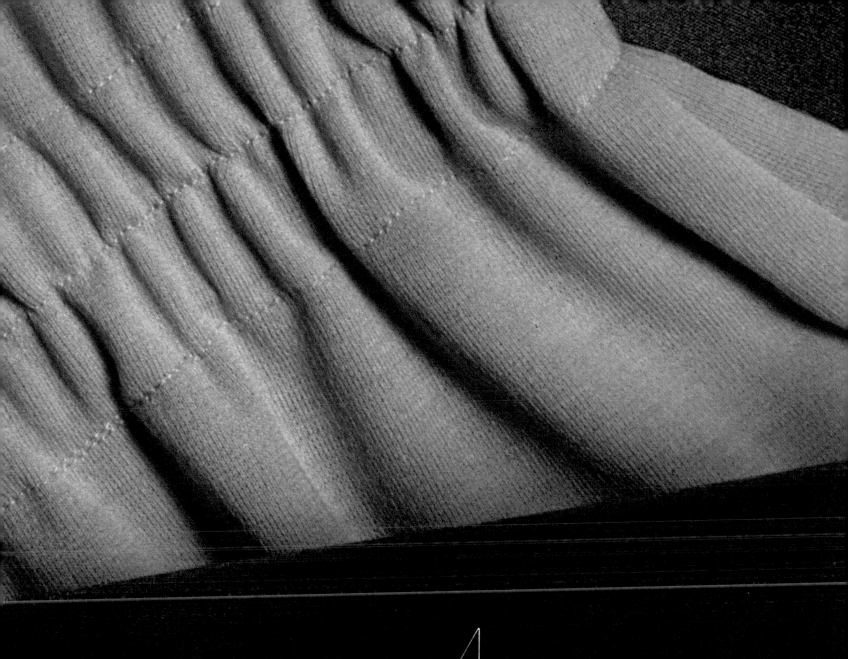

4
BETTER RESULTS FROM SIMPLE TECHNIQUES

Every home dressmaker pressed for time can find dozens of labor-saving devices to speed the work. And there are plenty of fabrics that are elegant without being difficult to handle. But neither equipment nor fabric will make the job easier if the project itself is too complicated. The sewer must be sure to select a design that has built-in shortcuts.

It might be a lounge dress with kimono sleeves or a simple shirtdress with an elas-

THE SHORTCUTS: FROM PATTERN TO COMPLETION

ticized waistline. These designs do not call for slapdash sewing; careful handling and preparation of fabric and seams are still absolutely necessary. The shortcut lies either in the construction of the garment or in simplification of the sewing process. You can, for example, make a dress from a pattern that has only a few pieces, with few seams or darts. Or you can substitute a comparatively easy technique for one that is more difficult and time-consuming.

Most pattern books are conveniently separated into various sections, one or more of which are usually labeled easy-to-make or very-easy-to-make. These patterns contain a minimum number of seams and darts. However, you may discover that many of them also tend to be limited in varieties of style. But you can escape limitations by studying the techniques outlined in this chapter. Once you understand them, you should be able to turn to the regular pattern sections of the books and zero in on those pattern designs that incorporate special timesaving shortcuts.

A careful reading of the pattern envelope can also help you select one of the simpler styles. On the back of most pattern envelopes there is a short paragraph describing in detail the various design elements—the cut of the sleeve, the shape of the neckline, the seaming in the skirt—as well as an outline of all the pattern pieces included for each garment and its variations. If this information proves too cursory for you to judge the degree of difficulty, take out the instruction sheet that accompanies every pattern (if the store permits such inspection) and see for yourself how each pattern element is constructed and sewn.

Always be sure you understand what you are looking for and what, in terms of your time and effort, you would like to avoid. Any design that requires fitting, with its shaped darts and seams is going to be much more time-consuming than one with loose, flowing lines that barely touch the body. A set-in sleeve always means more cutting, basting and sewing steps—not to mention more careful fitting procedures —than the wider-cut shirt sleeve or a kimono sleeve that is cut in one with the bodice. Collars that are constructed separately, often with interfacing, and then attached to the neckline require a good deal of patience and careful attention to detail. In fact, any details—such as topstitching or the matching of symmetrical design elements—mean a lot of preparatory basting and measuring. When you select your pattern you make the basic decision as to how much time you want to spend on your project.

Consider necklines, for instance. A number of flattering looks can be achieved without the trouble of making and sewing on a collar. The standing neckline (*pages 78-79*) provides a flattering high-necked look without the effort required for a turtleneck or a separate inset. It is cut in one with the bodice; you sew it together when you sew the shoulder seams, since its seams are an extension of the shoulder line. The only piece needed for finishing is the facing.

Another simple and attractive neckline requiring only a facing for finishing is the softly rounded bateau neck. A perfect background for pearls or a shoulder pin, this collar-bone-high neckline is finished off just by joining the shoulder seams.

Sleeves are another area where simpler styling can save sewing time and still produce elegant results. The easiest, of course, is the cap sleeve, which can either be a short piece stitched onto the bodice or a small extension of the shoulder or the bodice itself. But in many dresses it improves on the conventional sleeveless armhole, and it gives a pleasant softness and finish to an otherwise rather stark design line.

If you want a long sleeve, one of the simplest ones is the kimono, or T-, sleeve. This wide sleeve can either be cut in one with the bodice, requiring only two seam lines to assemble it, or it can be cut separately and then joined to the armhole in one long seam.

As you look at patterns with kimono sleeves, make sure you choose one of these simple versions. There are more complicated ones, usually narrower in fit and look, that require a gusset or some other underarm inset for ease of movement. Though handsome, these narrow-cut kimono sleeves require a number of painstaking steps to make them fit and hang properly. This is another case where the unpracticed eye might find the sketch difficult to decipher. Be sure you read the descriptive paragraph on the pattern envelope, and check to see how many pieces are required for the sleeve.

Not all the techniques included in this chapter can be found in the patterns. But they can be adapted to nearly any similar garment. The lettuce hem and the zigzag hem, for example (pages 115-117), both brainstorms of the talented young designer Stephen Burrows, can be used wherever you think appropriate. The lettuce hem is cut at the actual hemline and stitched in a zigzag row, close to the edge—if the fabric does not ravel easily. (If the fabric does ravel easily, the hem should be turned up about 1/8 inch and sewn with a straight machine stitch.) The lettuce hem is particularly suitable as a finishing decorative touch to the bottom of a long or short silky knit skirt. Or you can try it on the ends of a wide, uncuffed

kimono sleeve, preferably one that is made out of a soft, fluid fabric.

The zigzag hem is an ordinary, turned-up hem but with the blind hemming stitches replaced by zigzag stitching sewn so that it is in full view on the side of the fabric that shows. You can therefore use several rows of stitches in bright, contrasting colors to make a vivid design feature out of the hem, if you wish. Another attractive hemming idea is to use a row of decorative lace rather than the usual plain seam binding.

Not only are these simplified sewing techniques exceedingly flexible, but once you understand how they work, you might like to adapt, and at the same time simplify, some of your favorite patterns to include them. The procedure for constructing an extended elasticized casing for a waistline (pages 99-101), for instance, need not be used only at the waist. Any full sleeve that is originally designed to be pulled into a cuff may be made to fit at the wrist with an elasticized casing. Simply extend the sleeve to your wrist length, making sure to cut the fabric straight. Leave enough extra cloth to fold under for the casing, and proceed as you do for the waistline casing.

The drawstring tunnel technique (pages 101-102) is even more adaptable. It can be used both for long sleeves and for straight dresses that you would like to belt in an easy, stylish manner. If perhaps the garment you are making is waistless and the pattern does not indicate the position of the waistline, determine your natural waistline and mark it carefully around the circumference of the garment, and then proceed with the casing.

Similarly, any number of different fasteners can cut your working time considerably without sacrificing quality. The invisible zipper *(pages 106-109),* a fairly new addition to the sewing repertoire, is a quick, relatively easy alternative to the more conventional metal or nylon zipper. Use it anywhere you would a centered zipper—down the back or front of dresses or skirts. Since there is no visible stitching once the zipper is in place, it is especially useful with fabrics, both patterned and plain, on which you want to leave the surface undisturbed.

And the hook and eye need not be just hidden in waistbands or bodice fronts. Try it on any garment that meets or overlaps at the shoulder line. For patterns that use buttons and buttonholes to anchor shoulder straps —on a sun dress, for instance—substitute a strong hook and eye instead. It can be done in a fraction of the time required for making buttonholes and attaching buttons.

There are many ways to use such simplified design and sewing techniques. Some can be found in the patterns you buy, and it is well worth taking the time to search them out. Others can be adapted to your own individual requirements. But however they come to you, they should prove useful additions to your sewing expertise, and save you time and energy in the bargain.

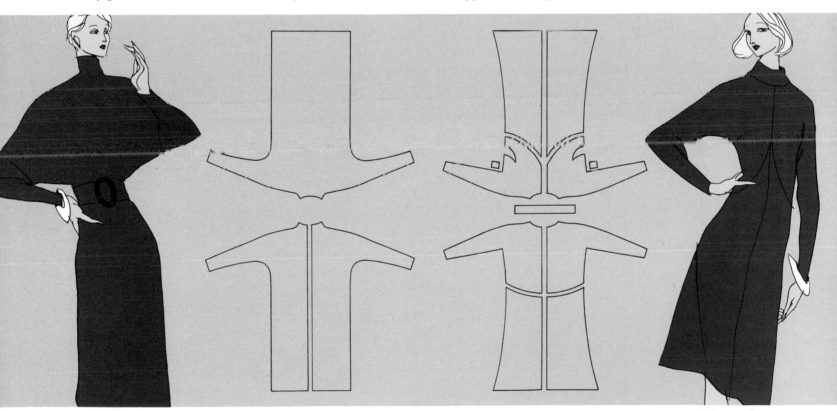

Both of these gowns are well-proportioned and handsome. But the long gown at left requires only three pattern pieces, while the one at right is made up of 12. The collar and sleeves of the first garment are merely extensions of the body section, and shape is achieved by the addition of a decorative belt. The collar of the gown at right must be made first and then attached, and the sleeves require an underarm inset for freedom of movement. The shape that the first gown achieves with a belt requires two darts in the second gown.

Two essential first steps

There are certain fundamental sewing steps that should not be shortcut. Two in particular are essential to an attractive, well-fitting garment —and in fact they should save time in the long run.

The first step is to adjust the pattern to your size. Few women have measurements that match the patterns precisely, so even the clothes that are easiest to make and need less fitting require some adjustments. They can quickly be made by following the procedures shown at right. If you compare your measurements to those printed on the pattern envelope, and then adjust the pattern, you will need fewer adjustments while you are sewing.

A mistaken notion of many home sewers is the assumption that transferring pattern markings to fabric takes too long. Not so. Once the pattern markings are on the fabric, every seam line, stitching line and notch will be right in front of you. You will save hours not having to measure countless times or having to judge by eye. The simplest method for transferring markings is shown on the opposite page. (All pattern markings are indicated in white in the drawings in the section that follows.) And devices for transferring markings onto fabrics that do not take tracing wheel markings are illustrated on pages 28-29.

MAKING PATTERN ADJUSTMENTS

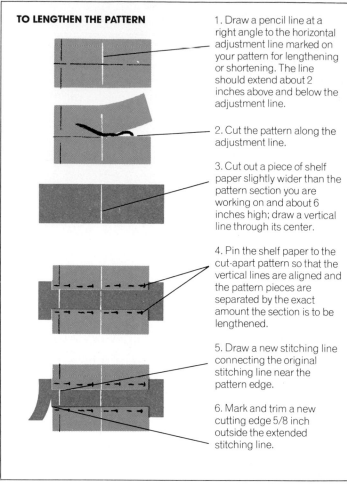

TO LENGTHEN THE PATTERN

1. Draw a pencil line at a right angle to the horizontal adjustment line marked on your pattern for lengthening or shortening. The line should extend about 2 inches above and below the adjustment line.

2. Cut the pattern along the adjustment line.

3. Cut out a piece of shelf paper slightly wider than the pattern section you are working on and about 6 inches high; draw a vertical line through its center.

4. Pin the shelf paper to the cut-apart pattern so that the vertical lines are aligned and the pattern pieces are separated by the exact amount the section is to be lengthened.

5. Draw a new stitching line connecting the original stitching line near the pattern edge.

6. Mark and trim a new cutting edge 5/8 inch outside the extended stitching line.

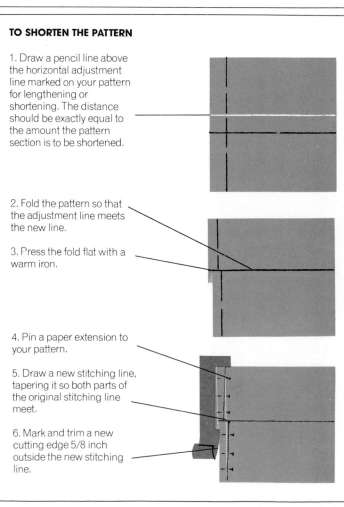

TO SHORTEN THE PATTERN

1. Draw a pencil line above the horizontal adjustment line marked on your pattern for lengthening or shortening. The distance should be exactly equal to the amount the pattern section is to be shortened.

2. Fold the pattern so that the adjustment line meets the new line.

3. Press the fold flat with a warm iron.

4. Pin a paper extension to your pattern.

5. Draw a new stitching line, tapering it so both parts of the original stitching line meet.

6. Mark and trim a new cutting edge 5/8 inch outside the new stitching line.

TO REDUCE THE PATTERN

1. At the point where you need to reduce your pattern piece, measure in from the stitching line and mark 1/4 of the total amount to be reduced on each side seam.

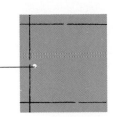

2. Draw a new stitching line, making a graduated curve from the point of reduction to the original stitching line.

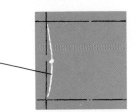

3. Mark and trim a new cutting edge 5/8 inch outside the new stitching line.

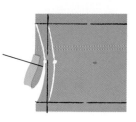

TO ENLARGE THE PATTERN

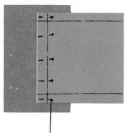

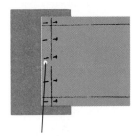

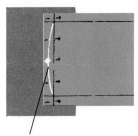

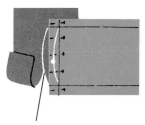

1. Lay your pattern piece on a strip of shelf paper cut to extend about 2 inches underneath the pattern and about 2 inches beyond the edge. Pin the pattern to the shelf paper.

2. At the point where you need to enlarge your pattern piece, measure out from the stitching line and mark 1/4 of the total amount to be enlarged on each seam. Measure onto the seam allowance or beyond it onto the shelf paper, if necessary.

3. Draw a new tapered stitching line from the point of enlargement into the original stitching line.

4. Mark and trim a new cutting edge 5/8 inch outside the new stitching line.

TRANSFERRING PATTERN MARKINGS

A

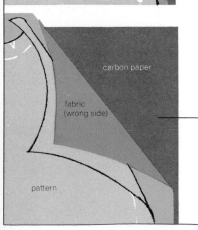

PREPARING TO MARK TWO LAYERS OF FABRIC

1A. After the pattern has been pinned to the fabric and the fabric pieces have been cut, remove just enough pins, from one piece at a time, so you can slip dressmaker's carbon paper between the layers of fabric and the pattern. Place one piece of carbon paper —carbon side up—under the bottom layer of fabric. Then place another piece of carbon paper—carbon side down—over the top layer of fabric. Pin the pattern back into position.

PREPARING TO MARK ONE LAYER OF FABRIC

1B. Place one piece of carbon paper—carbon side up—underneath the fabric.

B MARKING THE FABRIC

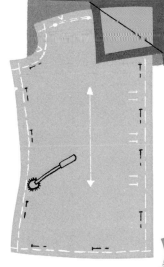

2. Run a tracing wheel along all stitching lines. Use a straightedge ruler as a guide for straight lines; trace curves freehand.

3. Trace the notches with a dull pencil.

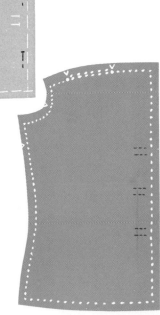

4. With the dull pencil, draw an X through the center of all circles and dots.

5. Remove the pattern from the fabric and baste along any markings that must show on both sides of the fabric—for example, the center front line and the placement lines for buttonholes, pockets and trimmings.

Variations on the plain seam

The plain seam *(top right)* serves for most tightly woven, light- or medium-weight fabrics like cotton or flannel. But many shortcut fabrics work best with a variation of the plain seam.

With felts, for example, a double seam can have unfinished outer edges *(left)*. On double-faced fabric a reversible seam like the one shown at bottom right gives you two finished garments—neither side looks like the wrong side. Knits can require both stretchable and stabilized seams—that is, seams that give and seams that keep the material from stretching. Very heavy fabrics, like those of upholstery weight, take a plain seam with a larger-than-usual seam allowance that must be ravel-proofed with tape edging or zigzag stitching.

All seam allowances should be trimmed, or "graded," to different widths when they are to be encased inside part of the finished garment, such as a collar. But the widths to which different weight fabrics are trimmed varies.

Wherever the fabric itself is appropriate, the seam variations that are recommended here can be incorporated into the sewing units shown in this section. Simply substitute the special seams and trimming instructions for the plain seams and average trimming widths described in these instructions.

THE PLAIN SEAM

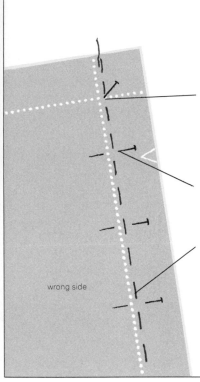

1. With the wrong sides of the fabric facing outward, pin together the pieces to be seamed, inserting the pins at right angles to the stitching line. Match and pin first where the seam-line markings intersect.

2. Match and pin next at the notch markings; add more pins at 1- to 2-inch intervals on a straight seam and at intervals as short as 1/4 inch on a curved seam.

3. Baste just outside the seam-line markings and remove the pins.

wrong side

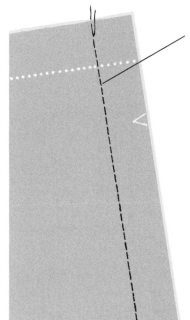

4. After trying on the garment for fit, machine stitch directly along the seam-line markings. Remove the bastings.

5. Press the seam open.

wrong side

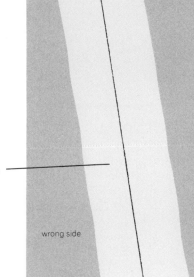

THE REVERSIBLE SEAM FOR DOUBLE-FACED FABRIC

A MAKING THE SEAM

1. Join the two pieces of fabric with a plain seam as illustrated in Steps 1-5 above, allowing a 3/4-inch seam allowance instead of the standard 5/8 inch.

wrong side

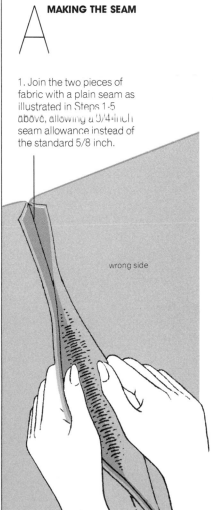

2. Separate the two layers that make up the seam allowance of the fabric along each side of the seam, snipping the bonding threads between the fabric layers with trimming scissors as you go.

B TRIMMING THE SEAM

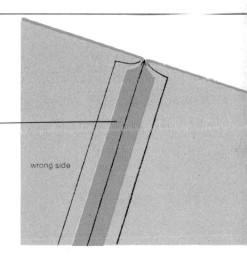

3. Spread open the four layers as a unit preparatory to trimming them as shown in the steps that follow.

wrong side

4. Leave one outer layer untrimmed.

5. Trim the second layer to 3/8 inch.

6. Trim the third layer slightly more than the second.

7. Trim the fourth layer slightly less than the third.

continued

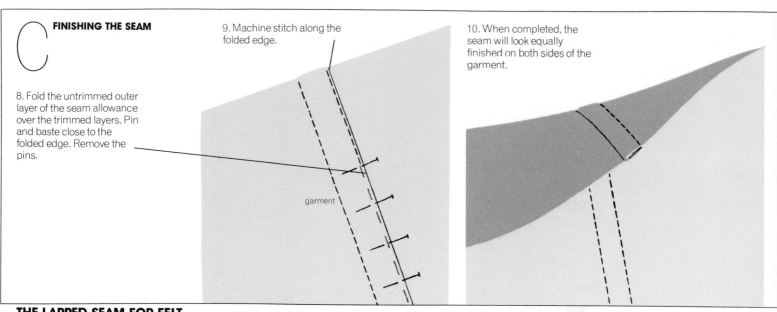

8. Fold the untrimmed outer layer of the seam allowance over the trimmed layers. Pin and baste close to the folded edge. Remove the pins.

9. Machine stitch along the folded edge.

10. When completed, the seam will look equally finished on both sides of the garment.

garment

THE LAPPED SEAM FOR FELT

A PREPARING THE SEAM

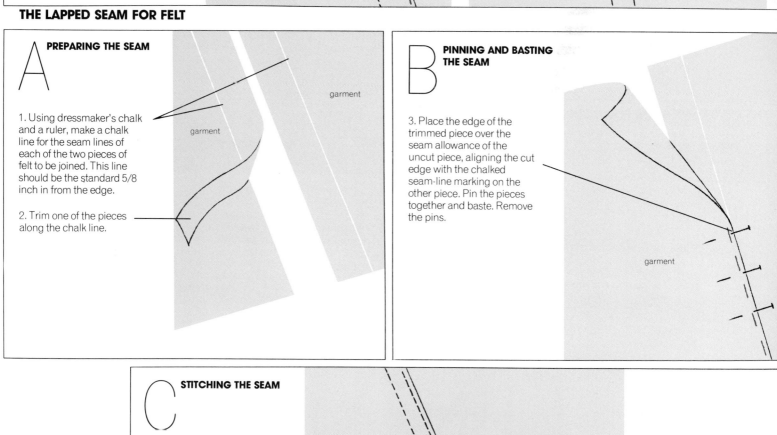

1. Using dressmaker's chalk and a ruler, make a chalk line for the seam lines of each of the two pieces of felt to be joined. This line should be the standard 5/8 inch in from the edge.

2. Trim one of the pieces along the chalk line.

garment

garment

B PINNING AND BASTING THE SEAM

3. Place the edge of the trimmed piece over the seam allowance of the uncut piece, aligning the cut edge with the chalked seam-line marking on the other piece. Pin the pieces together and baste. Remove the pins.

garment

C STITCHING THE SEAM

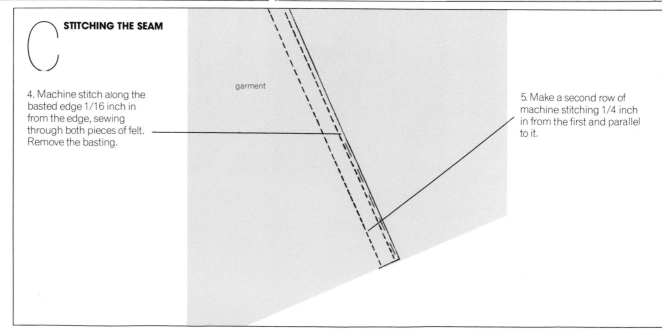

4. Machine stitch along the basted edge 1/16 inch in from the edge, sewing through both pieces of felt. Remove the basting.

garment

5. Make a second row of machine stitching 1/4 inch in from the first and parallel to it.

THE EXTRA-WIDE SEAM FOR HEAVY FABRICS

A | MAKING THE SEAM

1. Join the two pieces of fabric with a plain seam, as illustrated on page 63, leaving a 1-inch seam allowance instead of the standard 5/8 inch.

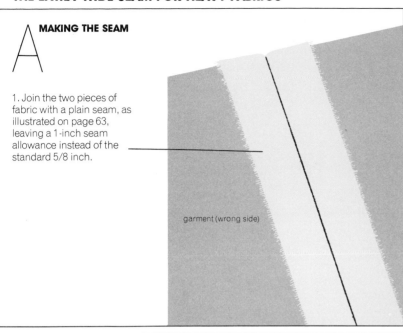

garment (wrong side)

B | ATTACHING TAPE TO THE SEAM

2. To give the wider seam allowance support, tape the seam. Unfold a strip of 1/2-inch-wide bias tape and pin one edge of the tape to the raw outside edge of one side of the seam allowance. Pin and baste close to the edge. Remove the pins.

3. Machine stitch the tape to the seam allowance along the outer fold line of the tape. Remove the basting.

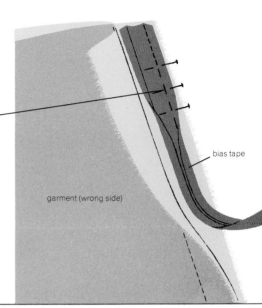

bias tape

garment (wrong side)

C | BINDING THE EDGE

4. Keeping the free edge of the tape unfolded, wrap the tape around the raw edge of the seam allowance.

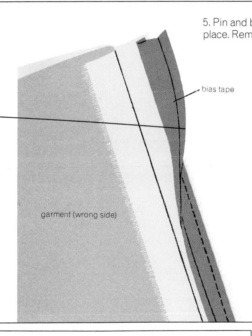

bias tape

garment (wrong side)

5. Pin and baste the tape in place. Remove the pins.

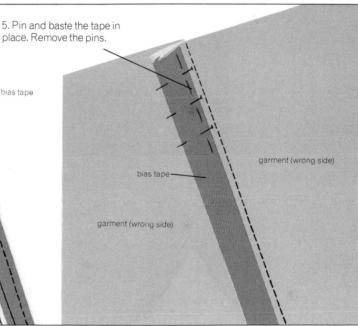

bias tape

garment (wrong side)

garment (wrong side)

D | FINISHING THE BINDING

6. Let the seam allowance lie open, and make a row of machine stitching along the fold of the tape, catching the tape lying underneath the seam allowance. Remove the bastings.

7. Bind the other half of the seam allowance in the same way.

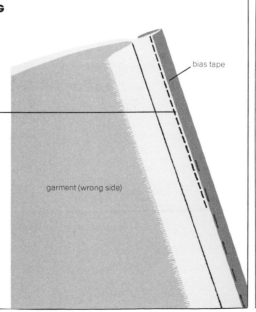

bias tape

garment (wrong side)

E | ALTERNATE SEAM FINISH FOR HEAVY FABRICS

7A. Finish both raw edges of the seam allowance with a zigzag stitch instead of binding them off with tape.

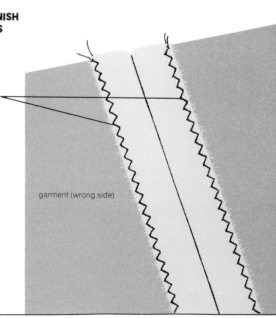

garment (wrong side)

THE STRETCH SEAM FOR KNITS

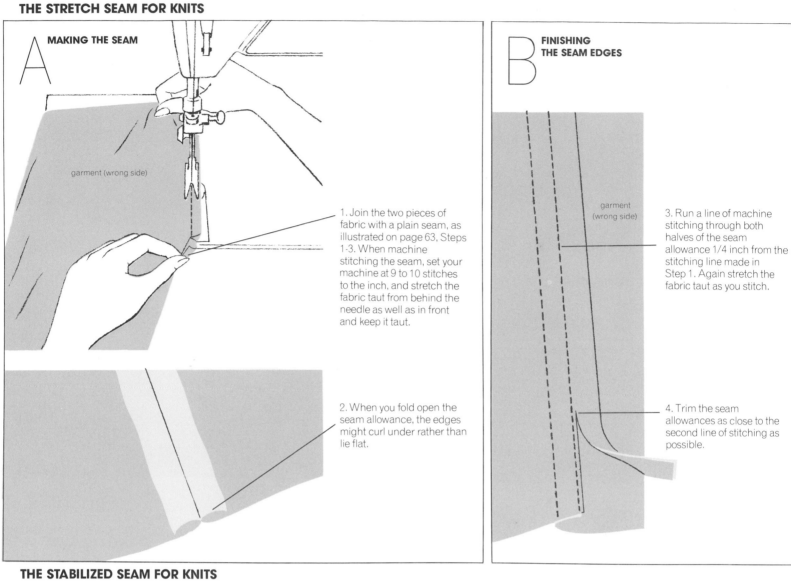

A MAKING THE SEAM

1. Join the two pieces of fabric with a plain seam, as illustrated on page 63, Steps 1-3. When machine stitching the seam, set your machine at 9 to 10 stitches to the inch, and stretch the fabric taut from behind the needle as well as in front and keep it taut.

garment (wrong side)

2. When you fold open the seam allowance, the edges might curl under rather than lie flat.

B FINISHING THE SEAM EDGES

garment (wrong side)

3. Run a line of machine stitching through both halves of the seam allowance 1/4 inch from the stitching line made in Step 1. Again stretch the fabric taut as you stitch.

4. Trim the seam allowances as close to the second line of stitching as possible.

THE STABILIZED SEAM FOR KNITS

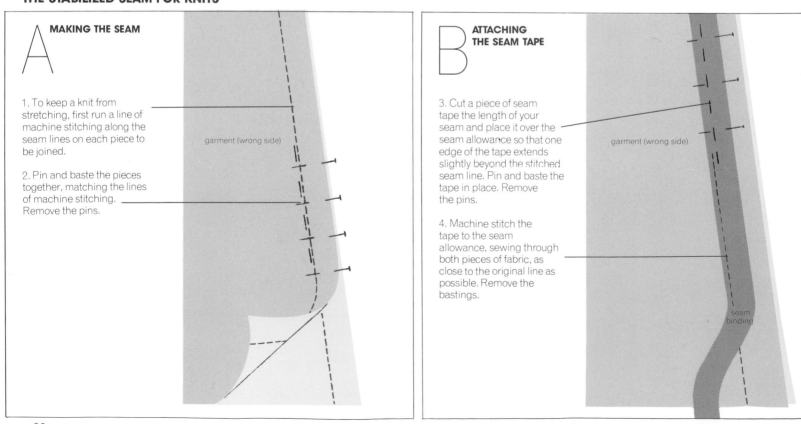

A MAKING THE SEAM

1. To keep a knit from stretching, first run a line of machine stitching along the seam lines on each piece to be joined.

2. Pin and baste the pieces together, matching the lines of machine stitching. Remove the pins.

garment (wrong side)

B ATTACHING THE SEAM TAPE

3. Cut a piece of seam tape the length of your seam and place it over the seam allowance so that one edge of the tape extends slightly beyond the stitched seam line. Pin and baste the tape in place. Remove the pins.

4. Machine stitch the tape to the seam allowance, sewing through both pieces of fabric, as close to the original line as possible. Remove the bastings.

garment (wrong side)

seam binding

TRIMMING SEAMS THAT INCLUDE FACINGS

LIGHTWEIGHT FABRIC

1A. If you include a facing in your seam, you should trim both the garment fabric and the facing to avoid bulging. When using lightweight fabric such as jersey, trim the seam allowance of the garment to 1/4 inch and the seam allowance of the facing to 1/8 inch.

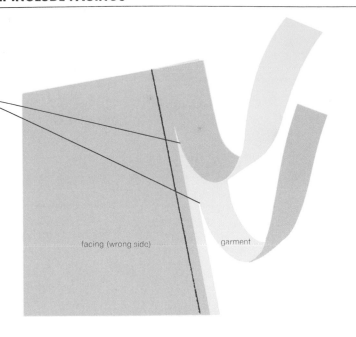

facing (wrong side)   garment

MEDIUM-WEIGHT FABRIC

1B. When using medium-weight fabric such as Lycra, stretch terry, spandex blends, polyester crepe, knits and felt, trim the seam allowance of the garment fabric to 3/8 inch and the seam allowance of the facing to 3/16 inch.

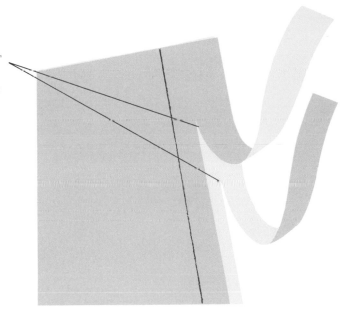

HEAVYWEIGHT FABRIC

1C. When using heavyweight fabrics such as upholstery fabric, trim the seam allowance of the garment fabric to 1/2 inch and the seam allowance of the facing to 3/8 inch.

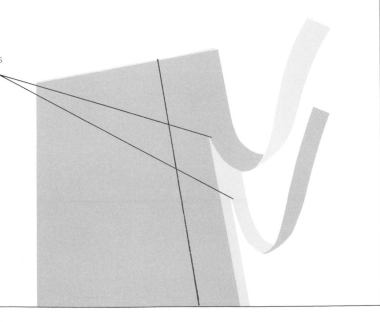

Necklines that have no collars

The necklines in this section save valuable time because they have no collars. With only one exception—the unfaced bateau neckline—all are variations on the basic technique that is used for the square neckline illustrated at right: they finish off the neck edge by reinforcing it with a hidden, fitted facing.

The elegance of simple necklines like these derives from the smooth perfection with which the facing is attached. Certain procedures are essential to ensure that the facing lies hidden, without puckering or buckling. Stay stitching along the bodice neckline prevents the fabric from stretching out of shape as the work progresses. Meticulous control of the machine when stitching seam corners and angles is necessary to create a crisply pointed "V" or to give a square neckline the required symmetry. Clipping into seam allowances is equally important: it releases the fabric tension that will otherwise produce unsightly wrinkles. Understitching the facing to the seam allowances restrains the facing and keeps it from slipping into view on the finished garment.

THE FACED SQUARE NECKLINE

A PREPARING THE BODICE

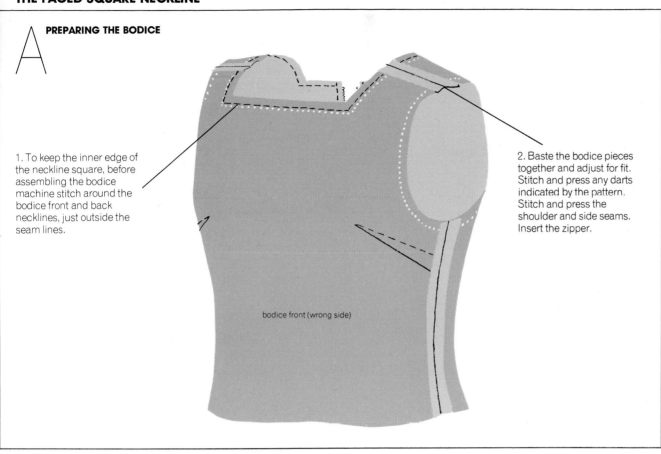

1. To keep the inner edge of the neckline square, before assembling the bodice machine stitch around the bodice front and back necklines, just outside the seam lines.

2. Baste the bodice pieces together and adjust for fit. Stitch and press any darts indicated by the pattern. Stitch and press the shoulder and side seams. Insert the zipper.

bodice front (wrong side)

B PREPARING THE FACING

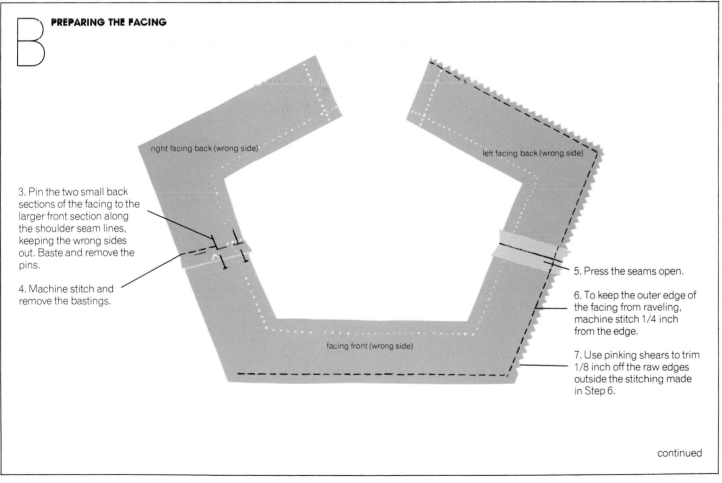

right facing back (wrong side)

left facing back (wrong side)

3. Pin the two small back sections of the facing to the larger front section along the shoulder seam lines, keeping the wrong sides out. Baste and remove the pins.

4. Machine stitch and remove the bastings.

5. Press the seams open.

6. To keep the outer edge of the facing from raveling, machine stitch 1/4 inch from the edge.

facing front (wrong side)

7. Use pinking shears to trim 1/8 inch off the raw edges outside the stitching made in Step 6.

continued

C ATTACHING THE FACING TO THE BODICE

8. Turn the bodice right side out.

9. Place the facing wrong side up over the bodice neckline, matching it to the bodice first at the shoulder seams and then at the corners.

10. Pin the facing to the bodice at 1-inch intervals around the neckline. Baste and remove the pins.

11. Machine stitch the facing to the bodice along the seam line. Stop about 1 inch from each corner and reset the machine to 15 stitches to the inch. Continue stitching to the corner. To make the corners square, stop the machine where the direction of the seam line changes. Raise the presser foot; pivot the fabric. Lower the presser foot; stitch for 1 inch. Stop, reset the machine to 12 stitches to the inch and continue to stitch. Remove the bastings.

12. To ensure a right angle at each corner, clip diagonally into the neckline seam allowances at each corner, cutting up to but not into the stitching.

13. Trim the seam allowance of the facing to 1/8 inch. Trim the seam allowance of the bodice to 1/4 inch.

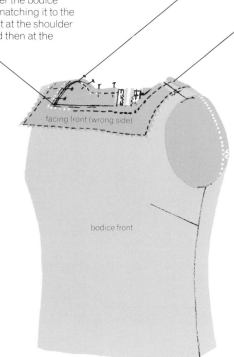

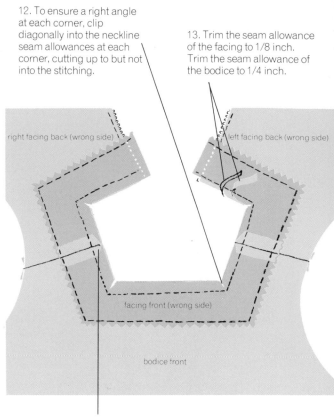

14. To reduce the bulk at the double seams, trim the facing shoulder seam allowances diagonally, above the machine stitching.

15. Repeat Step 14 on the garment shoulder seam allowances.

D FINISHING THE FACING

16. Turn the bodice wrong side out and pull the facing up above the neckline.

17. Press the neckline seam allowances toward the facing.

18. Turn the bodice right side out, keeping the facing pulled up above the neckline.

19. To prevent the facing from rolling out and showing on the finished garment, run a line of machine stitching—called understitching—around the facing, and through the seam allowances beneath, as close to the neckline seam as possible.

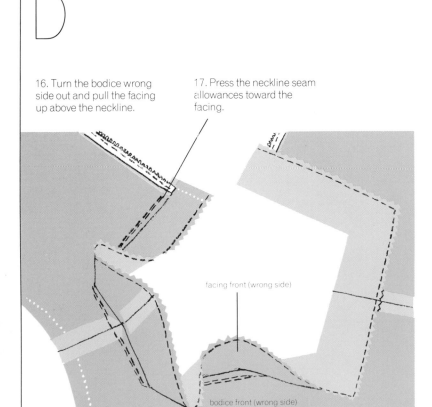

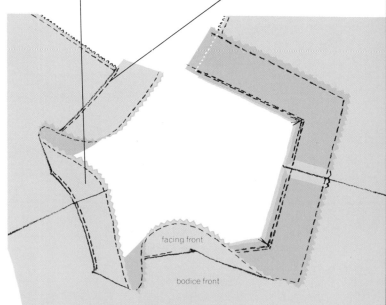

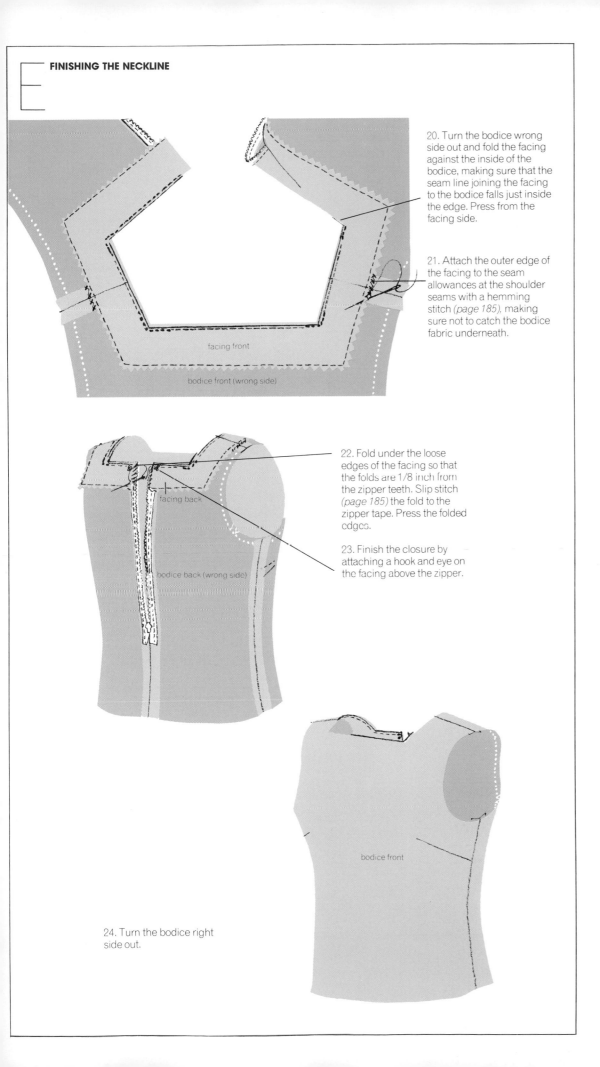

20. Turn the bodice wrong side out and fold the facing against the inside of the bodice, making sure that the seam line joining the facing to the bodice falls just inside the edge. Press from the facing side.

21. Attach the outer edge of the facing to the seam allowances at the shoulder seams with a hemming stitch *(page 185)*, making sure not to catch the bodice fabric underneath.

facing front

bodice front (wrong side)

22. Fold under the loose edges of the facing so that the folds are 1/8 inch from the zipper teeth. Slip stitch *(page 185)* the fold to the zipper tape. Press the folded edges.

23. Finish the closure by attaching a hook and eye on the facing above the zipper.

facing back

bodice back (wrong side)

bodice front

24. Turn the bodice right side out.

THE FACED CLOSED-FRONT V-NECKLINE

A — PREPARING THE BODICE

1. To hold the neckline of the bodice in a V-shape, before assembling the bodice machine stitch around the bodice front and back necklines just outside the seam lines.

2. Baste the bodice pieces together and adjust for fit. Stitch and press any darts indicated by the pattern. Stitch and press the shoulder and side seams. Insert the zipper.

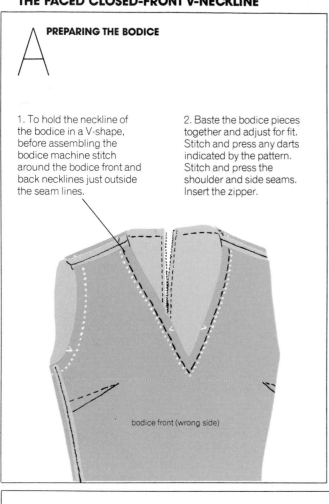

bodice front (wrong side)

B — PREPARING THE FACING

3. Pin the two small back sections of the facing to the larger front section along the shoulder seam lines, with the wrong sides out. Baste and remove the pins.

4. Machine stitch and remove the bastings.

5. Press the seams open.

6. To keep the outer edge of the facing from raveling, machine stitch it 1/4 inch from the edge.

7. Use pinking shears to trim 1/8 inch off the raw edges outside the stitching made in Step 6.

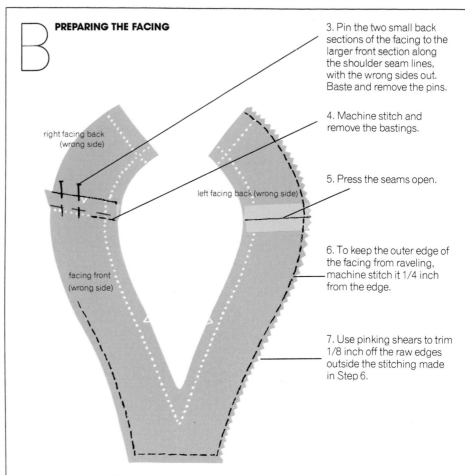

right facing back (wrong side)

left facing back (wrong side)

facing front (wrong side)

C — ATTACHING THE FACING TO THE BODICE

8. Turn the bodice right side out.

9. Place the facing wrong side up over the bodice neckline, matching it to the bodice first at the point of the V and then at the shoulder seams and notches.

10. Pin the facing to the bodice at 1-inch intervals around the neckline. Baste and remove the pins.

11. Machine stitch the facing to the bodice along the seam line, stitching the point of the V following the instructions on page 70, Box C, Step 11, with this exception: instead of pivoting at the corner as for the square, make one or two stitches across the point of the V; then continue in the new direction. Remove the basting.

12. To ensure a sharp V on the finished garment, clip straight into the neckline seam allowances at the point of the V, cutting up to but not into the stitching.

13. Trim the seam allowance of the facing to 1/8 inch. Trim the seam allowance of the bodice to 1/4 inch.

14. Clip straight into the seam allowances around the neckline curve at 1/2-inch intervals, cutting up to but not into the stitching.

15. To reduce the bulk at the double seams, trim the shoulder seam allowances of the facing diagonally, above the machine stitching.

16. Repeat Step 15 on the bodice shoulder seam allowances.

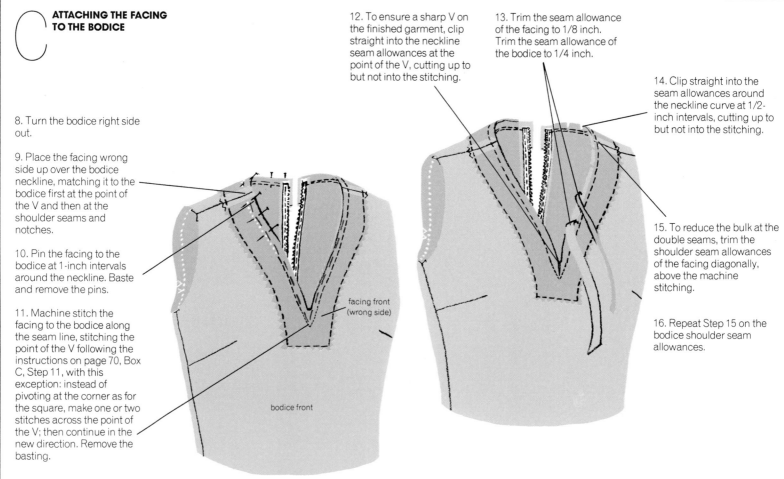

facing front (wrong side)

bodice front

FINISHING THE FACING

17. Turn the bodice wrong side out and pull the facing up above the neckline.

18. Press the neckline seam allowances toward the facing.

19. Turn the bodice right side out, keeping the facing pulled up above the neckline.

20. To prevent the facing from rolling out and showing on the finished garment, run a line of machine stitching—called understitching—around the facing, and through the seam allowances beneath, as close to the neckline seam as possible.

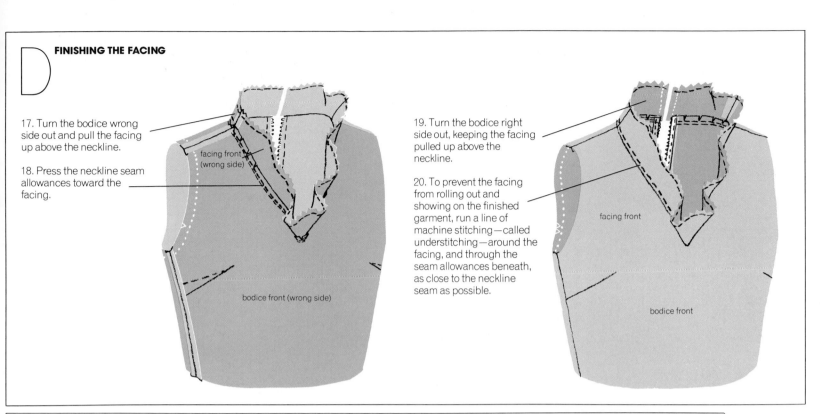

facing front (wrong side)

bodice front (wrong side)

facing front

bodice front

E

FINISHING THE NECKLINE

21. Turn the bodice wrong side out and fold the facing against the inside of the bodice, making sure that the seam line joining the facing to the bodice falls just inside the edge. Press from the facing side.

22. Attach the outer edge of the facing to the seam allowances at the shoulder seams with a hemming stitch (page 185), making sure not to catch the bodice fabric underneath.

23. Fold under the loose edges of the facing so that the folds are 1/8 inch from the zipper teeth. Slip stitch (page 185) the folds to the zipper tape. Press the folded edges.

24. Finish the closure by attaching a hook and eye on the facing above the zipper.

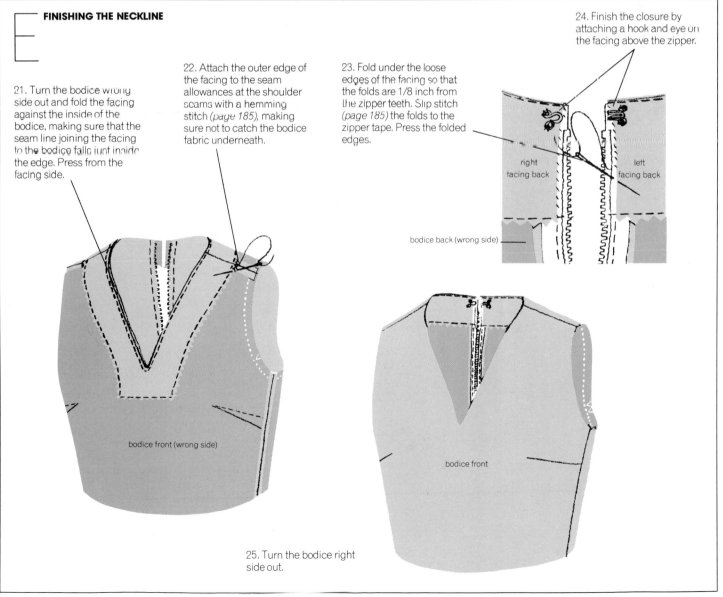

right facing back

left facing back

bodice back (wrong side)

bodice front (wrong side)

bodice front

25. Turn the bodice right side out.

THE FACED OPEN-FRONT V-NECKLINE

A. PREPARING THE BODICE

1. To hold the neckline of the bodice in a V-shape, before assembling the bodice machine stitch around the bodice front and back necklines just outside the seam lines.

2. Baste the bodice pieces together and adjust for fit. Stitch and press any darts indicated by the pattern. Stitch and press the shoulder and side seams.

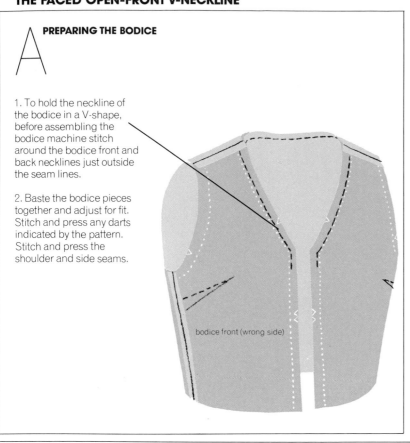

bodice front (wrong side)

B. PREPARING THE FACING

3. Pin the small back section of the facing to the larger front sections along the shoulder seam lines, keeping the wrong sides out. Baste and remove the pins.

4. Machine stitch and remove the bastings.

5. Press the seams open.

6. To keep the outer edge of the facing from raveling, machine stitch it 1/4 inch from the edge.

7. Use pinking shears to trim 1/8 inch off the raw edges outside the stitching made in Step 6.

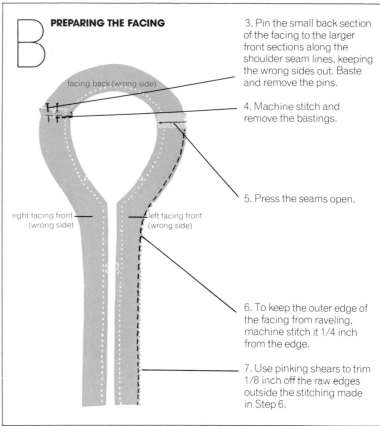

facing back (wrong side)

right facing front (wrong side)

left facing front (wrong side)

C. ATTACHING THE FACING TO THE BODICE

8. Turn the bodice right side out.

9. Place the facing wrong side up over the bodice neckline, matching it to the bodice first at the shoulder seams and then at the notches.

10. Pin the facing to the bodice at 1-inch intervals around the neckline and down the bodice front. Baste and remove the pins.

11. Machine stitch the facing to the bodice along the seam line. Remove the basting.

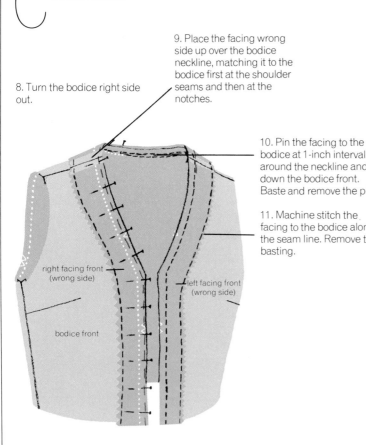

right facing front (wrong side)

left facing front (wrong side)

bodice front

12. Trim the seam allowance of the facing to 1/8 inch. Trim the seam allowance of the bodice to 1/4 inch.

13. Clip straight into the seam allowances around the neckline curve at 1/2-inch intervals, cutting up to but not into the stitching.

14. To reduce the bulk at the double seams, trim the shoulder seam allowances of the facing diagonally above the machine stitching.

15. Repeat Step 14 on the bodice shoulder seam allowances.

FINISHING THE FACING

16. Turn the bodice wrong side out and pull the facing up above the neckline and away from the bodice front opening.

17. Press the seam allowances around the neckline and bodice front toward the facing.

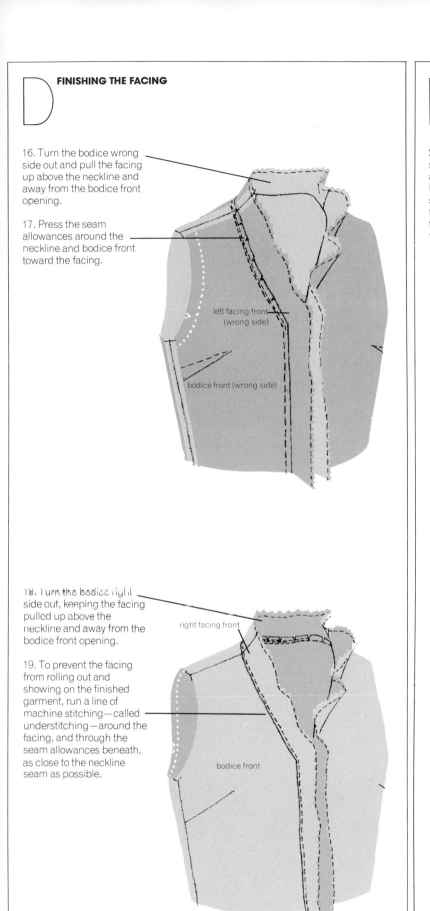

left facing front (wrong side)

bodice front (wrong side)

18. Turn the bodice right side out, keeping the facing pulled up above the neckline and away from the bodice front opening.

19. To prevent the facing from rolling out and showing on the finished garment, run a line of machine stitching—called understitching—around the facing, and through the seam allowances beneath, as close to the neckline seam as possible.

right facing front

bodice front

FINISHING THE NECKLINE

20. Turn the bodice wrong side out and fold the facing against the inside of the bodice, making sure that the seam line joining the facing to the bodice falls just inside the edge. Press from the facing side.

21. Attach the outer edge of the facing to the seam allowances at the shoulder seams with a hemming stitch (page 185), making sure not to catch the bodice fabric underneath.

right facing front

bodice front (wrong side)

22. Finish the bodice front closure with buttons or zipper as your pattern directs.

bodice front

23. Turn the bodice right side out.

THE FACED BATEAU NECKLINE

A PREPARING THE BODICE

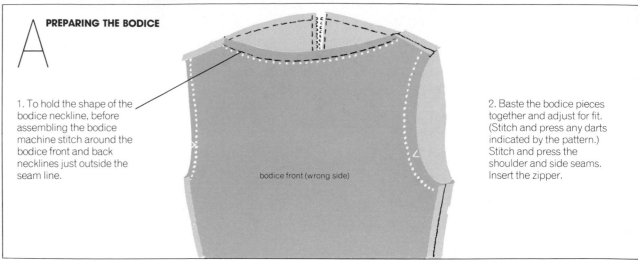

1. To hold the shape of the bodice neckline, before assembling the bodice machine stitch around the bodice front and back necklines just outside the seam line.

2. Baste the bodice pieces together and adjust for fit. (Stitch and press any darts indicated by the pattern.) Stitch and press the shoulder and side seams. Insert the zipper.

bodice front (wrong side)

B PREPARING THE FACING

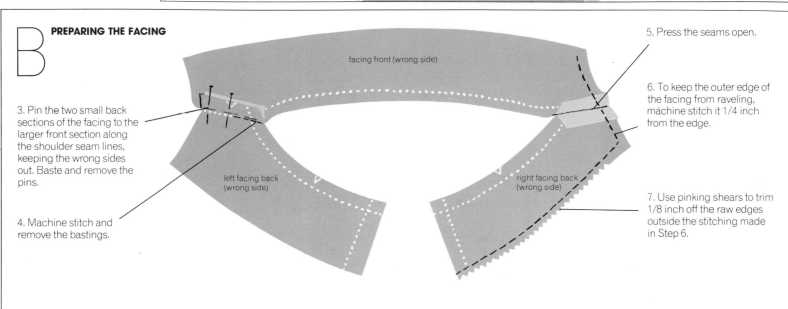

facing front (wrong side)

3. Pin the two small back sections of the facing to the larger front section along the shoulder seam lines, keeping the wrong sides out. Baste and remove the pins.

4. Machine stitch and remove the bastings.

left facing back (wrong side)

right facing back (wrong side)

5. Press the seams open.

6. To keep the outer edge of the facing from raveling, machine stitch it 1/4 inch from the edge.

7. Use pinking shears to trim 1/8 inch off the raw edges outside the stitching made in Step 6.

C ATTACHING THE FACING TO THE BODICE

8. Turn the bodice right side out.

9. Place the facing wrong side up over the bodice neckline, matching it to the bodice first at the shoulder seams and then at the notches.

10. Pin the facing to the bodice at 1-inch intervals around the neckline. Baste and remove the pins.

11. Machine stitch the facing to the bodice along the seam line, stitching each angle at the shoulders following the instructions on page 70, Box C, Step 11, with this exception: instead of pivoting at the corner as for the square, make one or two stitches straight across the point of the angle before continuing in the new direction. Remove the bastings.

12. To reinforce the sharp angles at the shoulder seams, run a second line of machine stitching directly over the first line, extending 1 inch along the front and back neckline seams.

13. Trim the seam allowance of the facing to 1/8 inch. Trim the seam allowance of the bodice to 1/4 inch.

14. To ensure sharp angles at the shoulder seams, clip straight into the seam allowances at each shoulder seam, and at 1/2-inch intervals for 2 inches on either side of the shoulders. Cut up to but not into the stitching.

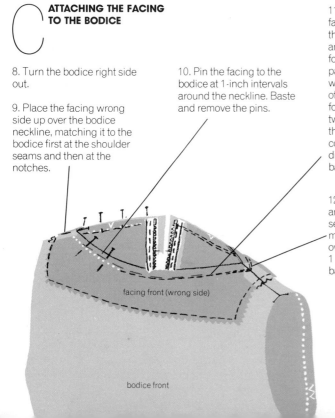

facing front (wrong side)

bodice front

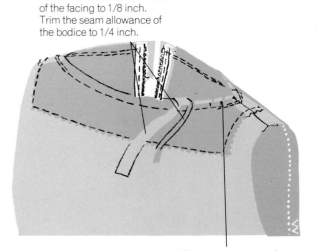

D | FINISHING THE FACING

15. Turn the bodice wrong side out and pull the facing up above the neckline.

16. Press the neckline seam allowances toward the facing.

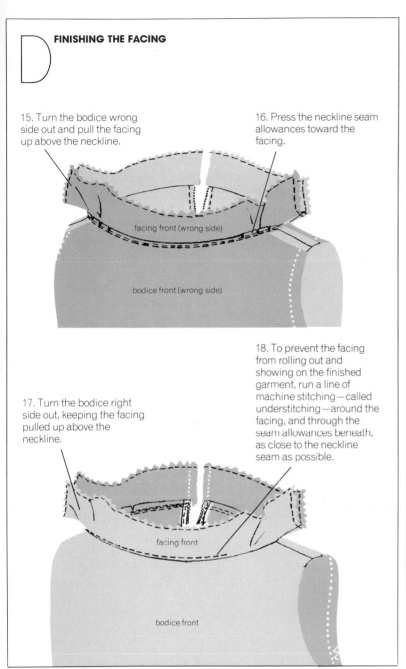

facing front (wrong side)

bodice front (wrong side)

17. Turn the bodice right side out, keeping the facing pulled up above the neckline.

18. To prevent the facing from rolling out and showing on the finished garment, run a line of machine stitching—called understitching—around the facing, and through the seam allowances beneath, as close to the neckline seam as possible.

facing front

bodice front

E | FINISHING THE NECKLINE

19. Turn the bodice wrong side out and fold the facing against the inside of the bodice, making sure that the seam line joining the facing to the bodice falls just inside the edge. Press from the facing side.

20. Attach the outer edge of the facing to the seam allowances at the shoulder seams with a hemming stitch (page 185), making sure not to catch the bodice fabric underneath.

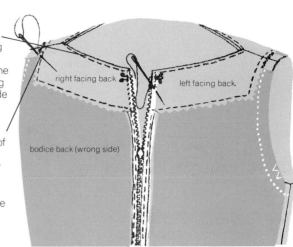

right facing back   left facing back

bodice back (wrong side)

21. Fold under the loose edges of the facing so that the folds are 1/8 inch from the zipper teeth. Slip stitch (page 185) the fold to the zipper tape. Press the folded edges.

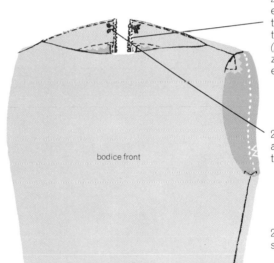

bodice front

22. Finish the closure by attaching a hook and eye on the facing above the zipper.

23. Turn the bodice right side out.

THE UNFACED BATEAU NECKLINE

A | PREPARING THE BODICE

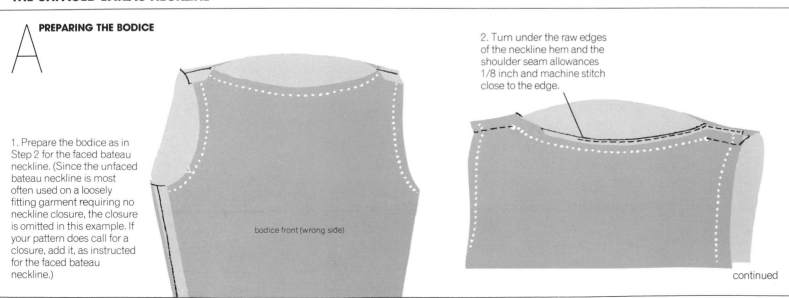

1. Prepare the bodice as in Step 2 for the faced bateau neckline. (Since the unfaced bateau neckline is most often used on a loosely fitting garment requiring no neckline closure, the closure is omitted in this example. If your pattern does call for a closure, add it, as instructed for the faced bateau neckline.)

bodice front (wrong side)

2. Turn under the raw edges of the neckline hem and the shoulder seam allowances 1/8 inch and machine stitch close to the edge.

continued

B FINISHING THE NECKLINE SEAM

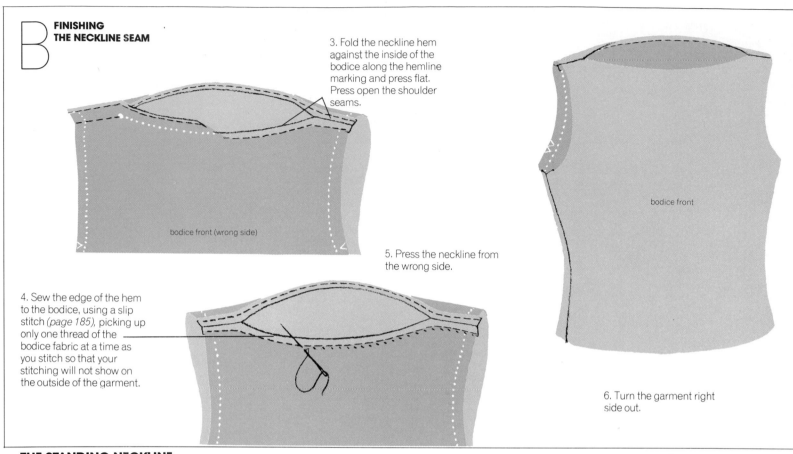

3. Fold the neckline hem against the inside of the bodice along the hemline marking and press flat. Press open the shoulder seams.

bodice front (wrong side)

4. Sew the edge of the hem to the bodice, using a slip stitch *(page 185)*, picking up only one thread of the bodice fabric at a time as you stitch so that your stitching will not show on the outside of the garment.

5. Press the neckline from the wrong side.

bodice front

6. Turn the garment right side out.

THE STANDING NECKLINE

A PREPARING THE BODICE

1. To hold the shape of the bodice neckline, before assembling the bodice machine stitch around the bodice front and back necklines just outside the seam line.

2. Baste the bodice pieces together and adjust for fit. Stitch and press any darts indicated by the pattern. Stitch and press the shoulder and side seams. Insert the zipper.

3. To free the neckline so it will stand up straight, clip into the shoulder seam allowances at the pattern markings—usually small circles—indicating the base of the neckline. Cut up to but not into the stitching.

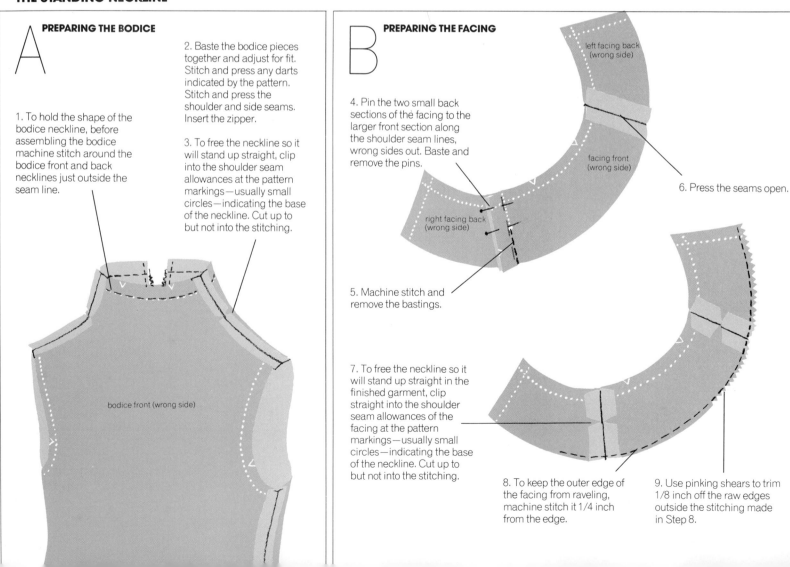

bodice front (wrong side)

B PREPARING THE FACING

left facing back (wrong side)

4. Pin the two small back sections of the facing to the larger front section along the shoulder seam lines, wrong sides out. Baste and remove the pins.

facing front (wrong side)

right facing back (wrong side)

6. Press the seams open.

5. Machine stitch and remove the bastings.

7. To free the neckline so it will stand up straight in the finished garment, clip straight into the shoulder seam allowances of the facing at the pattern markings—usually small circles—indicating the base of the neckline. Cut up to but not into the stitching.

8. To keep the outer edge of the facing from raveling, machine stitch it 1/4 inch from the edge.

9. Use pinking shears to trim 1/8 inch off the raw edges outside the stitching made in Step 8.

C ATTACHING THE FACING TO THE BODICE

10. Turn the bodice right side out.

11. Place the facing wrong side up over the bodice neckline, matching it to the bodice first at the shoulder seams and then at the notches.

12. Pin the facing to the bodice at 1-inch intervals around the neckline. Baste and remove the pins.

13. Machine stitch the facing to the bodice along the seam line and remove the bastings.

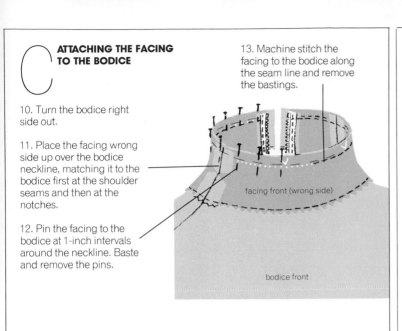

facing front (wrong side)

bodice front

14. Trim the seam allowance of the facing to 1/8 inch. Trim the seam allowance of the bodice to 1/4 inch.

15. Clip straight into the seam allowance at 1/2-inch intervals around the neckline, cutting up to but not into the stitching.

16. To reduce the bulk at the double seams, trim the shoulder seam allowances of the facing diagonally, above the machine stitching.

17. Repeat Step 16 on the bodice shoulder seam allowances.

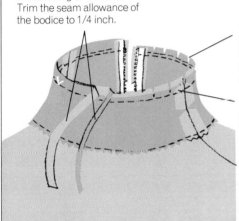

D FINISHING THE FACING

18. Turn the bodice wrong side out and pull the facing up above the neckline.

19. Press the neckline seam allowances toward the facing.

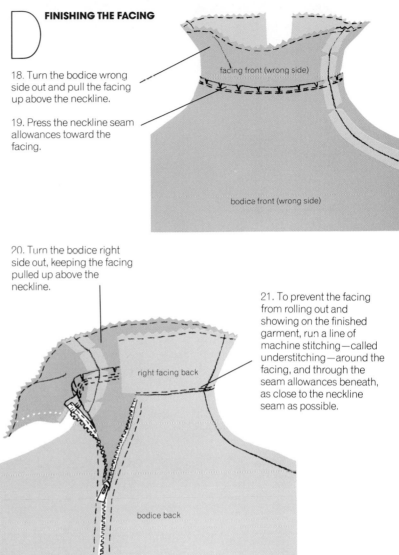

facing front (wrong side)

bodice front (wrong side)

20. Turn the bodice right side out, keeping the facing pulled up above the neckline.

21. To prevent the facing from rolling out and showing on the finished garment, run a line of machine stitching—called understitching—around the facing, and through the seam allowances beneath, as close to the neckline seam as possible.

right facing back

bodice back

E FINISHING THE NECKLINE

22. Turn the bodice wrong side out and fold the facing against the inside of the bodice, making sure that the seam line joining the facing to the bodice falls just inside the edge. Press from the facing side.

23. Attach the outer edges of the facing to the seam allowances at the shoulder seams with a hemming stitch (page 185), making sure not to catch the bodice fabric underneath.

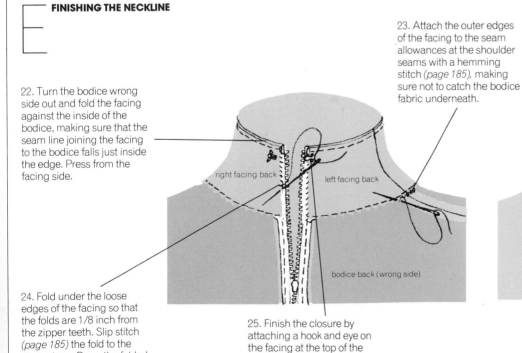

right facing back

left facing back

bodice back (wrong side)

24. Fold under the loose edges of the facing so that the folds are 1/8 inch from the zipper teeth. Slip stitch (page 185) the fold to the zipper tape. Press the folded edges.

25. Finish the closure by attaching a hook and eye on the facing at the top of the zipper.

bodice front

26. Turn the bodice right side out.

Accenting the shoulder gracefully

The attractive flow of a dress hangs, figuratively as well as literally, on its shoulder line, and an unusual shoulder can give even the simplest of dresses a special flair. The hook-and-eye shoulders and the one- and two-piece yoke shoulders shown on the following pages have enough design interest in themselves to bring elegance even to sleeveless dresses. Yet all three shoulder styles also qualify as shortcuts because they require none of the intricate fitting or dart adjustments that conventional shoulders demand.

To give the hook-and-eye shoulder a crisp outline, be sure to pull the stitching line of the shoulder points out to the edges with the tip of a needle before finishing the garment.

A shoulder yoke is, by definition, a garment part that crosses the shoulders and joins the front and back bodice. It can be made in one piece or two. And it can provide an extra accent by gathering—pulling some of the material together above the line where the yoke meets the front bodice. This detail creates a natural focus for the dress; it is particularly suited to lightweight fabrics that fall from the yoke and lie flat over the bustline. Stitching two rows of gathering threads, whether or not your pattern calls for them, ensures that the gathers will remain professionally perpendicular and even.

THE HOOK-AND-EYE SHOULDER

A PREPARING THE BODICE

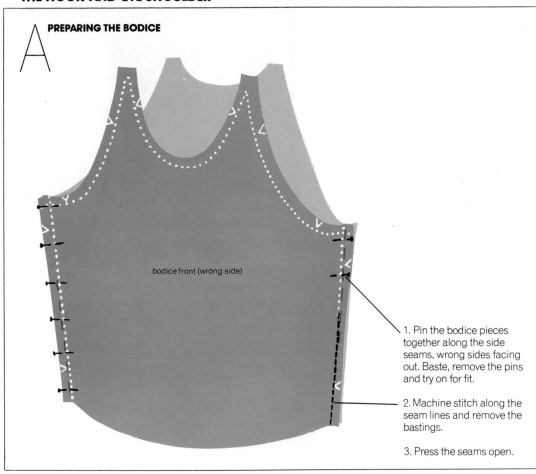

bodice front (wrong side)

1. Pin the bodice pieces together along the side seams, wrong sides facing out. Baste, remove the pins and try on for fit.

2. Machine stitch along the seam lines and remove the bastings.

3. Press the seams open.

B PREPARING THE FACING

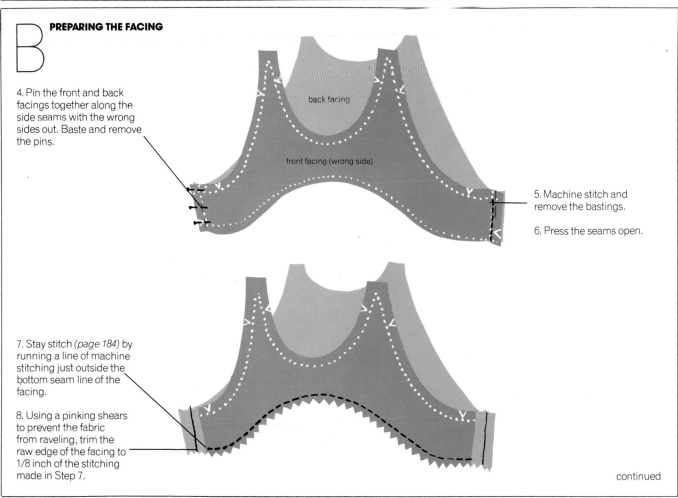

back facing

front facing (wrong side)

4. Pin the front and back facings together along the side seams with the wrong sides out. Baste and remove the pins.

5. Machine stitch and remove the bastings.

6. Press the seams open.

7. Stay stitch (page 184) by running a line of machine stitching just outside the bottom seam line of the facing.

8. Using a pinking shears to prevent the fabric from raveling, trim the raw edge of the facing to 1/8 inch of the stitching made in Step 7.

continued

C ATTACHING THE FACING TO THE BODICE

9. Turn the bodice right side out.

10. Pin the facing, wrong side out, to the bodice at 2-inch intervals all around the top edge of the garment, matching the pattern notches. Baste and remove the pins.

11. Machine stitch along the seam line.

12. As you approach each shoulder point, stop your machine 1 inch from the point and adjust the stitch size to 15 stitches to the inch.

13. Resume stitching until you reach the point. Then pivot the garment, make two or three stitches across the point and then continue to stitch down the other side for 1 inch.

14. Stop your machine and reset your stitch size to 12 stitches to the inch.

15. Continue machine stitching the facing to the bodice, following the procedures indicated in Steps 11-14.

16. Remove the basting and press the seams together.

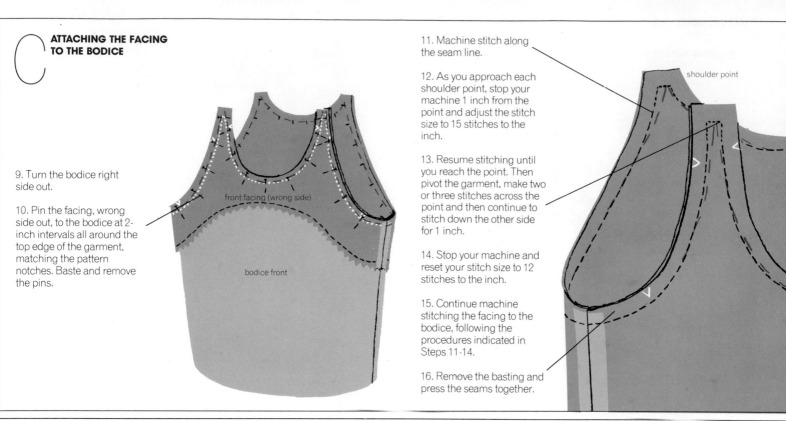

D FINISHING THE SEAMS

17. Trim the facing seam allowances around the armholes and neckline to 1/8 inch.

18. Trim the garment seam allowances around the armholes and neckline to 1/4 inch.

19. Trim straight across the four shoulder edges, cutting close to but not into the stitching.

20. Clip around the curved armholes and neckline at 1/2 inch intervals. Cut close to but not into the stitching.

21. Turn the facing inside the garment.

22. Use the tip of a needle to pull out the stitching line at each shoulder point.

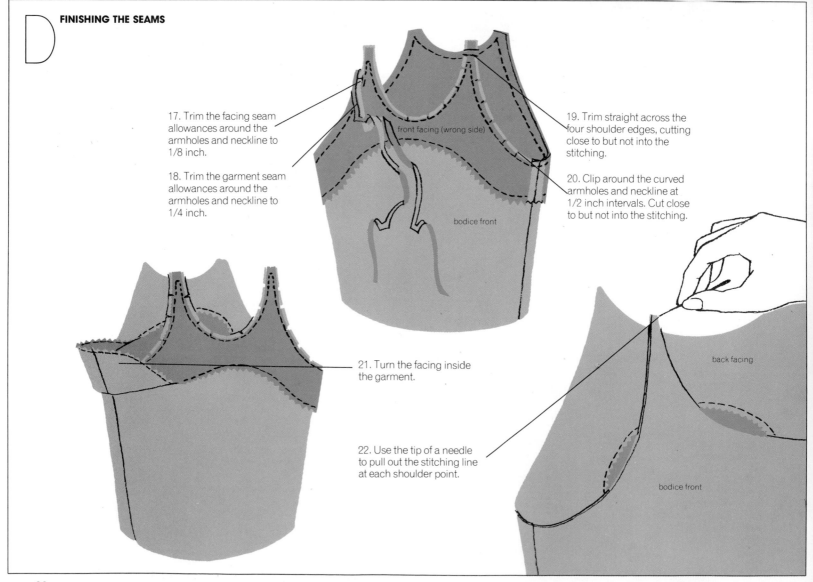

UNDERSTITCHING THE FACING

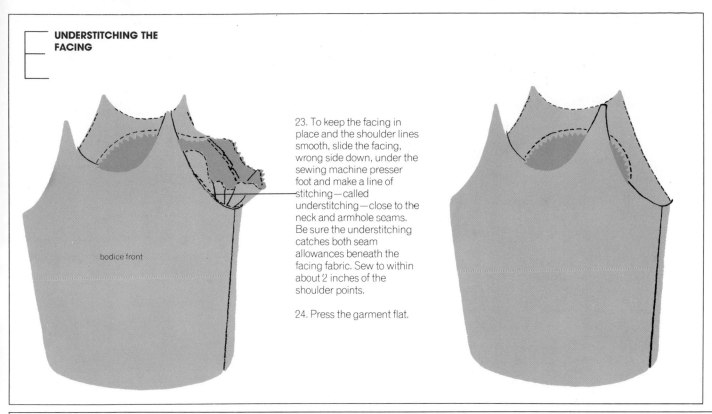

bodice front

23. To keep the facing in place and the shoulder lines smooth, slide the facing, wrong side down, under the sewing machine presser foot and make a line of stitching—called understitching—close to the neck and armhole seams. Be sure the understitching catches both seam allowances beneath the facing fabric. Sew to within about 2 inches of the shoulder points.

24. Press the garment flat.

F ATTACHING THE HOOKS AND EYES

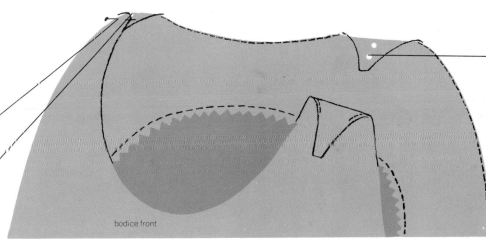

bodice front

25. Put the garment on.

26. Overlap each front shoulder point on each back shoulder point until they fit snugly. Pin them together.

27. To determine the placement of the eyes, use a dressmaker's marking pencil to mark the spot on the back bodice where the front shoulder points overlap the back shoulders. Remove the pins. Take off the garment.

28. Measure from the marks made in Step 27 a distance of 1/2 inch toward the back shoulder points and mark these points.

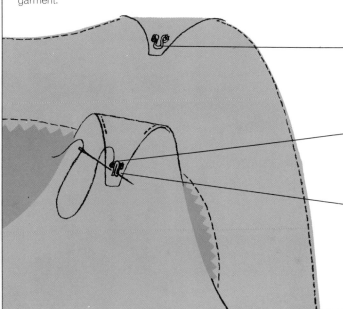

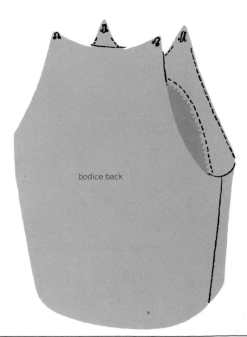

bodice back

29. Sew the round eyes on the right side—the side that is visible in the finished garment—at the marks made in Step 28, using a double strand of knotted thread. Stitch around each metal ring, catching only the facing fabric.

30. Sew the hooks to the undersides of the shoulder fronts 3/4 inch from the points. Sew around each metal ring as in Step 29.

31. Continue by sliding the needle under the hook and take a few stitches over the hook, under the bend. End with a fastening stitch.

32. Turn the bodice right side out.

THE ONE-PIECE YOKE ON A GATHERED BODICE

A — PREPARING THE BODICE

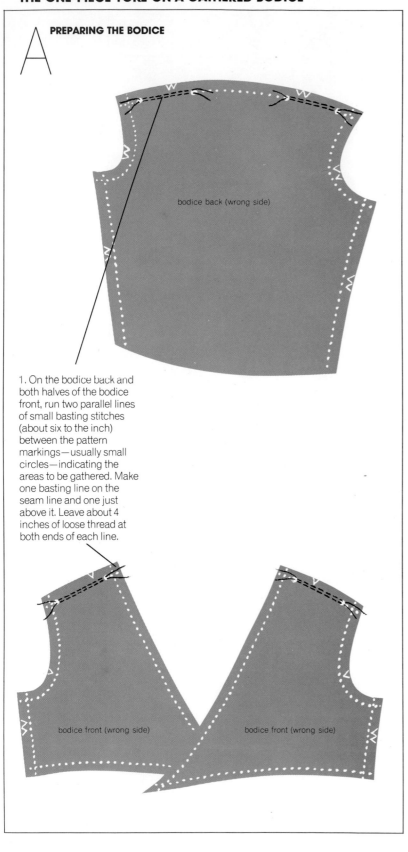

1. On the bodice back and both halves of the bodice front, run two parallel lines of small basting stitches (about six to the inch) between the pattern markings—usually small circles—indicating the areas to be gathered. Make one basting line on the seam line and one just above it. Leave about 4 inches of loose thread at both ends of each line.

B — ATTACHING THE BODICE BACK TO THE YOKE

2. Pull one end of each of the basted threads until the basted areas have been gathered enough to make the bodice back the same width as the yoke or shoulder section to which it is to be attached. (The space between the circles on the bodice back should now be equal to the space between the corresponding circles on the yoke.)

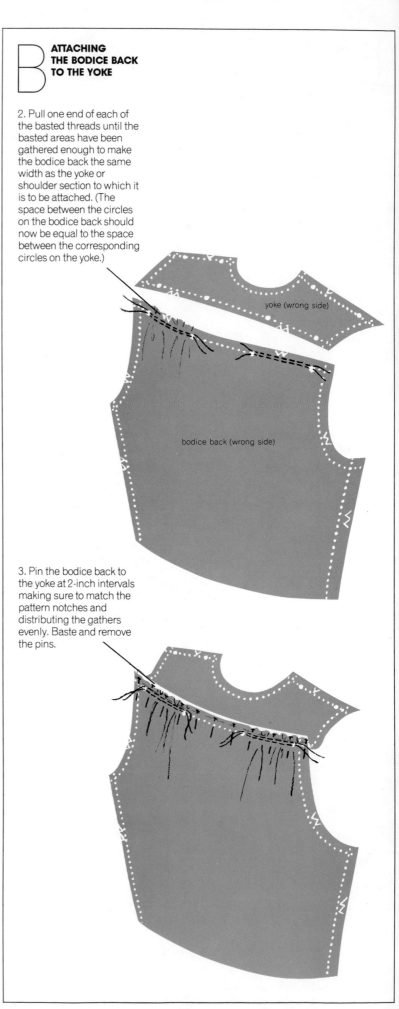

3. Pin the bodice back to the yoke at 2-inch intervals making sure to match the pattern notches and distributing the gathers evenly. Baste and remove the pins.

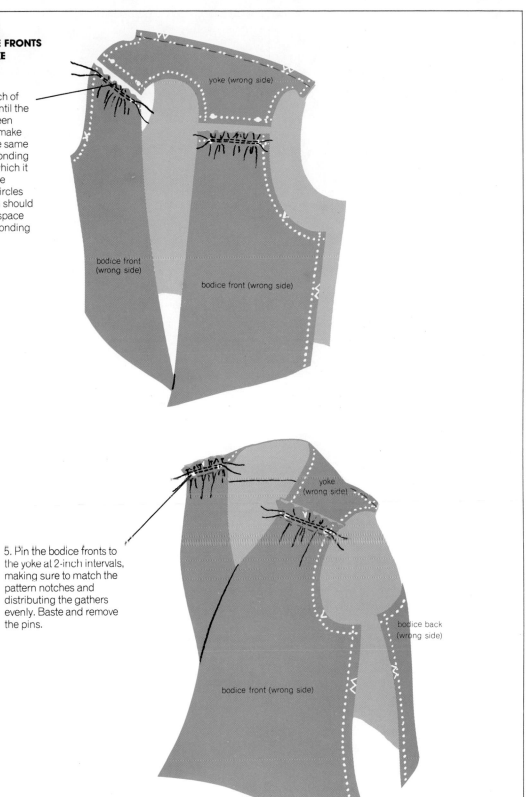

C ATTACHING THE BODICE FRONTS TO THE YOKE

4. Pull one end of each of the basted threads until the basted areas have been gathered enough to make each bodice front the same width as the corresponding edge of the yoke to which it is to be attached. (The space between the circles on each front section should now be equal to the space between the corresponding circles on the yoke.)

yoke (wrong side)

bodice front (wrong side)

bodice front (wrong side)

yoke (wrong side)

5. Pin the bodice fronts to the yoke at 2-inch intervals, making sure to match the pattern notches and distributing the gathers evenly. Baste and remove the pins.

bodice back (wrong side)

bodice front (wrong side)

continued

6. Machine stitch the yoke to the front and back bodice sections along the seam lines. Remove the bastings made in Steps 3 and 5.

7. Knot the loose ends of the basted gathering lines and cut off the excess threads. These bastings should remain in the finished garment.

8. Press the seams upward toward the yoke.

9. Pin the side seams together. Baste, remove the pins and try on for fit.

10. Machine stitch. Remove the bastings and press.

11. Attach the facing, following the instructions for the V-neckline, Box C, Steps 8-15, page 74.

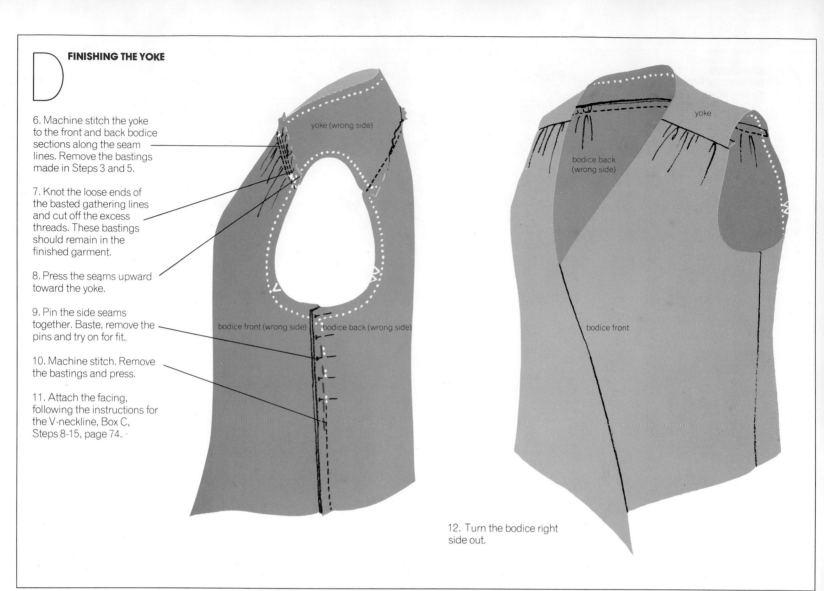

yoke (wrong side)

bodice front (wrong side)   bodice back (wrong side)

yoke

bodice back (wrong side)

bodice front

12. Turn the bodice right side out.

THE TWO-PIECE YOKE ON A GATHERED BODICE

A PREPARING THE BODICE

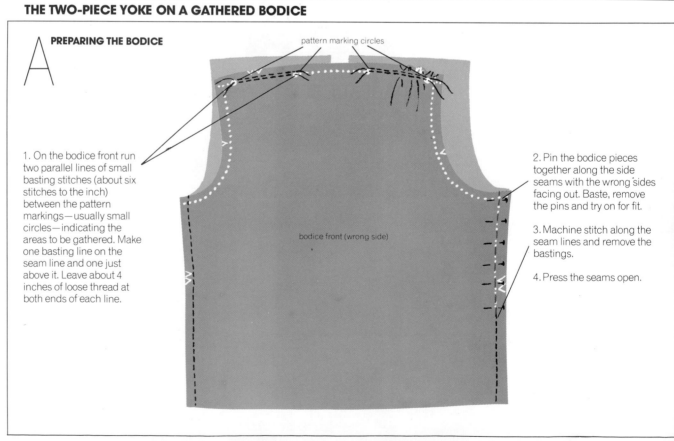

pattern marking circles

1. On the bodice front run two parallel lines of small basting stitches (about six stitches to the inch) between the pattern markings—usually small circles—indicating the areas to be gathered. Make one basting line on the seam line and one just above it. Leave about 4 inches of loose thread at both ends of each line.

bodice front (wrong side)

2. Pin the bodice pieces together along the side seams with the wrong sides facing out. Baste, remove the pins and try on for fit.

3. Machine stitch along the seam lines and remove the bastings.

4. Press the seams open.

ATTACHING THE BODICE FRONTS TO THE YOKE

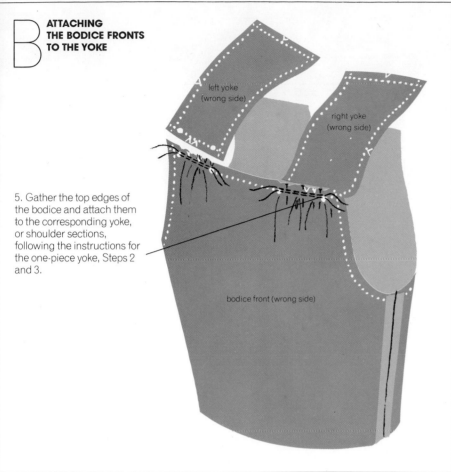

5. Gather the top edges of the bodice and attach them to the corresponding yoke, or shoulder sections, following the instructions for the one-piece yoke, Steps 2 and 3.

left yoke (wrong side)

right yoke (wrong side)

bodice front (wrong side)

ATTACHING THE BODICE BACK TO THE YOKE

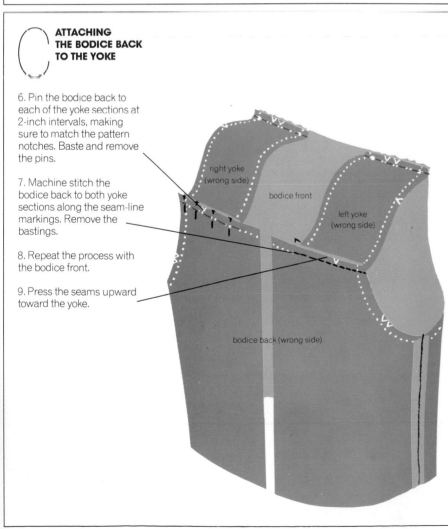

6. Pin the bodice back to each of the yoke sections at 2-inch intervals, making sure to match the pattern notches. Baste and remove the pins.

7. Machine stitch the bodice back to both yoke sections along the seam-line markings. Remove the bastings.

8. Repeat the process with the bodice front.

9. Press the seams upward toward the yoke.

right yoke (wrong side)

bodice front

left yoke (wrong side)

bodice back (wrong side)

FINISHING THE YOKE

10. Attach the facing, following the instructions for the square neckline, Box C, Steps 8-15, page 70. Turn the bodice right side out.

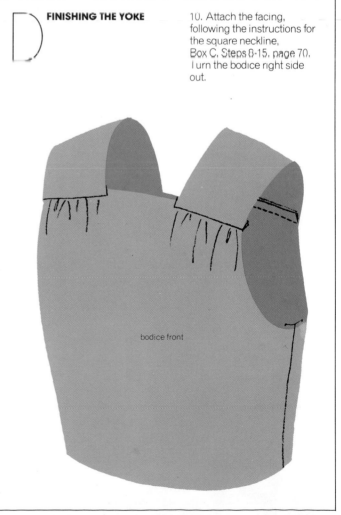

bodice front

Handsome but less difficult sleeves

One of the most complicated steps in dressmaking is the sleeve, but there are some attractive sleeves that require little effort. The cap, dolman and kimono sleeves are described on these pages. All of them can be attached before the side seams of the bodice are sewn, which means you can sew with the garment pieces flat instead of having to set the sleeve into a completed armhole. And two of them can be made from any fabric; for the cap sleeve, stiff fabrics are unsuitable.

The cap sleeve shown here is made from a separate piece of fabric, making it fuller than one that is an extension of the shoulder line. The dolman is even simpler—merely an extension of the bodice. It may be any length and narrows at the lower end. The wide sleeve of the T-shaped kimono may also be a bodice extension (in which case follow the directions for the dolman sleeve), or, as shown on pages 95-97, it may be a separate piece set at right angles to the bodice.

THE CAP SLEEVE

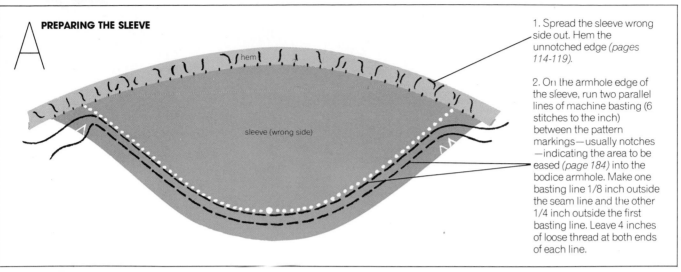

A PREPARING THE SLEEVE

hem

sleeve (wrong side)

1. Spread the sleeve wrong side out. Hem the unnotched edge *(pages 114-119)*.

2. On the armhole edge of the sleeve, run two parallel lines of machine basting (6 stitches to the inch) between the pattern markings—usually notches —indicating the area to be eased *(page 184)* into the bodice armhole. Make one basting line 1/8 inch outside the seam line and the other 1/4 inch outside the first basting line. Leave 4 inches of loose thread at both ends of each line.

B PINNING THE SLEEVE TO THE ARMHOLE

3. Stitch the shoulder seams to join the front and back of the bodice. Press the seams open. Make sure any darts are stitched and pressed. Spread the bodice out wrong side down.

4. With the wrong side facing out, pin the sleeve to the bodice at the shoulder seam with the pattern-indicated circle on the sleeve matched exactly to the shoulder seam.

5. To ease the sleeve so it will fit the bodice armhole, pull the two basting threads on the front half of the sleeve until the notch on the front half of the sleeve matches the corresponding notch on the bodice front. Pin the sleeve to the bodice at the notches. Adjust the easing evenly.

6. Pin the sleeve to the bodice front at 1/2-inch intervals along the seam line, starting at the pattern-indicated circle.

7. Repeat Steps 5 and 6 on the back half of the sleeve and the bodice back.

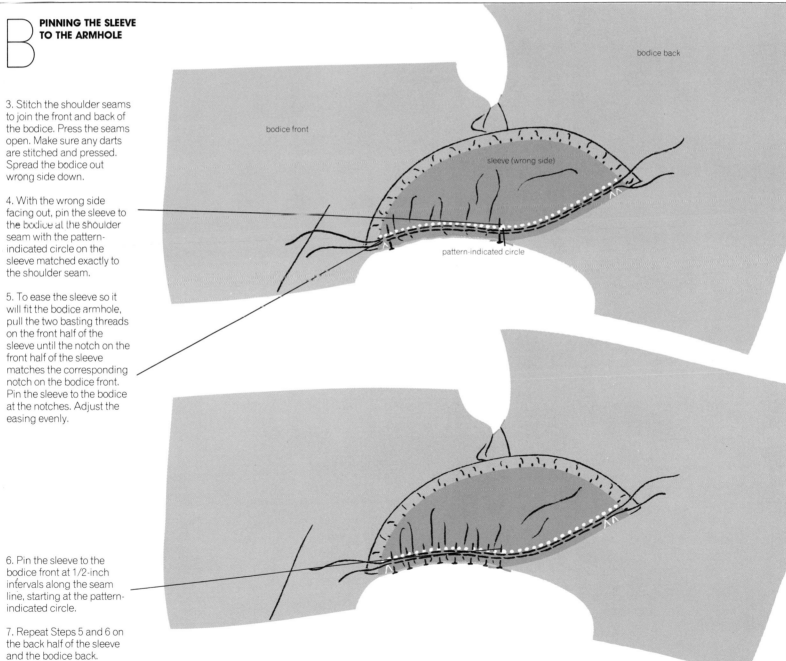

bodice back

bodice front

sleeve (wrong side)

pattern-indicated circle

continued

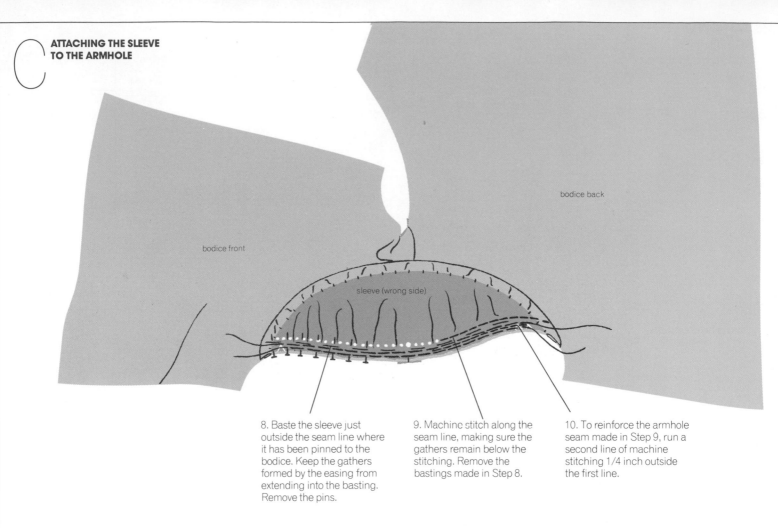

bodice back

bodice front

sleeve (wrong side)

8. Baste the sleeve just outside the seam line where it has been pinned to the bodice. Keep the gathers formed by the easing from extending into the basting. Remove the pins.

9. Machine stitch along the seam line, making sure the gathers remain below the stitching. Remove the bastings made in Step 8.

10. To reinforce the armhole seam made in Step 9, run a second line of machine stitching 1/4 inch outside the first line.

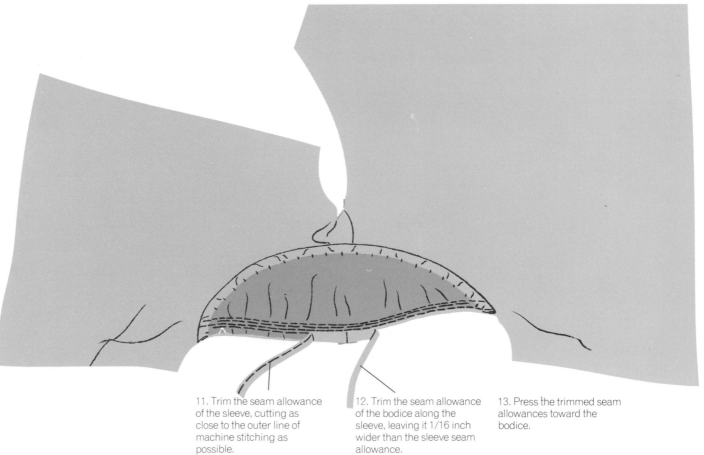

11. Trim the seam allowance of the sleeve, cutting as close to the outer line of machine stitching as possible.

12. Trim the seam allowance of the bodice along the sleeve, leaving it 1/16 inch wider than the sleeve seam allowance.

13. Press the trimmed seam allowances toward the bodice.

D | STITCHING THE SIDE SEAMS OF THE BODICE

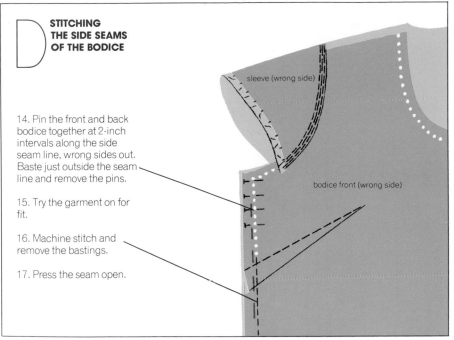

14. Pin the front and back bodice together at 2-inch intervals along the side seam line, wrong sides out. Baste just outside the seam line and remove the pins.

15. Try the garment on for fit.

16. Machine stitch and remove the bastings.

17. Press the seam open.

sleeve (wrong side)

bodice front (wrong side)

E | ATTACHING TAPE TO THE UNDERARM

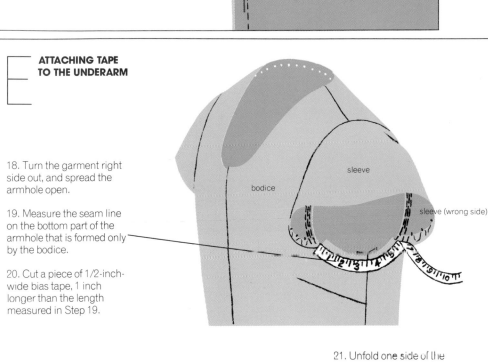

18. Turn the garment right side out, and spread the armhole open.

19. Measure the seam line on the bottom part of the armhole that is formed only by the bodice.

20. Cut a piece of 1/2-inch-wide bias tape, 1 inch longer than the length measured in Step 19.

sleeve

bodice

sleeve (wrong side)

21. Unfold one side of the bias tape and pin it to the underarm curve, matching the fold line of the tape to the seam line and extending the tape 1/2 inch onto the lower edge of the sleeve hem at both ends.

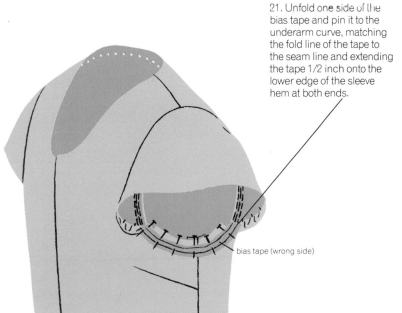

bias tape (wrong side)

22. Baste the bias tape to the underarm just above the fold line of the tape. Remove the pins.

23. Machine stitch along the fold line of the tape and remove the basting.

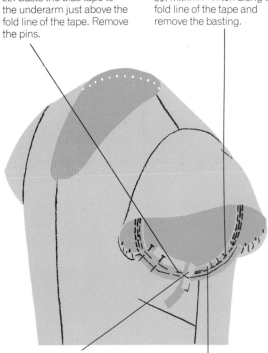

24. Trim the bodice underarm seam allowance to within 1/16 inch of the tape.

25. To keep the underarm seam allowance flat, clip straight into the tape and the bodice underarm seam allowance around the underarm at 1/2-inch intervals, cutting up to but not into the stitching.

continued

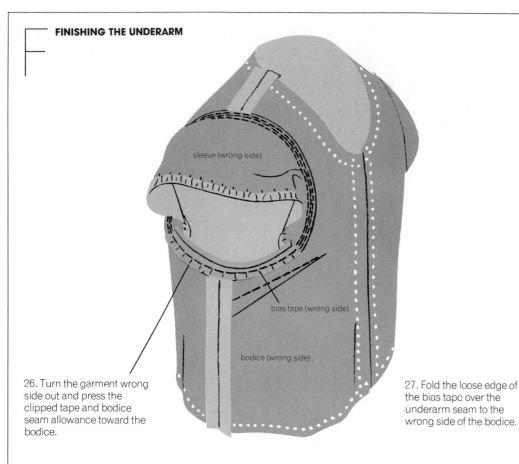

sleeve (wrong side)

bias tape (wrong side)

bodice (wrong side)

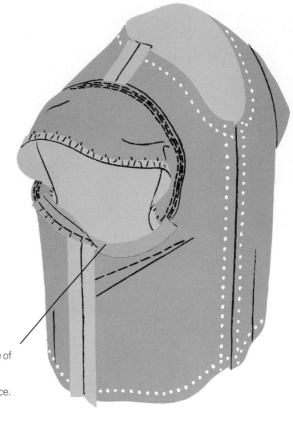

26. Turn the garment wrong side out and press the clipped tape and bodice seam allowance toward the bodice.

27. Fold the loose edge of the bias tape over the underarm seam to the wrong side of the bodice.

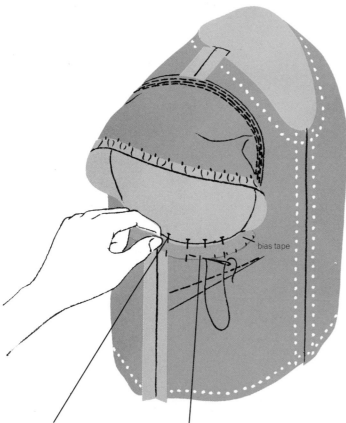

bias tape

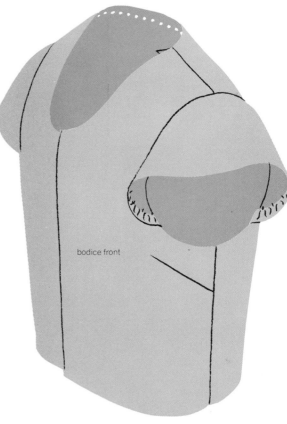

bodice front

28. Roll the seam line just below the fold and pin the tape in place along the underarm curve at 1/2-inch intervals.

29. Attach the folded edge of the tape to the bodice, using a slip stitch *(page 185)*. Remove the pins.

30. Press the tape flat from the wrong side.

31. Turn the garment right side out.

THE DOLMAN SLEEVE

A PREPARING THE BACK OF THE SLEEVE

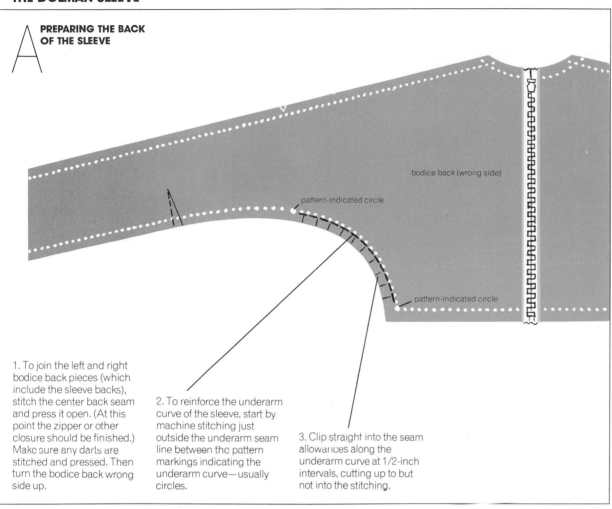

bodice back (wrong side)

pattern-indicated circle

pattern-indicated circle

1. To join the left and right bodice back pieces (which include the sleeve backs), stitch the center back seam and press it open. (At this point the zipper or other closure should be finished.) Make sure any darts are stitched and pressed. Then turn the bodice back wrong side up.

2. To reinforce the underarm curve of the sleeve, start by machine stitching just outside the underarm seam line between the pattern markings indicating the underarm curve—usually circles.

3. Clip straight into the seam allowances along the underarm curve at 1/2-inch intervals, cutting up to but not into the stitching.

B PREPARING THE FRONT OF THE SLEEVE

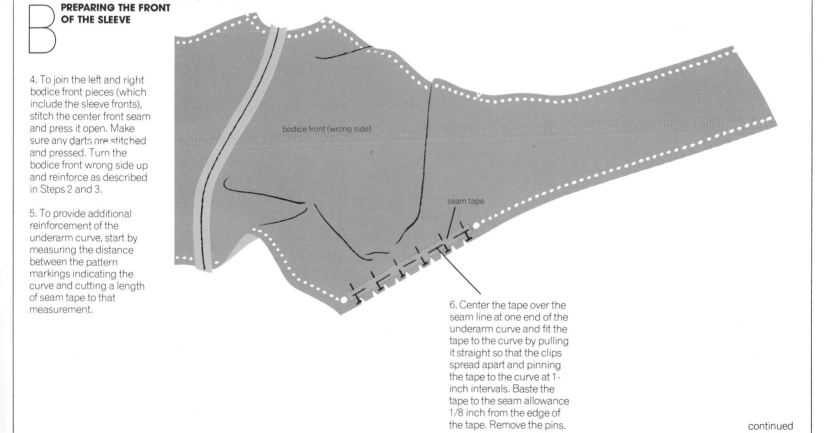

bodice front (wrong side)

seam tape

4. To join the left and right bodice front pieces (which include the sleeve fronts), stitch the center front seam and press it open. Make sure any darts are stitched and pressed. Turn the bodice front wrong side up and reinforce as described in Steps 2 and 3.

5. To provide additional reinforcement of the underarm curve, start by measuring the distance between the pattern markings indicating the curve and cutting a length of seam tape to that measurement.

6. Center the tape over the seam line at one end of the underarm curve and fit the tape to the curve by pulling it straight so that the clips spread apart and pinning the tape to the curve at 1-inch intervals. Baste the tape to the seam allowance 1/8 inch from the edge of the tape. Remove the pins.

continued

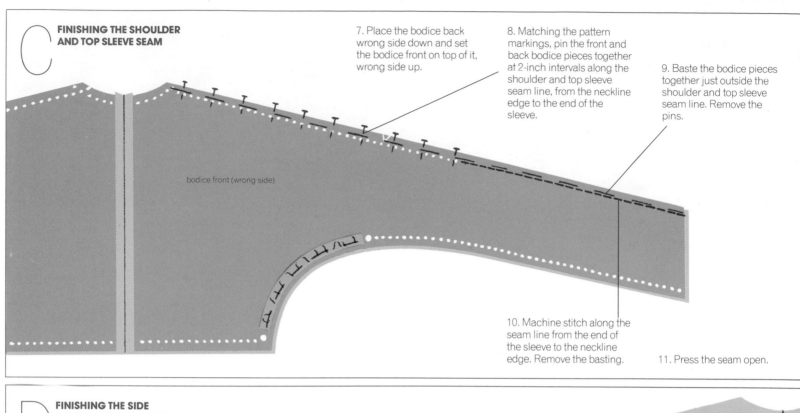

C FINISHING THE SHOULDER AND TOP SLEEVE SEAM

7. Place the bodice back wrong side down and set the bodice front on top of it, wrong side up.

8. Matching the pattern markings, pin the front and back bodice pieces together at 2-inch intervals along the shoulder and top sleeve seam line, from the neckline edge to the end of the sleeve.

9. Baste the bodice pieces together just outside the shoulder and top sleeve seam line. Remove the pins.

bodice front (wrong side)

10. Machine stitch along the seam line from the end of the sleeve to the neckline edge. Remove the basting.

11. Press the seam open.

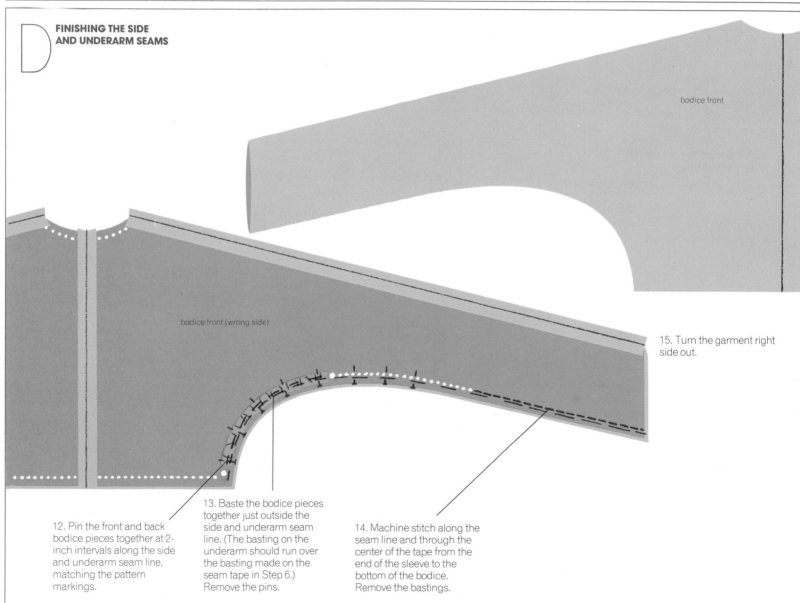

D FINISHING THE SIDE AND UNDERARM SEAMS

bodice front

bodice front (wrong side)

15. Turn the garment right side out.

12. Pin the front and back bodice pieces together at 2-inch intervals along the side and underarm seam line, matching the pattern markings.

13. Baste the bodice pieces together just outside the side and underarm seam line. (The basting on the underarm should run over the basting made on the seam tape in Step 6.) Remove the pins.

14. Machine stitch along the seam line and through the center of the tape from the end of the sleeve to the bottom of the bodice. Remove the bastings.

THE T-SHAPED KIMONO SLEEVE

A ATTACHING THE SLEEVE TO THE BODICE

1. Stitch the bodice shoulder seams and press them open. Make sure any darts are stitched and pressed. Spread out the bodice, wrong side down.

2. Place the right sleeve wrong side up over the right half of the bodice, matching the notches and making sure that the pattern-indicated circle in the middle of the armhole seam line of the sleeve falls at the shoulder seam of the bodice and that the two end circles on the sleeve match the corresponding circles on the bodice.

3. Pin the sleeve to the bodice between the end circles along the edge of the armhole. Baste just outside the seam line. Remove the pins.

4. Machine stitch along the seam line, making sure not to stitch beyond the circles at the ends of the sleeve. Remove the basting.

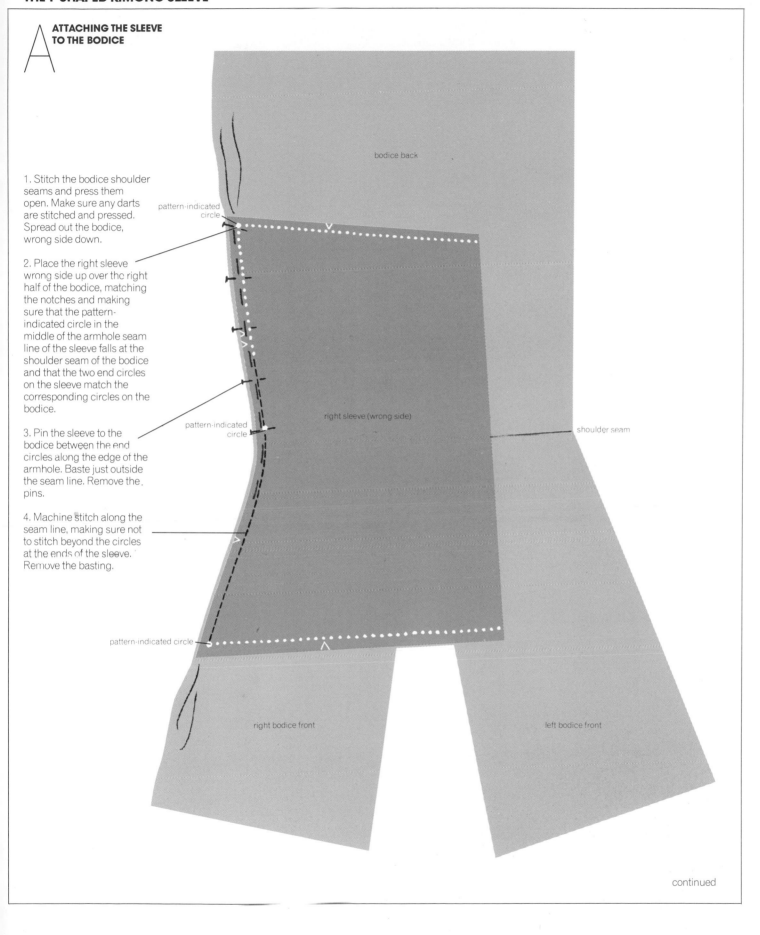

bodice back

pattern-indicated circle

right sleeve (wrong side)

pattern-indicated circle

shoulder seam

pattern-indicated circle

right bodice front

left bodice front

continued

B STITCHING THE SIDE SEAM OF THE BODICE

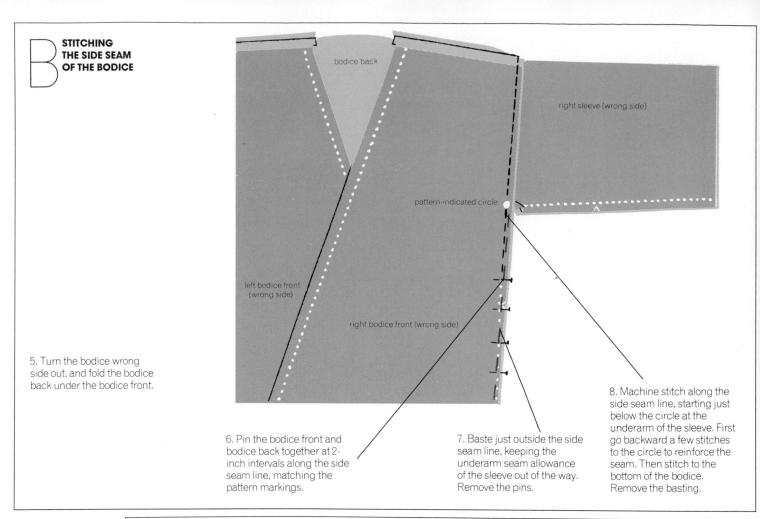

5. Turn the bodice wrong side out, and fold the bodice back under the bodice front.

6. Pin the bodice front and bodice back together at 2-inch intervals along the side seam line, matching the pattern markings.

7. Baste just outside the side seam line, keeping the underarm seam allowance of the sleeve out of the way. Remove the pins.

8. Machine stitch along the side seam line, starting just below the circle at the underarm of the sleeve. First go backward a few stitches to the circle to reinforce the seam. Then stitch to the bottom of the bodice. Remove the basting.

C STITCHING THE UNDERARM SEAM OF THE SLEEVE

9. Pin the underarm edges of the sleeve together at 2-inch intervals along the seam line, matching the pattern markings.

10. Baste just outside the underarm seam line, keeping the side seam allowance out of the way. Remove the pins.

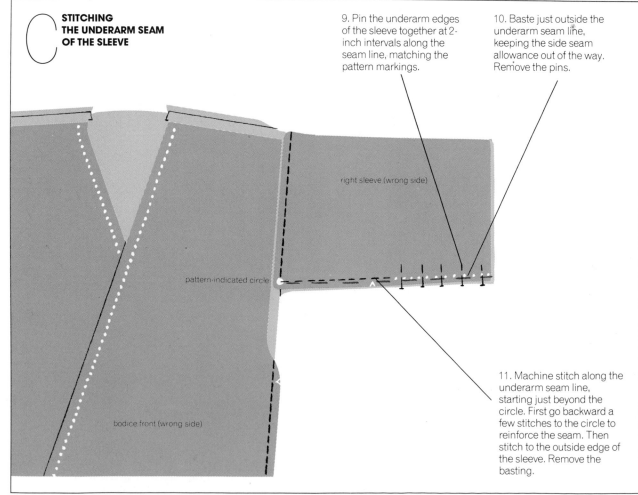

11. Machine stitch along the underarm seam line, starting just beyond the circle. First go backward a few stitches to the circle to reinforce the seam. Then stitch to the outside edge of the sleeve. Remove the basting.

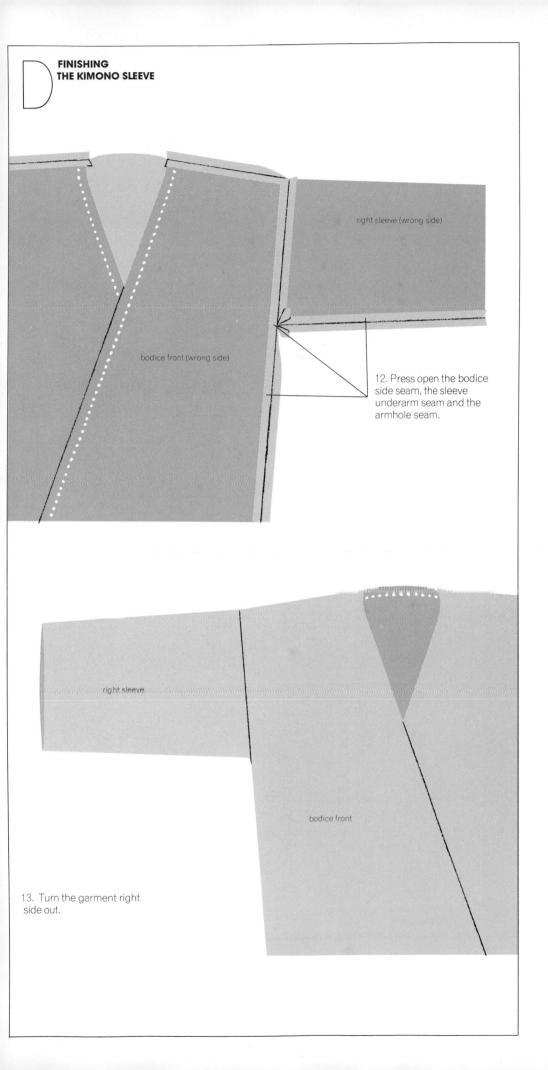

right sleeve (wrong side)

bodice front (wrong side)

12. Press open the bodice
side seam, the sleeve
underarm seam and the
armhole seam.

right sleeve

bodice front

13. Turn the garment right
side out.

Waistlines with the fit built in

It is not always necessary to go through the time-consuming process of making and attaching the usual tailored waistband with zipper in order to have a dress, skirt or tunic hug the waist. There are easier methods for accomplishing an attractive, well-fitting waistline, and the instructions for them are shown on the following pages.

One method is to use elastic or a drawstring. A tie belt can be attached to the garment as a wraparound; or a waistband can have loose ends that tie.

Elastic and drawstring can be slipped through a tunnel of fabric attached on the inside of a dress. The tunnel, also called a casing, is usually made of the same fabric as the garment. If the fabric is heavyweight, use a lighter-weight fabric for the casing. With skirts or pants the top edge of the garment itself can be folded over to serve as the casing.

The key to success in making flat, professional-looking tie ends and drawstrings is the method you use to turn them right side out after they have been stitched. For fairly wide tie ends, use a ruler; for a narrower version, use the eraser end of an ordinary pencil (page 104).

THE SINGLE-ELASTICIZED WAIST FOR A DRESS OR TUNIC

A SEAMING THE CASING STRIP

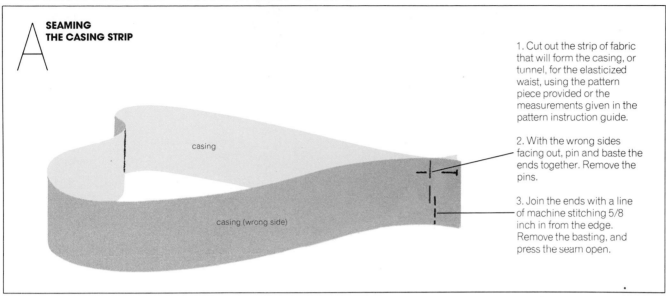

1. Cut out the strip of fabric that will form the casing, or tunnel, for the elasticized waist, using the pattern piece provided or the measurements given in the pattern instruction guide.

2. With the wrong sides facing out, pin and baste the ends together. Remove the pins.

3. Join the ends with a line of machine stitching 5/8 inch in from the edge. Remove the basting, and press the seam open.

B PREPARING THE EDGES OF THE CASING STRIP

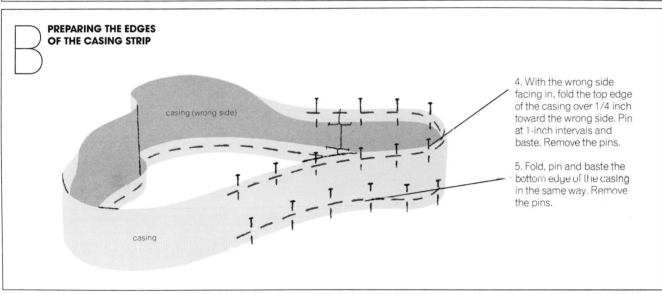

4. With the wrong side facing in, fold the top edge of the casing over 1/4 inch toward the wrong side. Pin at 1-inch intervals and baste. Remove the pins.

5. Fold, pin and baste the bottom edge of the casing in the same way. Remove the pins.

C BASTING THE CASING STRIP INSIDE THE GARMENT

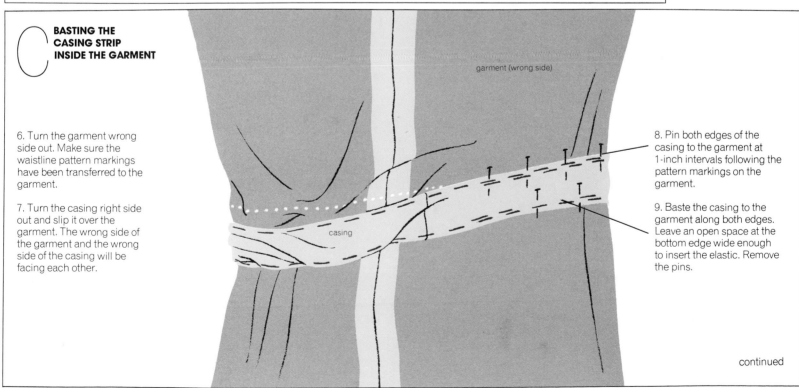

6. Turn the garment wrong side out. Make sure the waistline pattern markings have been transferred to the garment.

7. Turn the casing right side out and slip it over the garment. The wrong side of the garment and the wrong side of the casing will be facing each other.

8. Pin both edges of the casing to the garment at 1-inch intervals following the pattern markings on the garment.

9. Baste the casing to the garment along both edges. Leave an open space at the bottom edge wide enough to insert the elastic. Remove the pins.

continued

FINISHING THE CASING

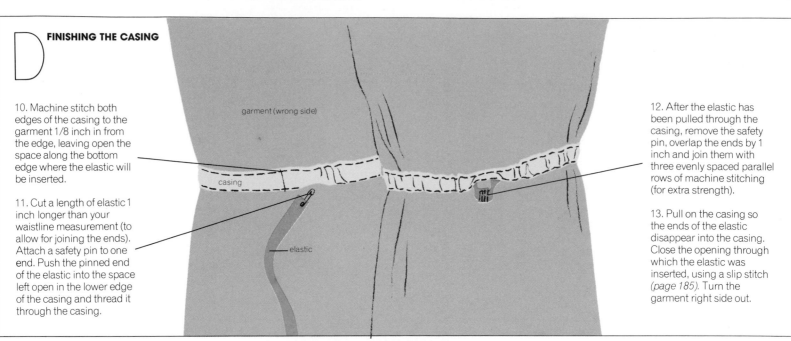

10. Machine stitch both edges of the casing to the garment 1/8 inch in from the edge, leaving open the space along the bottom edge where the elastic will be inserted.

11. Cut a length of elastic 1 inch longer than your waistline measurement (to allow for joining the ends). Attach a safety pin to one end. Push the pinned end of the elastic into the space left open in the lower edge of the casing and thread it through the casing.

12. After the elastic has been pulled through the casing, remove the safety pin, overlap the ends by 1 inch and join them with three evenly spaced parallel rows of machine stitching (for extra strength).

13. Pull on the casing so the ends of the elastic disappear into the casing. Close the opening through which the elastic was inserted, using a slip stitch (page 185). Turn the garment right side out.

THE DOUBLE-ELASTICIZED WAIST FOR A DRESS OR TUNIC

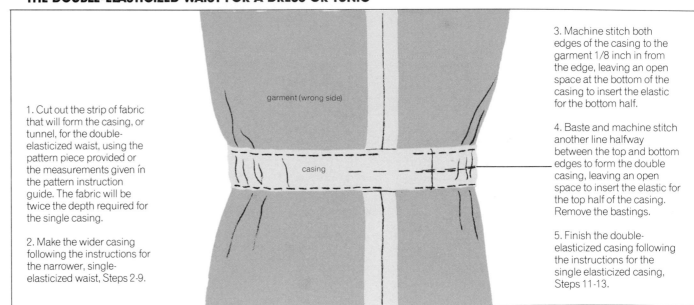

1. Cut out the strip of fabric that will form the casing, or tunnel, for the double-elasticized waist, using the pattern piece provided or the measurements given in the pattern instruction guide. The fabric will be twice the depth required for the single casing.

2. Make the wider casing following the instructions for the narrower, single-elasticized waist, Steps 2-9.

3. Machine stitch both edges of the casing to the garment 1/8 inch in from the edge, leaving an open space at the bottom of the casing to insert the elastic for the bottom half.

4. Baste and machine stitch another line halfway between the top and bottom edges to form the double casing, leaving an open space to insert the elastic for the top half of the casing. Remove the bastings.

5. Finish the double-elasticized casing following the instructions for the single elasticized casing, Steps 11-13.

THE ELASTICIZED WAIST FOR A SKIRT

A **MEASURING AND BASTING THE CASING**

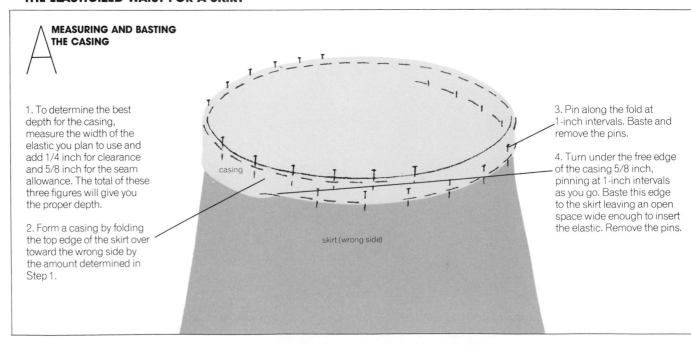

1. To determine the best depth for the casing, measure the width of the elastic you plan to use and add 1/4 inch for clearance and 5/8 inch for the seam allowance. The total of these three figures will give you the proper depth.

2. Form a casing by folding the top edge of the skirt over toward the wrong side by the amount determined in Step 1.

3. Pin along the fold at 1-inch intervals. Baste and remove the pins.

4. Turn under the free edge of the casing 5/8 inch, pinning at 1-inch intervals as you go. Baste this edge to the skirt leaving an open space wide enough to insert the elastic. Remove the pins.

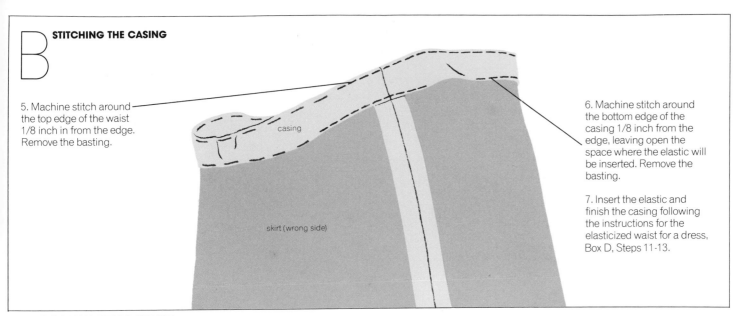

B STITCHING THE CASING

5. Machine stitch around the top edge of the waist 1/8 inch in from the edge. Remove the basting.

casing

skirt (wrong side)

6. Machine stitch around the bottom edge of the casing 1/8 inch from the edge, leaving open the space where the elastic will be inserted. Remove the basting.

7. Insert the elastic and finish the casing following the instructions for the elasticized waist for a dress, Box D, Steps 11-13.

THE DRAWSTRING WAIST

A MAKING THE DRAWSTRING OPENING

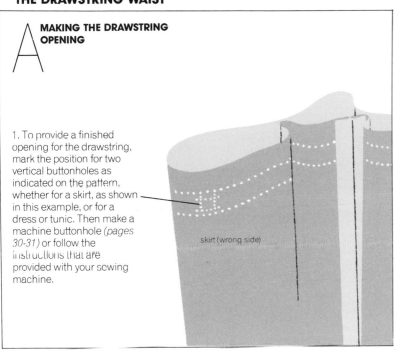

1. To provide a finished opening for the drawstring, mark the position for two vertical buttonholes as indicated on the pattern, whether for a skirt, as shown in this example, or for a dress or tunic. Then make a machine buttonhole (pages 30-31) or follow the instructions that are provided with your sewing machine.

skirt (wrong side)

B PREPARING THE CASING

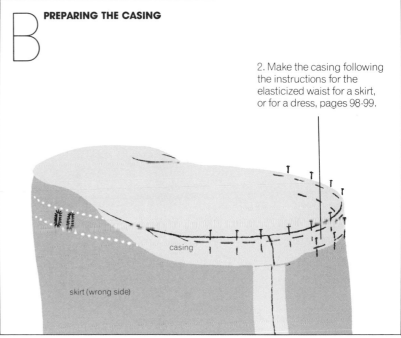

2. Make the casing following the instructions for the elasticized waist for a skirt, or for a dress, pages 98-99.

casing

skirt (wrong side)

C MAKING THE DRAWSTRING

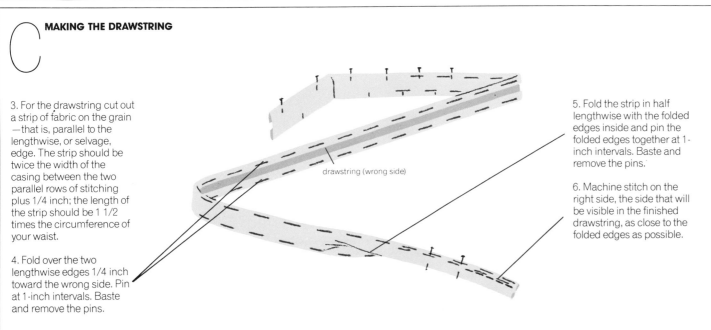

3. For the drawstring cut out a strip of fabric on the grain —that is, parallel to the lengthwise, or selvage, edge. The strip should be twice the width of the casing between the two parallel rows of stitching plus 1/4 inch; the length of the strip should be 1 1/2 times the circumference of your waist.

4. Fold over the two lengthwise edges 1/4 inch toward the wrong side. Pin at 1-inch intervals. Baste and remove the pins.

drawstring (wrong side)

5. Fold the strip in half lengthwise with the folded edges inside and pin the folded edges together at 1-inch intervals. Baste and remove the pins.

6. Machine stitch on the right side, the side that will be visible in the finished drawstring, as close to the folded edges as possible.

D FINISHING THE DRAWSTRING CASING

7. Pull the drawstring through the casing by attaching a safety pin to one end and inserting it into one of the buttonholes. Then push the drawstring through the casing until the safety pin end comes out of the other buttonhole.

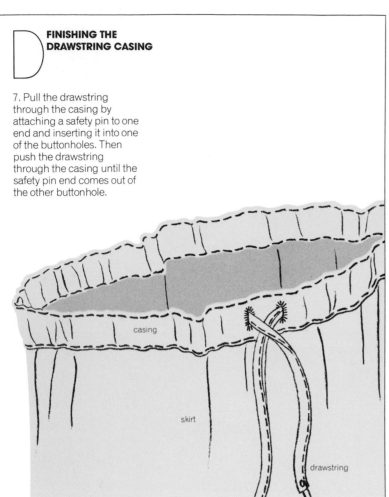

E FINISHING THE ENDS OF THE DRAWSTRING

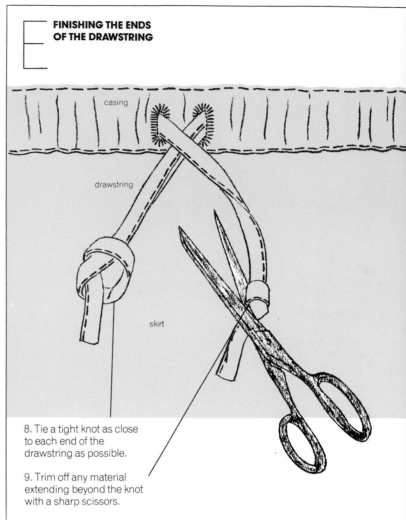

8. Tie a tight knot as close to each end of the drawstring as possible.

9. Trim off any material extending beyond the knot with a sharp scissors.

THE ATTACHED TIE BELT

A PINNING AND BASTING THE BELT

1. Cut out the halves of the tie belt pieces from the garment fabric, following the pattern instructions.

2. Fold the belt pieces in half, lengthwise, with the wrong sides facing out.

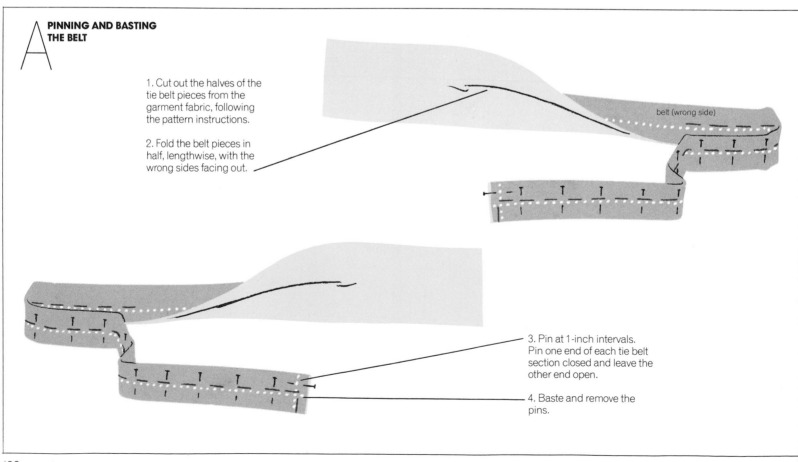

3. Pin at 1-inch intervals. Pin one end of each tie belt section closed and leave the other end open.

4. Baste and remove the pins.

B STITCHING THE BELT

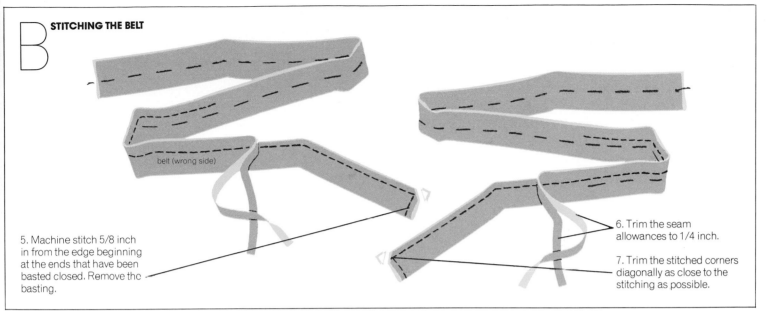

belt (wrong side)

5. Machine stitch 5/8 inch in from the edge beginning at the ends that have been basted closed. Remove the basting.

6. Trim the seam allowances to 1/4 inch.

7. Trim the stitched corners diagonally as close to the stitching as possible.

C TURNING THE BELT

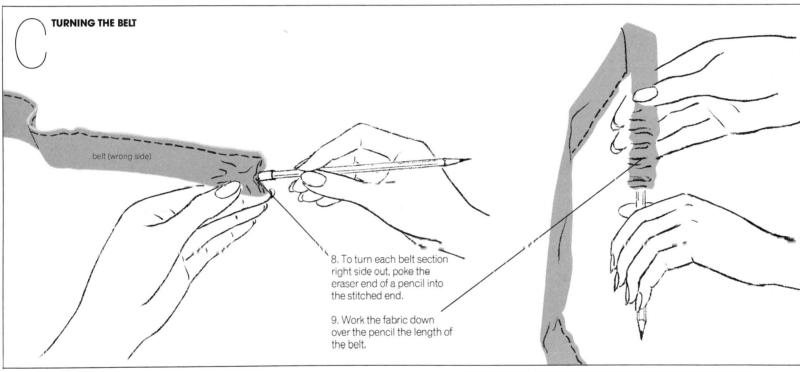

belt (wrong side)

8. To turn each belt section right side out, poke the eraser end of a pencil into the stitched end.

9. Work the fabric down over the pencil the length of the belt.

D FINISHING THE BELT

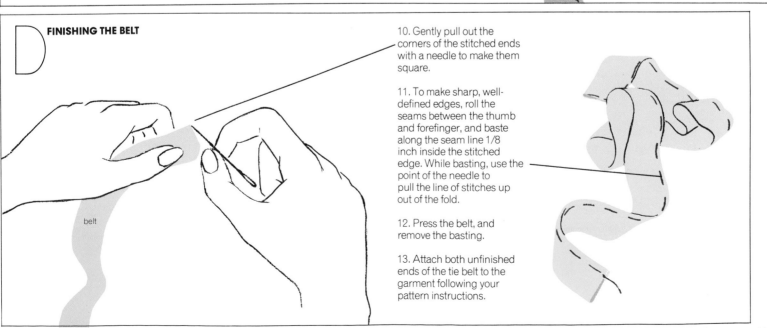

belt

10. Gently pull out the corners of the stitched ends with a needle to make them square.

11. To make sharp, well-defined edges, roll the seams between the thumb and forefinger, and baste along the seam line 1/8 inch inside the stitched edge. While basting, use the point of the needle to pull the line of stitches up out of the fold.

12. Press the belt, and remove the basting.

13. Attach both unfinished ends of the tie belt to the garment following your pattern instructions.

THE TIE-END WAISTBAND

A PINNING AND BASTING THE BELT

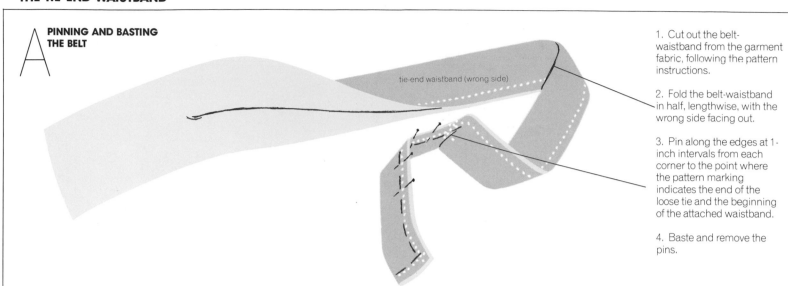

1. Cut out the belt-waistband from the garment fabric, following the pattern instructions.

2. Fold the belt-waistband in half, lengthwise, with the wrong side facing out.

3. Pin along the edges at 1-inch intervals from each corner to the point where the pattern marking indicates the end of the loose tie and the beginning of the attached waistband.

4. Baste and remove the pins.

B STITCHING THE TIE ENDS

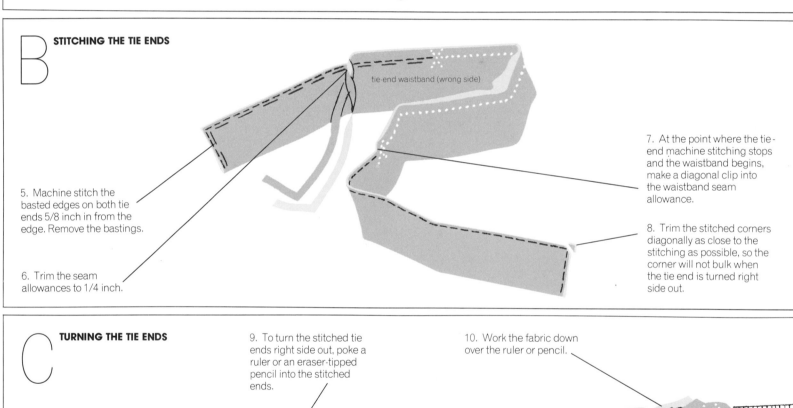

5. Machine stitch the basted edges on both tie ends 5/8 inch in from the edge. Remove the bastings.

6. Trim the seam allowances to 1/4 inch.

7. At the point where the tie-end machine stitching stops and the waistband begins, make a diagonal clip into the waistband seam allowance.

8. Trim the stitched corners diagonally as close to the stitching as possible, so the corner will not bulk when the tie end is turned right side out.

C TURNING THE TIE ENDS

9. To turn the stitched tie ends right side out, poke a ruler or an eraser-tipped pencil into the stitched ends.

10. Work the fabric down over the ruler or pencil.

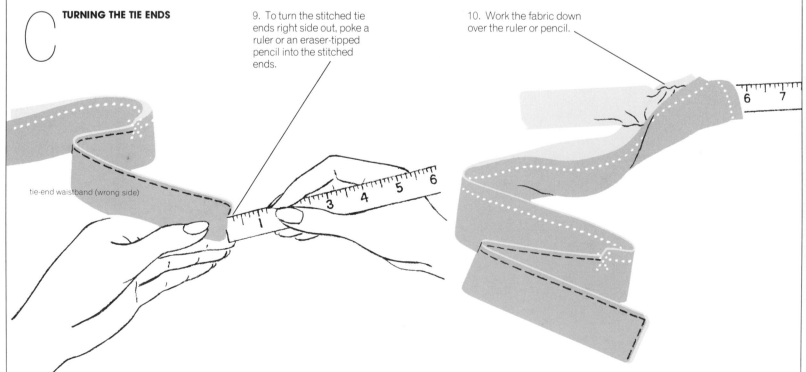

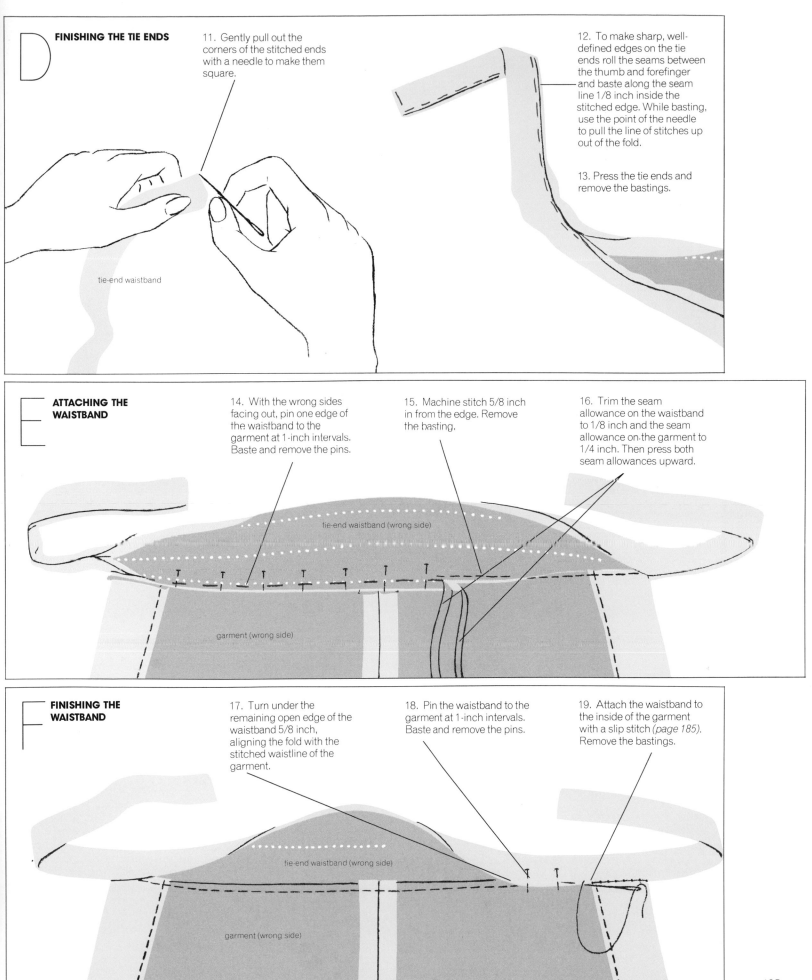

D **FINISHING THE TIE ENDS**

11. Gently pull out the corners of the stitched ends with a needle to make them square.

12. To make sharp, well-defined edges on the tie ends roll the seams between the thumb and forefinger and baste along the seam line 1/8 inch inside the stitched edge. While basting, use the point of the needle to pull the line of stitches up out of the fold.

13. Press the tie ends and remove the bastings.

tie-end waistband

E **ATTACHING THE WAISTBAND**

14. With the wrong sides facing out, pin one edge of the waistband to the garment at 1-inch intervals. Baste and remove the pins.

15. Machine stitch 5/8 inch in from the edge. Remove the basting.

16. Trim the seam allowance on the waistband to 1/8 inch and the seam allowance on the garment to 1/4 inch. Then press both seam allowances upward.

tie-end waistband (wrong side)

garment (wrong side)

F **FINISHING THE WAISTBAND**

17. Turn under the remaining open edge of the waistband 5/8 inch, aligning the fold with the stitched waistline of the garment.

18. Pin the waistband to the garment at 1-inch intervals. Baste and remove the pins.

19. Attach the waistband to the inside of the garment with a slip stitch *(page 185)*. Remove the bastings.

tie-end waistband (wrong side)

garment (wrong side)

Elegantly closing the gap

Buttonholes, clasps and zippers often demand detailed workmanship —but quite similar closures can be made with far less effort. A special kind of slide fastener called an "invisible zipper," for example, takes minutes to sew; yet it achieves the elegant look of a softly pressed seam, as shown on the dress at right.

Unlike the conventional zipper, which reveals a telltale bulge and stitching, the invisible zipper is set into the seam with the aid of a special zipper foot *(page 32)* that can be attached to any sewing machine. The finished zipper is barely visible. An essential part of the procedure is that the zipper must be open when it is inserted into a seam.

An easy way to avoid bound buttonholes is to make in-seam buttonholes, which are created by leaving gaps while stitching the seam line. To make an in-seam buttonhole, simply stitch a narrow extension to the center front or center back edge of the garment, as shown on pages 109-110, thus creating a seam for the buttonholes to appear in an inch or so away from the edge.

With slightly more delicate maneuvers decorative buttonhole loops can be made out of narrow strips of fabric. This technique is even easier if you use a loop turner *(page 36)*.

A PREPARING THE GARMENT FOR THE ZIPPER

right garment back
(wrong side)

1. Place the right half of the garment back on a flat surface, wrong side up.

2. Lay the closed zipper on top of the garment along the markings for the center back seam line, positioning it so that the zipper tab falls 5/8 inch below the neckline edge.

3. Mark the position of the zipper tab and the bottom end of the zipper with pins. Then set the zipper aside.

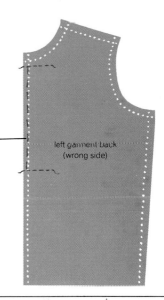

4. Mark the position of the pins with a horizontal running stitch (page 185) and remove the pins.

5. Run a line of basting stitches along the seam-line marking of the garment section between the horizontal markings made in Step 4. This line indicates exactly where the zipper will be inserted.

6. Repeat Steps 1-5 on the left half of the garment back.

left garment back
(wrong side)

B PREPARING THE ZIPPER

7. Open the zipper and lay it face down on your ironing board. The inside edges where the zipper coils are located will be folded over a fraction of an inch toward you.

8. With the tip of your iron press the inside edges of the zipper flat so that the folded-over coil edge is turned toward the other side.

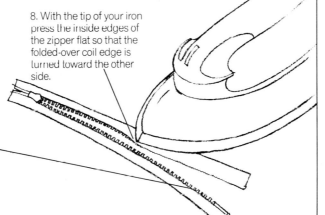

C ATTACHING THE ZIPPER TO THE RIGHT HALF OF THE GARMENT

9. Place the right half of the garment back on a flat surface, wrong side down.

10. Place the open zipper face down on the garment back so that the top and bottom ends of the coils are aligned with the horizontal basted markings made in Step 4. The coils of the left half of the zipper should be flush against the vertical basted markings made in Step 5.

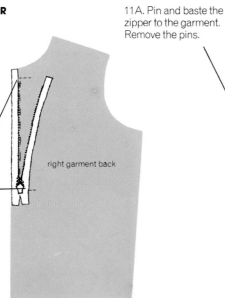

right garment back

11A. Pin and baste the zipper to the garment. Remove the pins.

11B. Alternately, attach the zipper to the garment with adhesive basting tape following the instructions on page 34.

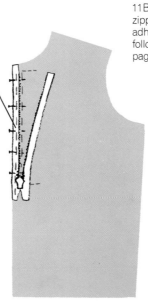

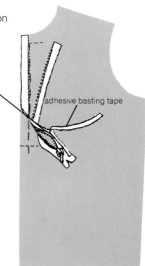

adhesive basting tape

continued

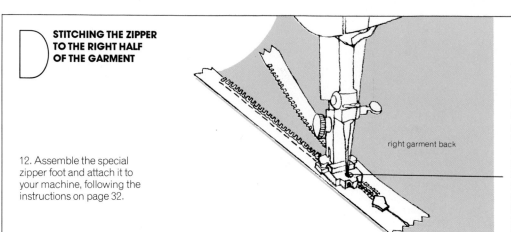

D STITCHING THE ZIPPER TO THE RIGHT HALF OF THE GARMENT

12. Assemble the special zipper foot and attach it to your machine, following the instructions on page 32.

13. Making sure that the zipper coil feeds into the right-hand groove of the zipper foot (as you face it), stitch the zipper to the garment beginning at the neck edge and continuing until the zipper foot touches and is stopped by the pull tab. Then stitch backward a few stitches before removing the garment from the machine. Remove all bastings and the adhesive basting tape, if used.

E ATTACHING THE ZIPPER TO THE LEFT HALF OF THE GARMENT

14. Place the left half of the garment back on a flat surface, wrong side down.

15. Place the remaining free side of the zipper tab face down on the left garment back so that the top end of the coil is aligned with the horizontal basted marking made in Step 4. The coiled edge should be flush against the vertical basted markings made in Step 6.

16A. Pin and baste the zipper to the garment. Remove the pins.

16B. Alternately, attach the zipper to the garment with adhesive basting tape following the instructions on page 34.

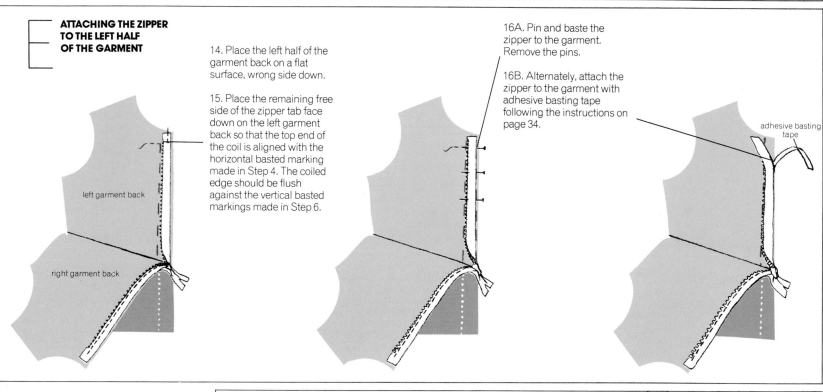

F STITCHING THE ZIPPER TO THE LEFT HALF OF THE GARMENT

17. Making sure that the zipper coil feeds into the left-hand groove of the zipper foot (as you face it), stitch the zipper to the garment beginning at the neck edge and continuing until the zipper foot touches and is stopped by the pull tab. Then stitch backward a few stitches before removing the garment from the machine. Remove all bastings and the adhesive basting tape, if used. Close the zipper before proceeding to the next step.

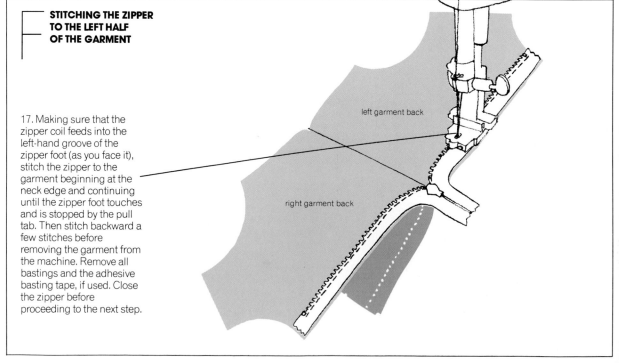

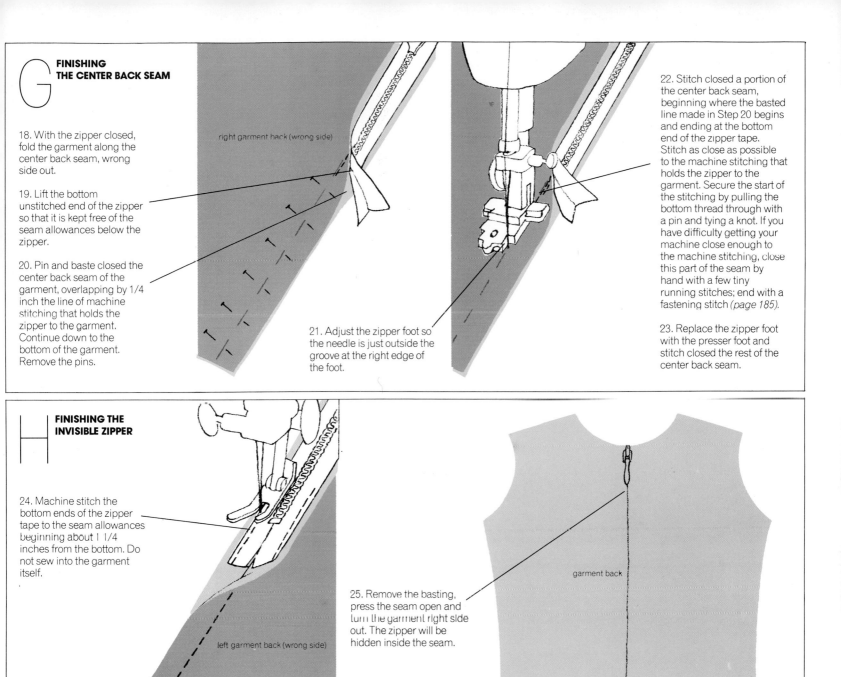

G FINISHING THE CENTER BACK SEAM

18. With the zipper closed, fold the garment along the center back seam, wrong side out.

19. Lift the bottom unstitched end of the zipper so that it is kept free of the seam allowances below the zipper.

20. Pin and baste closed the center back seam of the garment, overlapping by 1/4 inch the line of machine stitching that holds the zipper to the garment. Continue down to the bottom of the garment. Remove the pins.

right garment back (wrong side)

21. Adjust the zipper foot so the needle is just outside the groove at the right edge of the foot.

22. Stitch closed a portion of the center back seam, beginning where the basted line made in Step 20 begins and ending at the bottom end of the zipper tape. Stitch as close as possible to the machine stitching that holds the zipper to the garment. Secure the start of the stitching by pulling the bottom thread through with a pin and tying a knot. If you have difficulty getting your machine close enough to the machine stitching, close this part of the seam by hand with a few tiny running stitches; end with a fastening stitch (page 185).

23. Replace the zipper foot with the presser foot and stitch closed the rest of the center back seam.

H FINISHING THE INVISIBLE ZIPPER

24. Machine stitch the bottom ends of the zipper tape to the seam allowances beginning about 1 1/4 inches from the bottom. Do not sew into the garment itself.

left garment back (wrong side)

25. Remove the basting, press the seam open and turn the garment right side out. The zipper will be hidden inside the seam.

garment back

IN-SEAM BUTTONHOLES

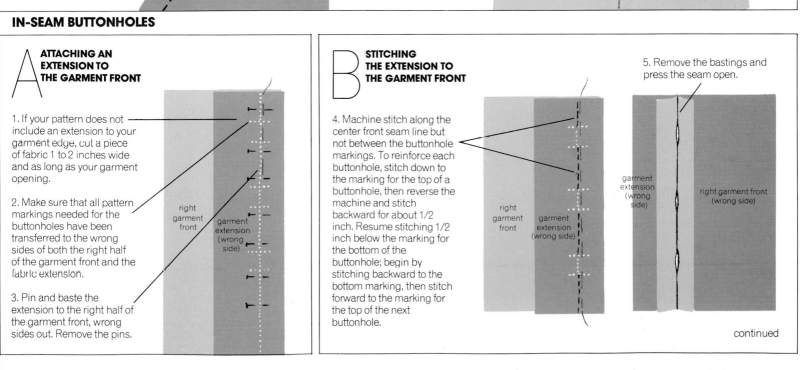

A ATTACHING AN EXTENSION TO THE GARMENT FRONT

1. If your pattern does not include an extension to your garment edge, cut a piece of fabric 1 to 2 inches wide and as long as your garment opening.

2. Make sure that all pattern markings needed for the buttonholes have been transferred to the wrong sides of both the right half of the garment front and the fabric extension.

3. Pin and baste the extension to the right half of the garment front, wrong sides out. Remove the pins.

right garment front

garment extension (wrong side)

B STITCHING THE EXTENSION TO THE GARMENT FRONT

4. Machine stitch along the center front seam line but not between the buttonhole markings. To reinforce each buttonhole, stitch down to the marking for the top of a buttonhole, then reverse the machine and stitch backward for about 1/2 inch. Resume stitching 1/2 inch below the marking for the bottom of the buttonhole; begin by stitching backward to the bottom marking, then stitch forward to the marking for the top of the next buttonhole.

5. Remove the bastings and press the seam open.

right garment front

garment extension (wrong side)

garment extension (wrong side)

right garment front (wrong side)

continued

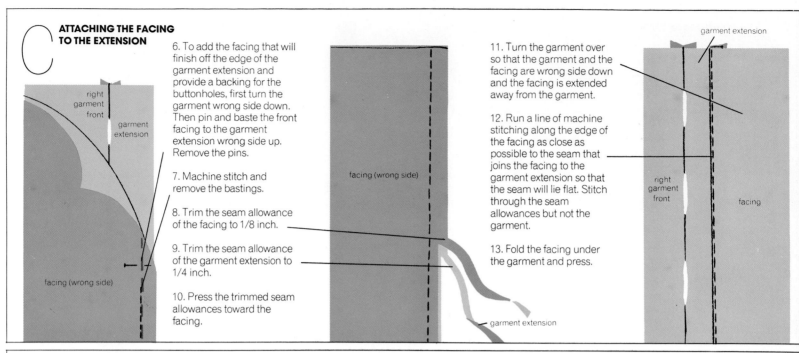

C ATTACHING THE FACING TO THE EXTENSION

6. To add the facing that will finish off the edge of the garment extension and provide a backing for the buttonholes, first turn the garment wrong side down. Then pin and baste the front facing to the garment extension wrong side up. Remove the pins.

7. Machine stitch and remove the bastings.

8. Trim the seam allowance of the facing to 1/8 inch.

9. Trim the seam allowance of the garment extension to 1/4 inch.

10. Press the trimmed seam allowances toward the facing.

11. Turn the garment over so that the garment and the facing are wrong side down and the facing is extended away from the garment.

12. Run a line of machine stitching along the edge of the facing as close as possible to the seam that joins the facing to the garment extension so that the seam will lie flat. Stitch through the seam allowances but not the garment.

13. Fold the facing under the garment and press.

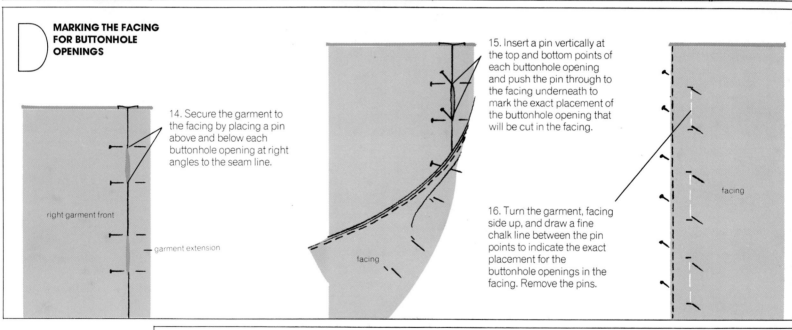

D MARKING THE FACING FOR BUTTONHOLE OPENINGS

14. Secure the garment to the facing by placing a pin above and below each buttonhole opening at right angles to the seam line.

15. Insert a pin vertically at the top and bottom points of each buttonhole opening and push the pin through to the facing underneath to mark the exact placement of the buttonhole opening that will be cut in the facing.

16. Turn the garment, facing side up, and draw a fine chalk line between the pin points to indicate the exact placement for the buttonhole openings in the facing. Remove the pins.

E FINISHING THE BUTTONHOLE OPENINGS ON THE FACING

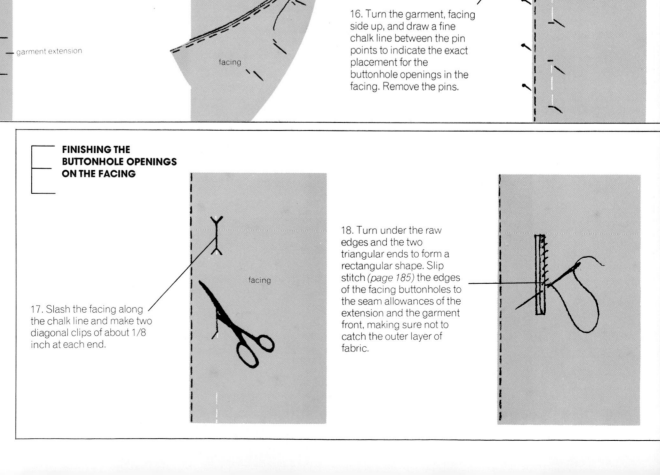

17. Slash the facing along the chalk line and make two diagonal clips of about 1/8 inch at each end.

18. Turn under the raw edges and the two triangular ends to form a rectangular shape. Slip stitch (page 185) the edges of the facing buttonholes to the seam allowances of the extension and the garment front, making sure not to catch the outer layer of fabric.

LOOPS FOR BUTTONS

A CUTTING OUT THE LOOPS

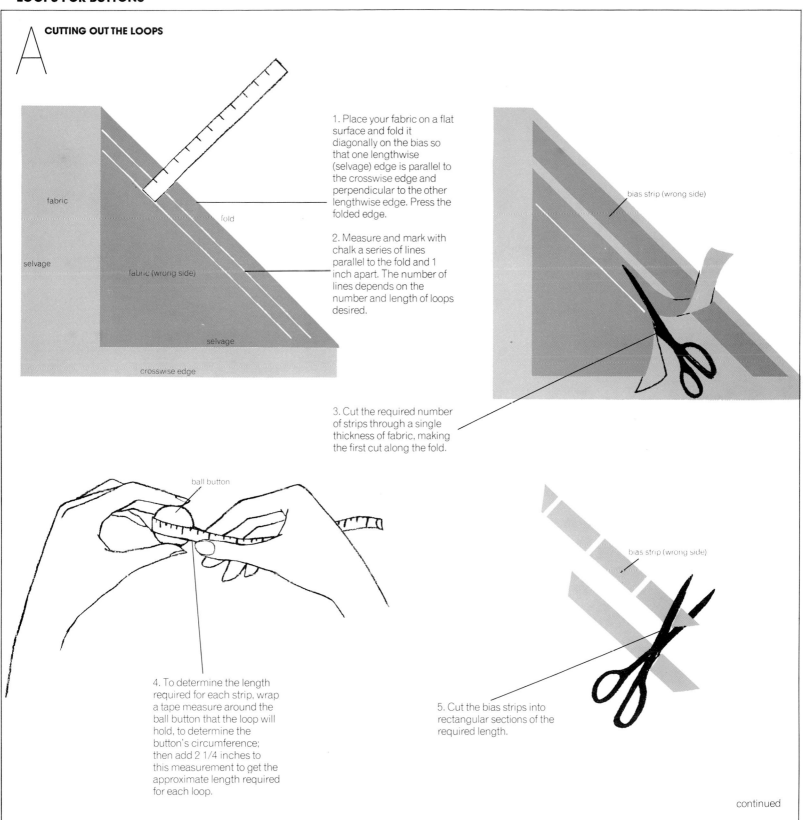

1. Place your fabric on a flat surface and fold it diagonally on the bias so that one lengthwise (selvage) edge is parallel to the crosswise edge and perpendicular to the other lengthwise edge. Press the folded edge.

2. Measure and mark with chalk a series of lines parallel to the fold and 1 inch apart. The number of lines depends on the number and length of loops desired.

3. Cut the required number of strips through a single thickness of fabric, making the first cut along the fold.

fabric

selvage

fabric (wrong side)

fold

selvage

crosswise edge

bias strip (wrong side)

ball button

4. To determine the length required for each strip, wrap a tape measure around the ball button that the loop will hold, to determine the button's circumference; then add 2 1/4 inches to this measurement to get the approximate length required for each loop.

bias strip (wrong side)

5. Cut the bias strips into rectangular sections of the required length.

continued

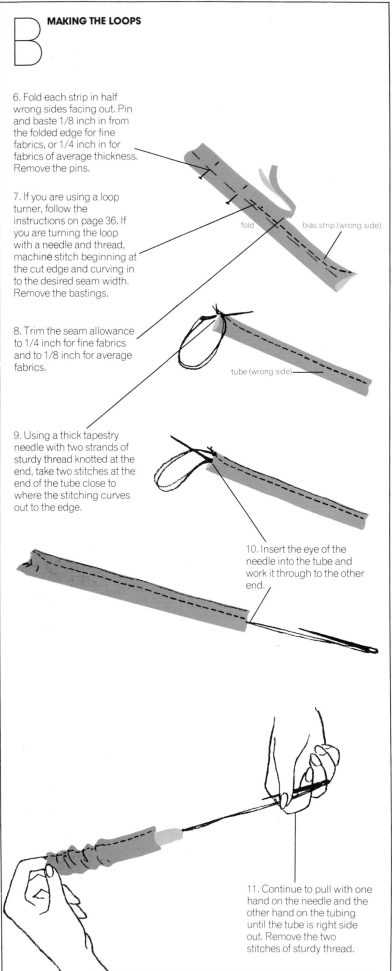

B   MAKING THE LOOPS

6. Fold each strip in half wrong sides facing out. Pin and baste 1/8 inch in from the folded edge for fine fabrics, or 1/4 inch in for fabrics of average thickness. Remove the pins.

7. If you are using a loop turner, follow the instructions on page 36. If you are turning the loop with a needle and thread, machine stitch beginning at the cut edge and curving in to the desired seam width. Remove the bastings.

fold

bias strip (wrong side)

8. Trim the seam allowance to 1/4 inch for fine fabrics and to 1/8 inch for average fabrics.

tube (wrong side)

9. Using a thick tapestry needle with two strands of sturdy thread knotted at the end, take two stitches at the end of the tube close to where the stitching curves out to the edge.

10. Insert the eye of the needle into the tube and work it through to the other end.

11. Continue to pull with one hand on the needle and the other hand on the tubing until the tube is right side out. Remove the two stitches of sturdy thread.

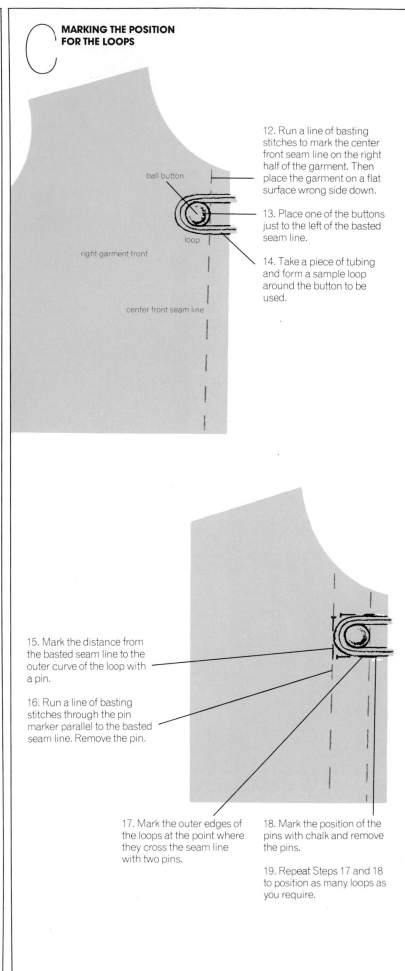

C   MARKING THE POSITION FOR THE LOOPS

12. Run a line of basting stitches to mark the center front seam line on the right half of the garment. Then place the garment on a flat surface wrong side down.

ball button

right garment front

loop

center front seam line

13. Place one of the buttons just to the left of the basted seam line.

14. Take a piece of tubing and form a sample loop around the button to be used.

15. Mark the distance from the basted seam line to the outer curve of the loop with a pin.

16. Run a line of basting stitches through the pin marker parallel to the basted seam line. Remove the pin.

17. Mark the outer edges of the loops at the point where they cross the seam line with two pins.

18. Mark the position of the pins with chalk and remove the pins.

19. Repeat Steps 17 and 18 to position as many loops as you require.

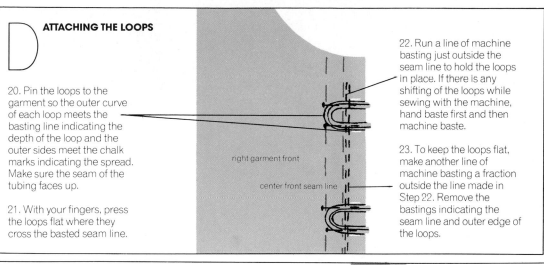

D ATTACHING THE LOOPS

20. Pin the loops to the garment so the outer curve of each loop meets the basting line indicating the depth of the loop and the outer sides meet the chalk marks indicating the spread. Make sure the seam of the tubing faces up.

21. With your fingers, press the loops flat where they cross the basted seam line.

22. Run a line of machine basting just outside the seam line to hold the loops in place. If there is any shifting of the loops while sewing with the machine, hand baste first and then machine baste.

23. To keep the loops flat, make another line of machine basting a fraction outside the line made in Step 22. Remove the bastings indicating the seam line and outer edge of the loops.

right garment front

center front seam line

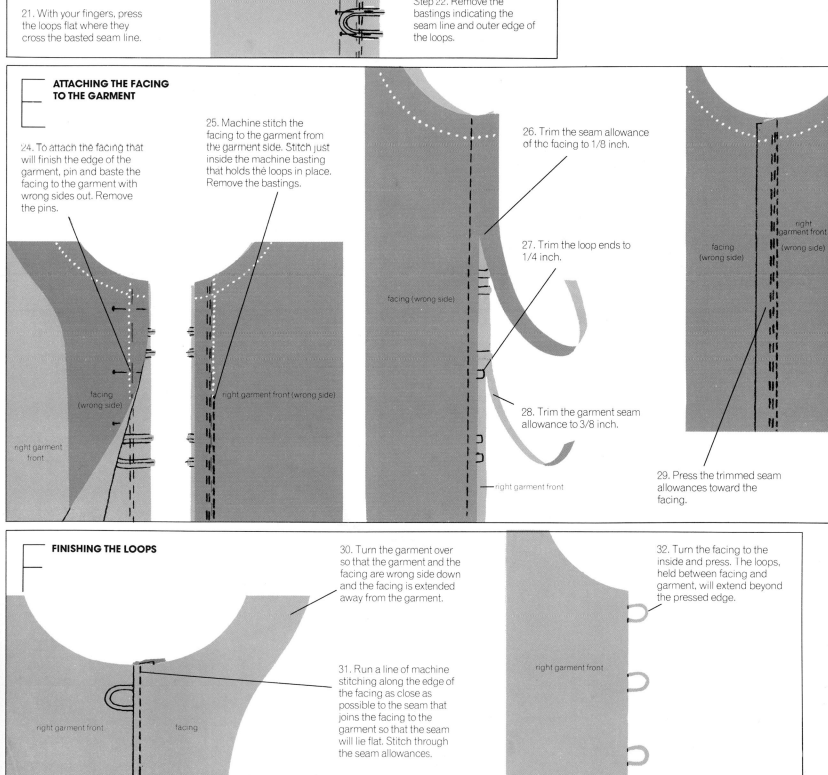

E ATTACHING THE FACING TO THE GARMENT

24. To attach the facing that will finish the edge of the garment, pin and baste the facing to the garment with wrong sides out. Remove the pins.

25. Machine stitch the facing to the garment from the garment side. Stitch just inside the machine basting that holds the loops in place. Remove the bastings.

26. Trim the seam allowance of the facing to 1/8 inch.

27. Trim the loop ends to 1/4 inch.

28. Trim the garment seam allowance to 3/8 inch.

29. Press the trimmed seam allowances toward the facing.

facing (wrong side)

right garment front (wrong side)

facing (wrong side)

right garment front

right garment front

facing (wrong side)

right garment front (wrong side)

F FINISHING THE LOOPS

30. Turn the garment over so that the garment and the facing are wrong side down and the facing is extended away from the garment.

31. Run a line of machine stitching along the edge of the facing as close as possible to the seam that joins the facing to the garment so that the seam will lie flat. Stitch through the seam allowances.

32. Turn the facing to the inside and press. The loops, held between facing and garment, will extend beyond the pressed edge.

right garment front

facing

right garment front

Decorative and simple hems

Some shortcut techniques provide useful and decorative edgings by omitting a few steps required to make the basic hem. Other hemming techniques take advantage of shortcut fabrics. All can also be used for edging sleeves and pant legs.

The zigzag hem requires no seam tape; the hem is simply turned up and sewn through the garment with a zigzag stitch that decorates the visible side. It is especially useful on fluid fabrics like jerseys and knits.

The lettuce hem can also be made without tape. If the fabric is nonravelly, the hem does not even have to be turned up; a zigzag stitch along the raw edge creates a loose, rippling effect. The lettuce hem is suitable only for fabrics resilient enough to spring back after stretching.

If you prefer a plain hemmed edge but are working with a fluid fabric, you should use a lightweight seam tape on the inside—a good one is scallop-edged stretch lace *(page 117)*. The conventional heavier tape might stretch the material out of shape. To make a simple hem and still keep knits from raveling or sagging, use the double finish *(page 118)*. Hems on double-faced fabrics can be made unobtrusive with the fold-under method shown on page 119. But be sure to let skirts hang for 24 hours, to find their natural shape, before starting any hem.

THE LETTUCE HEM

A PREPARING THE HEM

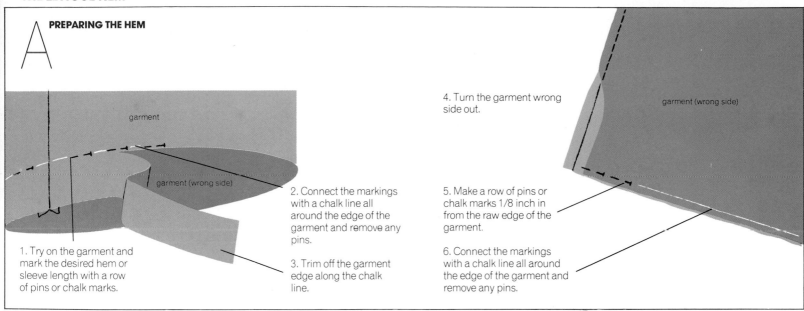

garment

garment (wrong side)

1. Try on the garment and mark the desired hem or sleeve length with a row of pins or chalk marks.

2. Connect the markings with a chalk line all around the edge of the garment and remove any pins.

3. Trim off the garment edge along the chalk line.

4. Turn the garment wrong side out.

garment (wrong side)

5. Make a row of pins or chalk marks 1/8 inch in from the raw edge of the garment.

6. Connect the markings with a chalk line all around the edge of the garment and remove any pins.

B STITCHING THE HEM

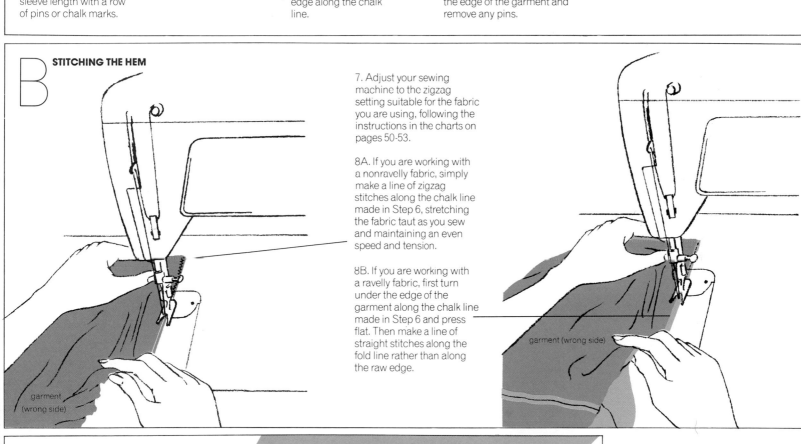

7. Adjust your sewing machine to the zigzag setting suitable for the fabric you are using, following the instructions in the charts on pages 50-53.

8A. If you are working with a nonravelly fabric, simply make a line of zigzag stitches along the chalk line made in Step 6, stretching the fabric taut as you sew and maintaining an even speed and tension.

8B. If you are working with a ravelly fabric, first turn under the edge of the garment along the chalk line made in Step 6 and press flat. Then make a line of straight stitches along the fold line rather than along the raw edge.

garment (wrong side)

garment (wrong side)

C FINISHING THE HEM

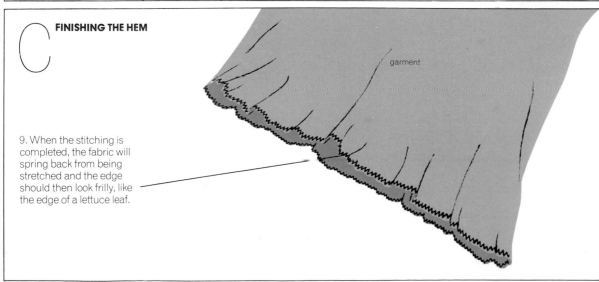

garment

9. When the stitching is completed, the fabric will spring back from being stretched and the edge should then look frilly, like the edge of a lettuce leaf.

THE ZIGZAG HEM

A PREPARING THE GARMENT

1. Try on the garment and mark the desired hem or sleeve length with a row of pins or chalk marks.

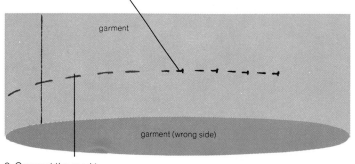

2. Connect the markings with a line of basting stitches. Remove any pins.

3. Turn the garment wrong side out.

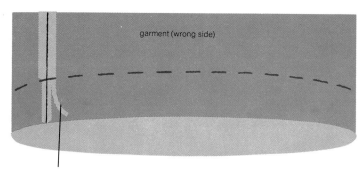

4. To avoid a bulge under the hem, trim the seam allowances of any seams below the hemline markings to a width of 1/4 inch.

5. Measure down from the basted hemline markings the hem depth called for by your pattern and make a row of pins or chalk marks.

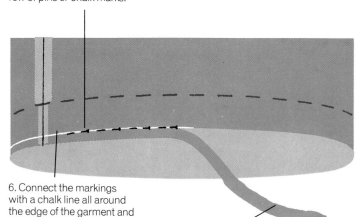

6. Connect the markings with a chalk line all around the edge of the garment and remove any pins.

7. Trim off the garment edge along the chalk line.

B TURNING UP THE HEM

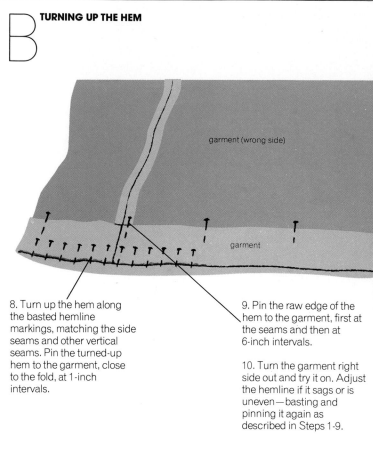

8. Turn up the hem along the basted hemline markings, matching the side seams and other vertical seams. Pin the turned-up hem to the garment, close to the fold, at 1-inch intervals.

9. Pin the raw edge of the hem to the garment, first at the seams and then at 6-inch intervals.

10. Turn the garment right side out and try it on. Adjust the hemline if it sags or is uneven—basting and pinning it again as described in Steps 1-9.

C PINNING AND BASTING THE HEM

11. Turn the garment wrong side out.

12. Run a line of basting stitches all around the garment 1/4 inch in from the folded edge of the hem, sewing through both layers of the fabric. Remove the pins along the folded edge.

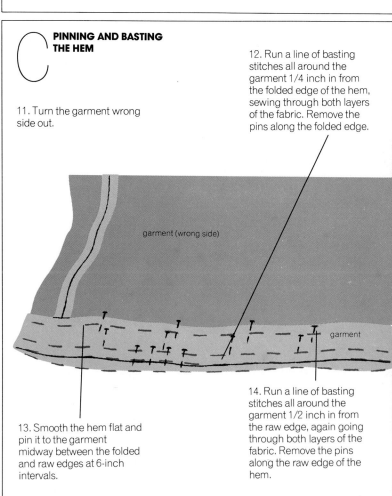

13. Smooth the hem flat and pin it to the garment midway between the folded and raw edges at 6-inch intervals.

14. Run a line of basting stitches all around the garment 1/2 inch in from the raw edge, again going through both layers of the fabric. Remove the pins along the raw edge of the hem.

D STITCHING THE HEM

15. Adjust your sewing machine to the zigzag setting suitable for the fabric you are using, following the instructions in the charts on pages 50-53.

16. Make a line of zigzag stitches as close to the hem edge as possible without going over it. Remove the pins and bastings.

17. When the zigzag stitching is completed, turn the garment right side out. There will be a line of decorative zigzag stitches visible on the outside of the finished garment.

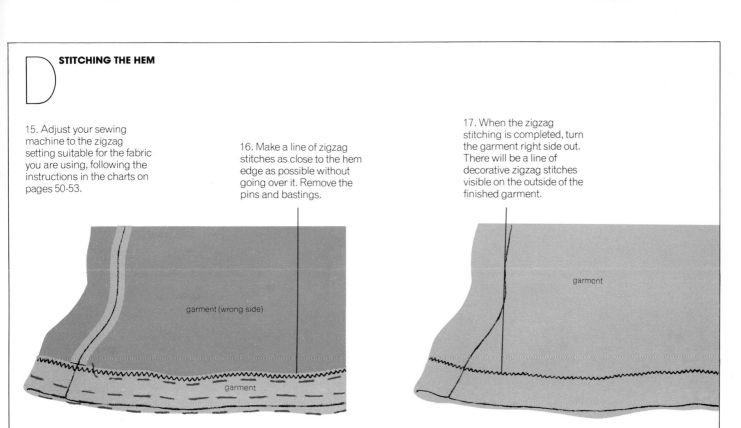

THE LACE-EDGED HEM

A PREPARING THE HEM

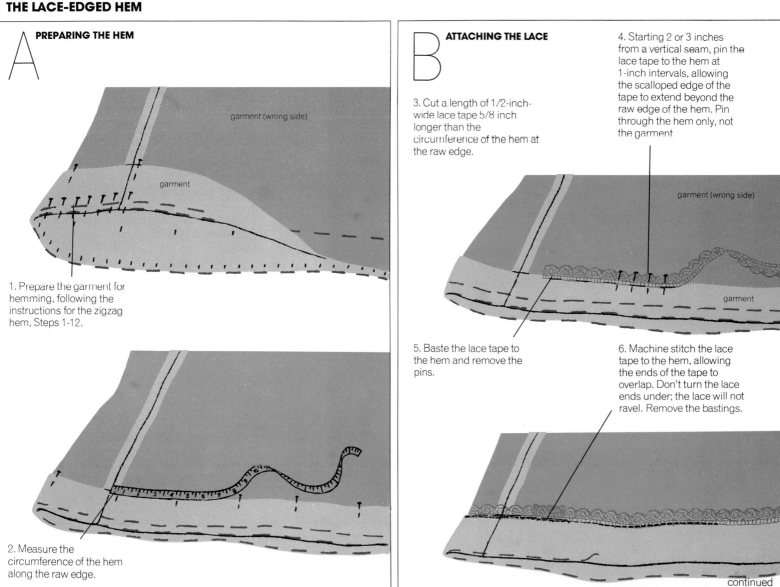

1. Prepare the garment for hemming, following the instructions for the zigzag hem, Steps 1-12.

2. Measure the circumference of the hem along the raw edge.

B ATTACHING THE LACE

3. Cut a length of 1/2-inch-wide lace tape 5/8 inch longer than the circumference of the hem at the raw edge.

4. Starting 2 or 3 inches from a vertical seam, pin the lace tape to the hem at 1-inch intervals, allowing the scalloped edge of the tape to extend beyond the raw edge of the hem. Pin through the hem only, not the garment.

5. Baste the lace tape to the hem and remove the pins.

6. Machine stitch the lace tape to the hem, allowing the ends of the tape to overlap. Don't turn the lace ends under; the lace will not ravel. Remove the bastings.

continued

FINISHING THE HEM

7. Pin the lace tape through the hem to the garment at 1-inch intervals.

8. Hand stitch the scalloped edge of the lace tape to the garment, using the slip stitch *(page 185),* which will not show on the visible side of the garment. Remove the pins and bastings and press on the wrong side.

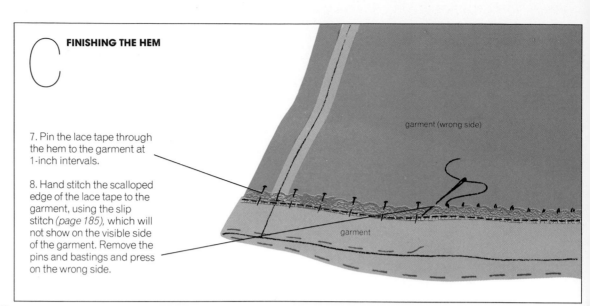

THE DOUBLE HEM FOR KNITS

A **MAKING THE HEM**

1. Prepare the hem following the instructions for the zigzag hem, Steps 1-11. Remove the pins.

2. Run a line of machine stitching close to the trimmed raw edge of the garment.

3. Working on the inside of the garment, insert a row of pins all around the hem, midway between the top and bottom edges.

4. Fold back the hem over the row of pins and sew along the fold all around the garment, using loose catch stitches *(page 185).*

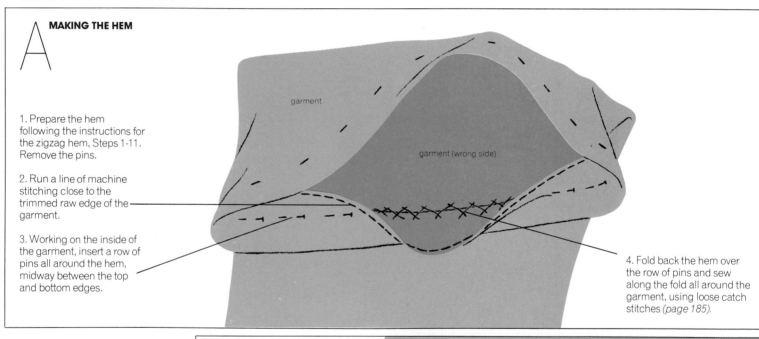

B **FINISHING THE HEM**

5. Catch stitch *(page 185)* the hem edge to the garment. Remove the basting.

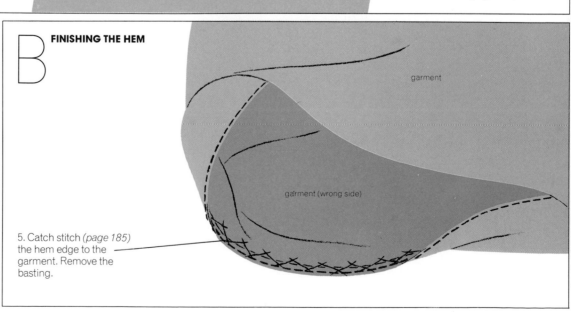

HEMMING DOUBLE-FACED FABRIC

A PREPARING THE HEM

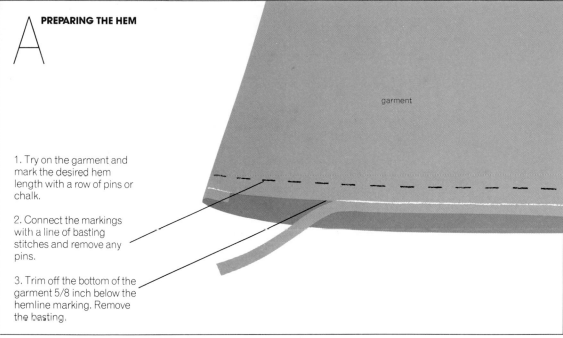

garment

1. Try on the garment and mark the desired hem length with a row of pins or chalk.

2. Connect the markings with a line of basting stitches and remove any pins.

3. Trim off the bottom of the garment 5/8 inch below the hemline marking. Remove the basting.

B SEPARATING THE DOUBLE-FACED FABRIC

4. Separate the two layers of the double-faced fabric to a depth of about 1 1/4 inches by snipping the bonding threads between the layers with scissors.

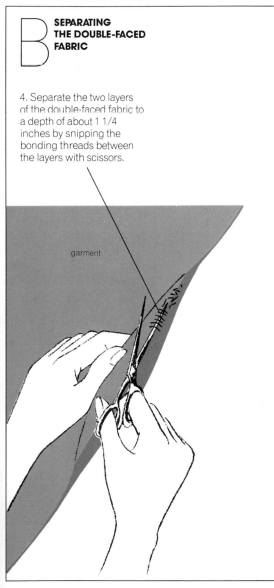

garment

C FINISHING THE HEM

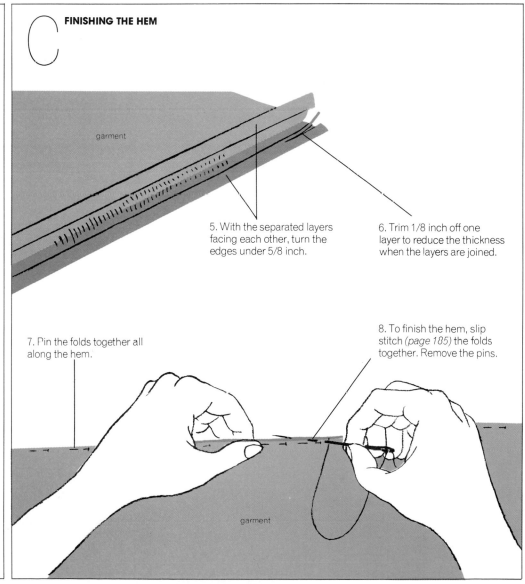

garment

5. With the separated layers facing each other, turn the edges under 5/8 inch.

6. Trim 1/8 inch off one layer to reduce the thickness when the layers are joined.

7. Pin the folds together all along the hem.

8. To finish the hem, slip stitch (*page 185*) the folds together. Remove the pins.

garment

5
A SYMPHONY OF SHAPES AND FORMS

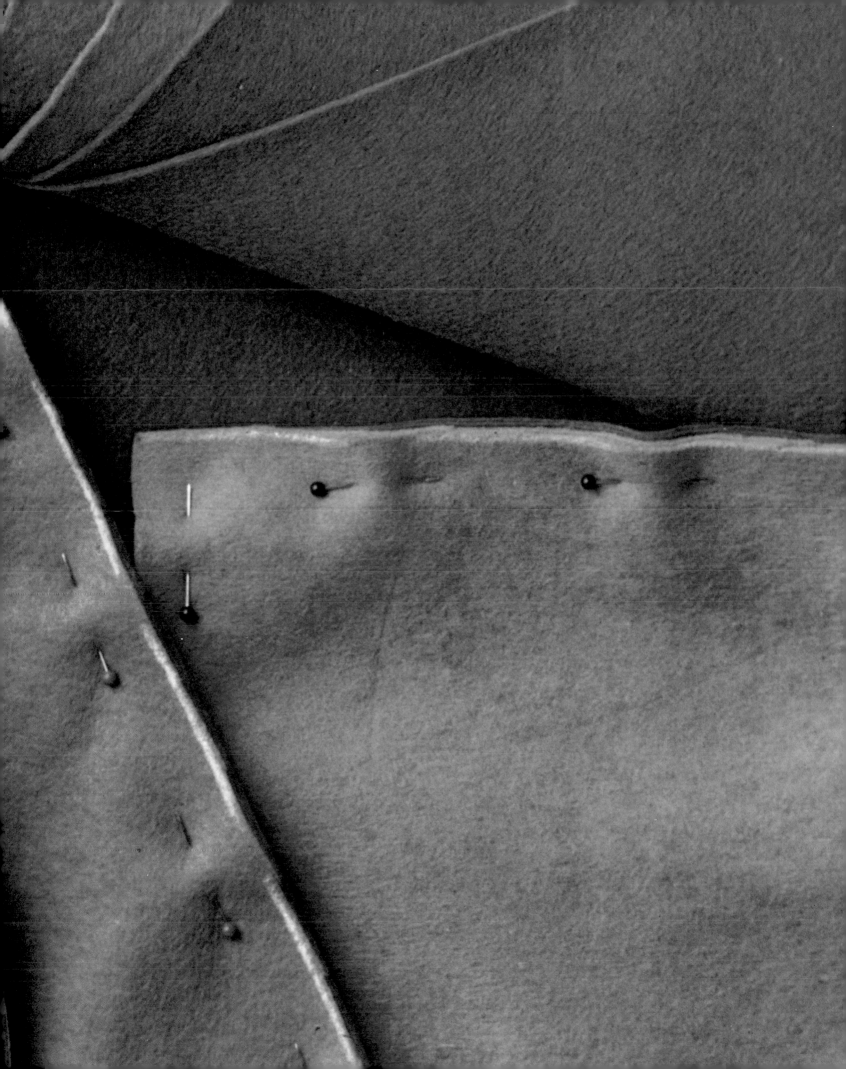

Euclid would never have dreamed of the imaginative 20th Century transformations of circles, squares and triangles when he devised the basic principles of geometry some 2,000 years ago. In fact, as the designs on pages 128-155 illustrate, even the straightest lines can be changed into the most enticing curves; a perfect circle can become the flatteringly imperfect straight lines of floor-length pants. And anyone who thinks

USING THE GEOMETRY AROUND YOU

geometric shapes have to be uninteresting need only regard the triangular bikini.

All the same, perhaps it is natural for most of us to be leery of geometrics. The mere thought of geometry conjures up unselling visions of endless hours sitting in high school mathematics classes memorizing theorems and trying to get our right angles to materialize properly. πr^2 became not the stuff of dreams but rather of nightmares; and our logarithms went bump in the night.

But those unpleasant memories may be a bit unfair to the science of geometry which, in its pure form, is literally all around us—and pleasantly too, in nearly all its forms, including fashions. Almost everything we see has some kind of geometric shape. Moreover, geometry has lately been experiencing an exuberant renaissance, in the fine and graphic arts as much as in fashion. And along with this widespread use and display of geometrics has come a heightened public awareness of the potentials of the pure, geometric form as a logical vehicle for creativity and artistry.

Not that this should come as any news. Geometric shapes have long enthralled the artist as well as his public. The Parthenon in Athens is a supreme triumph of geometry with its triangles and rectangles and the ingenious superimposition of one shape upon the other. The modern-day skyscraper, with its stretched-out rectangles, is in its own way as much a monument to geometrics as a Gothic cathedral. And there is also the breathtaking use of geometrics by modern artists—from Frank Stella (pages 126-127) to Mondrian to Picasso.

For the fact is that the clean, pure lines that characterize geometric shapes lend themselves to an infinite variety of uses and embellishments. The artist starts with something basic—even if it is only a straight line—and takes off from there. The possibilities before him are endless: color is added or not; embellishments are added or not; shapes are juxtaposed or repeated.

It is the artist, indeed, who has led the dressmaker to the use of geometrics. We need only look at the human body, and the artist's depictions of it long before the advent of the designer's sketchbooks. The artists' representations are filled with the translation of the human body into geometric forms. Standing, we are rectangles; seated, we become triangles. Each shape contains a series of circles within circles. Da Vinci, Dürer, Charles Le Brun and Le Corbusier all utilized geometrics to explain our human anatomy. Then along came the Cubist painters of the 20th Century. They proceeded to take those venerable sketchbooks—indeed they took the entire human body—and turn them inside out, literally reassembling them, and us, along starkly geometric lines. Consider, in this category, Marcel Duchamp's startling and revolutionary Nude Descending a Staircase.

Just as one artist sees the human body as a rectangle, another artist might envision a skirt as a circle. The point is, both are perceiving that in the final analysis the fundamental shapes and forms in fashion, as in art, amount to nothing more or less than geometrics. In the 1920s French designer Gabrielle "Coco" Chanel dramatically demonstrated this fundamental fact of life and fashion. She took the pure geometric form—the basic rectangle—and made it three-dimensional, thus forming the perfect envelope for the human body. What she did was to translate geometric lines and planes and angles into the chic, comfortable and completely free clothing that became her lifelong trademark.

Other designers were less successful. The harsh, stark geometric fashions of the

1960s were an overreaction to the geometric influence that was engulfing the art world at the time. Women found themselves not so much enveloped as encased in hard-edge rectangles, trapezoids and triangles. The construction of these garments was incredibly rigid, and some of the designers of this period, dealing in welt seaming and interfacing and underlining, could have been called the hardhats of the clothing construction industry. Parisians André Courrèges and Paco Rabanne were but two of the fashion designers of the 1960s whose obsession with geometry led them into enthusiastic yet impractical styles (*below and opposite*).

For all their faults, enthusiastic styles were a plunge into something very different and very daring. As with every new movement or modification of an old movement, the clothes of the '60s can be seen as experimental steps in the direction of a useful technique. The human form is roughly symmetrical, but it certainly is not made up solely of rectangles and squares and triangles. The curves of the body cannot be clothed in straight lines alone. Still, the attempt to achieve this provided an interesting approach to an ever-present problem—even if it turned out to be the wrong approach.

Which, of course, brings us right back to the original use of geometric mathematics: a solution to a problem. And to the basic and intriguing idea that geometrics, while not the solution in themselves, are indeed the

Parisian designer Paco Rabanne originated a geometric version of chain mail in the 1960s when he designed a do-it-yourself disk dress. By buying boxes of pierced plastic circles and metal connecting rings, a dedicated fad follower could link the circles and make a personalized garment that was guaranteed to garner attention.

beginning of the solution. By starting with these pure forms—with all their esthetic and functional values—we can move on to something quite different and altogether pleasing. By superimposing these forms onto the human body, we can then begin to translate them into flexible, adaptable and comfortable shapes and designs that are both reminiscent of their origins and suggestive of infinite possibilities.

It is but a short step from the rectangle to the skirt, from the triangle to the scarf and from the circle to the shawl. Almost magically, rectangles have the potential to become ruffles, circles can become sleeves, triangles turn into collars. Pleat the rectangles, shirr the circles, trim the triangles

—the possibilities are just as endless as they are intriguing.

Just as there is artistry on canvas or in stone, so there is artistry in fabric and design. For what, after all, is art? It is at once as simple and as complicated as the most basic dictionary definition: "Systematic application of knowledge or skill in effecting a desired result." By this definition, the pursuit of art is wide open—from building bridges to knitting socks. For if art is indeed the systematic application of knowledge, aimed at a specific end, be it a canvas or a statue or a coat, the home sewer is indeed an artist—and in the process of creation she has accomplished a great deal more than merely covering a human body.

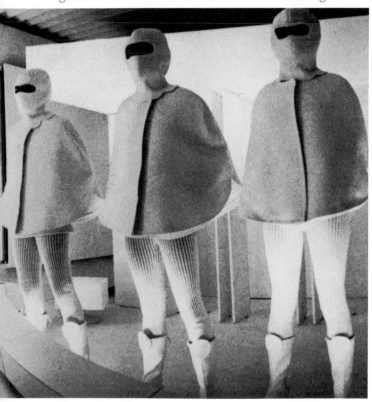

Geometrics have occasionally been carried to extremes. Designer André Courrèges garbed mannequins in simple circular capes and then converted them to unisex

oddities with spacesuit hoods (left). Courrèges' metal bikinis, also made from circles, inspired photographer Bert Stern to mimic the style with models in microdresses.

Inspiration from the world of art

The painting at the top is entitled *Takht-i-Sulay-man 1,* the one below *Saskatoon 1.* The two paintings are as divergent as the Islamic and Canadian names given them by their artist, Frank Stella; yet both are composed entirely of semicircles. And both exhibit the infinite variety of designs that are available in the world of geometrics.

Stella says the top painting was inspired by ancient circular cities of Asia Minor. In a bold abstract design recalling the intricate symmetry of an Oriental gate, the semicircles are silhouetted to create the shape of the painting itself. The bottom painting emphasizes subtle colors rather than form, which is provided by the solid background, to achieve a very different effect. Here the look is reminiscent of flower petals.

When Stella began to paint, in the mid-1950s, he found the art world in flux: "The field was sort of open. All you had to do was do it." The same might be said of fashion today: rigid rules are bowing to individual style. Thus the sewer, like the painter, can use a simple shape to create an original look, as shown on the pages that follow.

One of 93 geometric paintings that Frank Stella subdivided into three

By setting semicircles against a background of soft green, Stella

groups of interlaces, rainbows and fans, this work is a major example of interlaced semicircles.

achieved a purely decorative effect that contrasts with his structural use of the semicircles at top.   127

A dress and scarf of triangles

The gown at left has a cool Euclidean beauty that is flattering to nearly any figure. And when it is worn with a head-wrapping scarf in a handsome print, it becomes a striking evening costume. Both gown and scarf are extremely simple to make, because they are based on a single geometric form: the triangle. Using the instructions on the following pages, you can quickly make an individual pattern with only three basic measurements. And you can modify the pattern for a street-length dress, or for a fingertip-length top that can be worn with pants.

A lightweight knit fabric, such as matte jersey, at least 45 inches wide is recommended. The scarf may be made with any lightweight woven material. Buy a piece of fabric that is twice the total length of the basic dress triangle *(Steps 5-7 of the directions)*, plus 6 or 8 inches to allow for waste. Resist the urge to change the cutting layout shown: knit fabrics, like napped fabrics, normally must be cut with all pattern pieces facing in the same direction. Use an even-feed sewing machine foot on slippery knit fabrics. Either a marked throat plate or a seam guide *(page 33)* will help you machine stitch a straight 5/8-inch seam without preliminary marking.

THE TRIANGLE DRESS

A TAKING BODY MEASUREMENTS

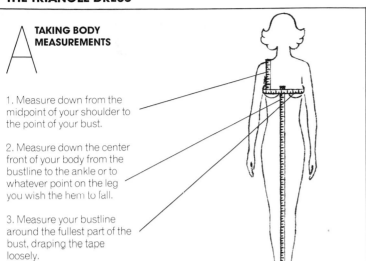

1. Measure down from the midpoint of your shoulder to the point of your bust.

2. Measure down the center front of your body from the bustline to the ankle or to whatever point on the leg you wish the hem to fall.

3. Measure your bustline around the fullest part of the bust, draping the tape loosely.

B MAKING THE PAPER PATTERN FOR THE DRESS

4. To make the triangle dress, you will need to make one triangular pattern piece from which you will cut four identical triangles. To do this, cut a large sheet of paper, or piece together several sheets, at least as long as the sum of the measurements taken in Steps 1 and 2 plus about 6 inches. The width should be about 30 inches.

5. To mark the length of the basic triangle needed, rule a vertical line down the center of the paper the length of the shoulder-to-bust measurement taken in Step 1. Mark the bottom of the line with a small dot to indicate the bustline.

6. Then extend this vertical line down beyond the dot by the length of the bust-to-hem measurement taken in Step 2; mark the bottom of the line with a small dot to indicate the finished hem edge.

7. Extend the vertical line beyond the hemline dot by the number of inches desired for the hem allowance, usually 2 1/2 inches.

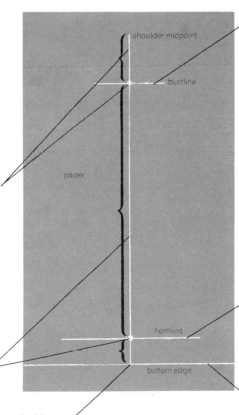

8. To mark the width of the basic triangle needed at the bustline, first take the total bust measurement made in Step 3, add 2 inches for ease and divide by 4. Then rule a horizontal line through the bustline dot the length of this measurement. Make this line perpendicular to the vertical line and of equal length on either side of the vertical line.

9. To mark the width of the basic triangle needed at the hemline, rule a horizontal line running through the hemline dot one fourth of the length of the desired hemline circumference—a total ranging from 72 inches to 88 inches depending on the fullness desired. Make this line perpendicular to the vertical line and of equal length on either side of the vertical line.

10. To mark the bottom edge of the basic triangle, rule a horizontal line across the paper at the base of the vertical line and perpendicular to it.

11. To mark the sides of the basic triangle from the top point to the bustline, rule two lines connecting the ends of the horizontal line indicating the bustline with the top of the vertical line.

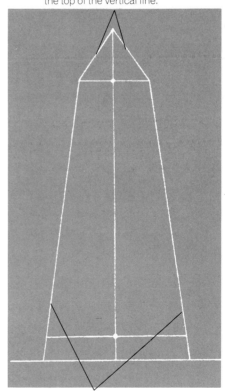

12. To mark the sides of the basic triangle from the bustline to the bottom edge, rule two lines connecting the ends of the horizontal bustline marking with the ends of the horizontal hemline marking. Then extend these two lines until they meet the horizontal line indicating the bottom edge.

continued

C FINISHING THE PAPER PATTERN FOR THE DRESS

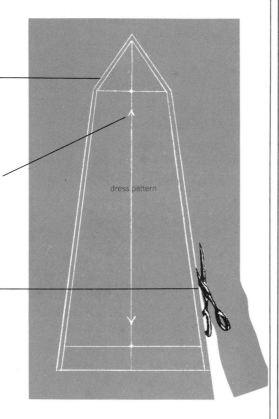

13. To provide for seam allowances, rule a second line 5/8 inch outside the lines made in Steps 11 and 12.

14. Mark the vertical center line of the basic triangle with arrows.

15. Cut out the basic triangle pattern along the outer lines. Then make a duplicate of it.

dress pattern

D MAKING THE PAPER PATTERN FOR THE FACING

16. To make a pattern for a facing for the upper portion of the triangle dress, trace the upper portion of the paper pattern completed in Step 15 from the apex of the triangle to a point 2 inches below the horizontal line marking the bustline.

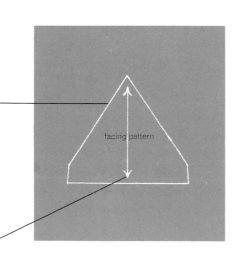

facing pattern

17. Mark the vertical center of the triangle with arrows.

18. Cut out the pattern for the facing along the traced markings. Then make a duplicate of it.

E CUTTING OUT THE DRESS

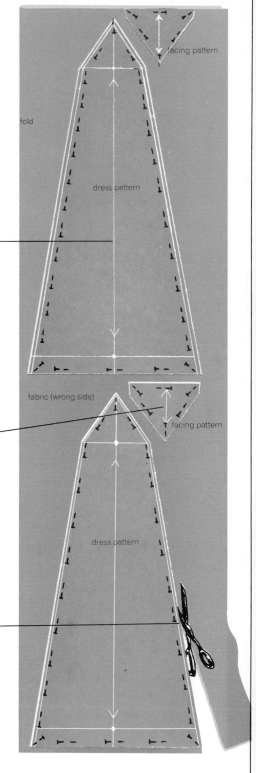

facing pattern

fold

dress pattern

19. Fold your fabric in half lengthwise, wrong sides out, and pin the two pattern pieces for the dress, completed in Step 15, to the fabric, with the arrows indicating the vertical centers of the triangles parallel to the lengthwise edges.

20. Pin the two pattern pieces for the facing to the folded fabric, with the arrows parallel to the lengthwise edges.

fabric (wrong side)

facing pattern

dress pattern

21. Cut out the four dress triangles and the four facing triangles from the garment fabric.

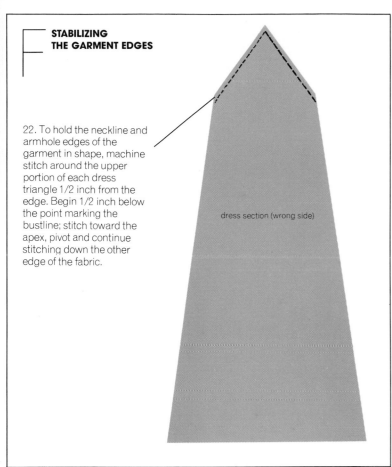

F STABILIZING THE GARMENT EDGES

22. To hold the neckline and armhole edges of the garment in shape, machine stitch around the upper portion of each dress triangle 1/2 inch from the edge. Begin 1/2 inch below the point marking the bustline; stitch toward the apex, pivot and continue stitching down the other edge of the fabric.

dress section (wrong side)

G STITCHING THE DRESS

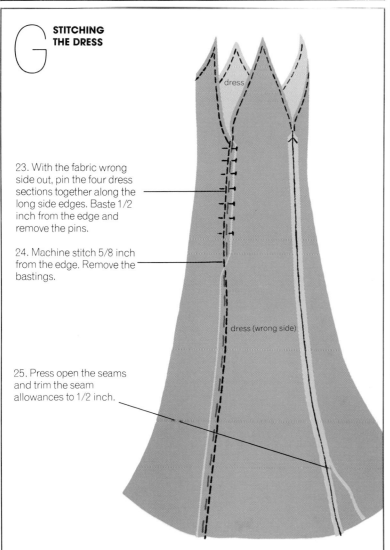

23. With the fabric wrong side out, pin the four dress sections together along the long side edges. Baste 1/2 inch from the edge and remove the pins.

24. Machine stitch 5/8 inch from the edge. Remove the bastings.

25. Press open the seams and trim the seam allowances to 1/2 inch.

dress

dress (wrong side)

H STITCHING THE FACING

26. With the facing wrong side out, pin the four facing triangles together along the short side edges. Baste 1/2 inch from the edge and remove the pins.

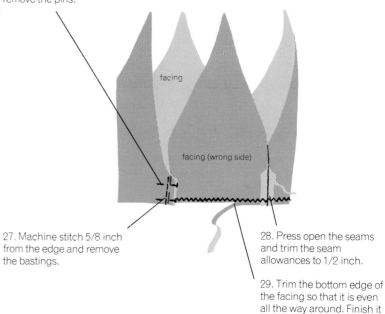

facing

facing (wrong side)

27. Machine stitch 5/8 inch from the edge and remove the bastings.

28. Press open the seams and trim the seam allowances to 1/2 inch.

29. Trim the bottom edge of the facing so that it is even all the way around. Finish it with a zigzag stitch.

continued

ATTACHING THE FACING TO THE DRESS

30. Turn the dress right side out and slip the facing over it, wrong side out.

31. Pin the facing to the dress, matching first at the side seams, then pinning at 1-inch intervals along the V-shaped armhole and neckline edges. Baste 1/2 inch from the edge and remove the pins.

32. Machine stitch 5/8 inch from the edge, pivoting at the base of each V and at each tip. Remove the bastings.

dress (wrong side)

facing (wrong side)

dress

33. Trim the seam allowances along the stitched edges to 1/4 inch.

34. Trim the seam allowances diagonally at the tip of each of the triangles.

35. Clip straight into the seam allowances at the base of each V, cutting up to but not into the stitching.

36. Turn the dress wrong side out. Fold the facing to the inside of the dress and press.

37. Pin the facing to the seam allowances of the four side seams and attach with a line of overcast stitches. Do not catch the garment fabric in the stitching.

dress

facing

dress (wrong side)

FINISHING THE DRESS

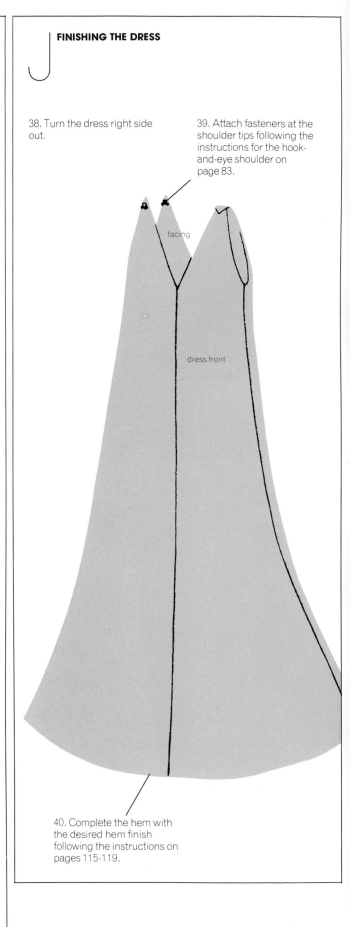

38. Turn the dress right side out.

39. Attach fasteners at the shoulder tips following the instructions for the hook-and-eye shoulder on page 83.

facing

dress front

40. Complete the hem with the desired hem finish following the instructions on pages 115-119.

THE SELF-LINED WRAPAROUND SCARF

A PREPARING THE FABRIC

1. For an average size triangle wraparound scarf, take 36-inch-wide fabric and cut a 40- to 42-inch length, allowing 4 to 6 inches for wastage in straightening the fabric. To make a larger scarf, use 45-inch wide fabric.

2. To make sure one crosswise edge of the fabric is straight, make a small cut into one of the finished, or selvage, edges. Then snag a crosswise thread with a pin. Gently pull the thread so that it shows up as a puckered line along the width of the fabric.

3. Cut along the puckered line from one lengthwise edge to the other.

4. Place the fabric wrong side down on a flat surface and fold it diagonally so that the crosswise edge straightened in Steps 2 and 3 lines up against the bottom selvage edge.

5. Pin the two layers of fabric together along the matched edges.

6. Smooth out the folded fabric with your hand and press along the diagonal fold.

7. Pin the two layers of fabric together along the second selvage edge.

8. Trim away the excess fabric from the second crosswise edge so that it is even with the second selvage edge.

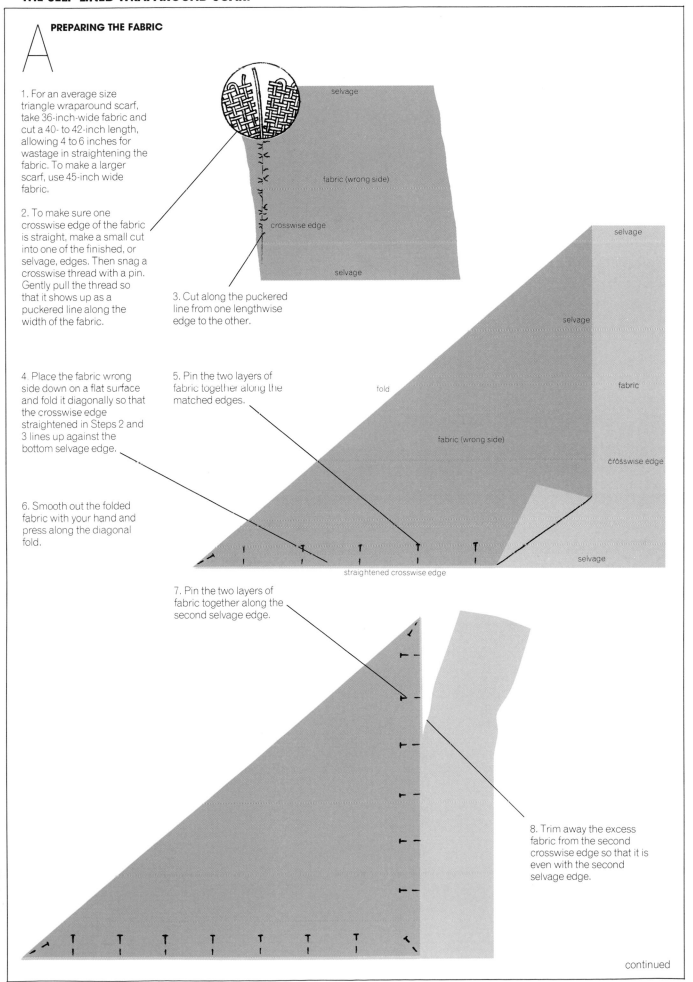

continued

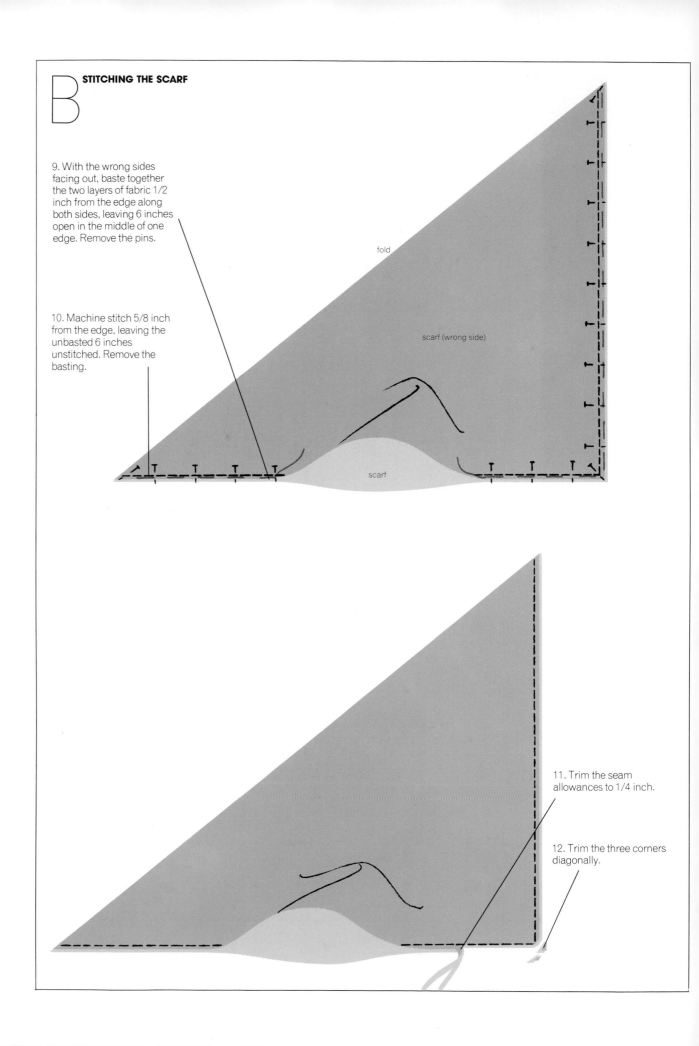

9. With the wrong sides facing out, baste together the two layers of fabric 1/2 inch from the edge along both sides, leaving 6 inches open in the middle of one edge. Remove the pins.

10. Machine stitch 5/8 inch from the edge, leaving the unbasted 6 inches unstitched. Remove the basting.

fold

scarf (wrong side)

scarf

11. Trim the seam allowances to 1/4 inch.

12. Trim the three corners diagonally.

FINISHING THE SCARF

13. Turn the scarf right side out by pulling the fabric through the 6-inch opening. Press.

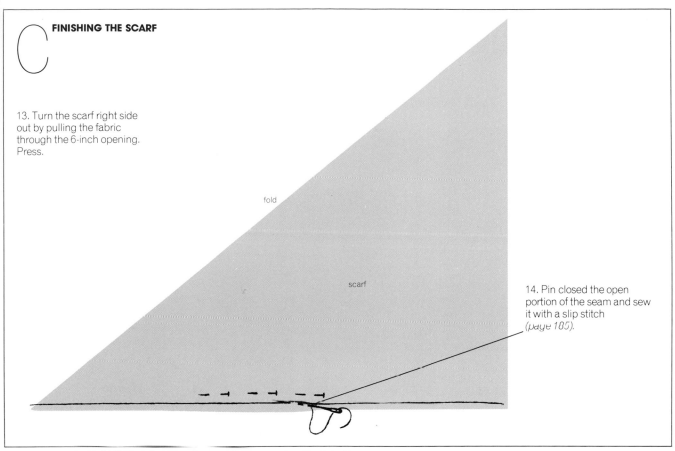

fold

scarf

14. Pin closed the open portion of the seam and sew it with a slip stitch (page 185).

THE WRAPAROUND SCARF WITH CONTRASTING LINING

1. To make a triangle wraparound scarf with a contrasting lining, make two separate triangles instead of one folded over, following the instructions for the self-lined scarf in Steps 1-8. Pin one of the lining triangles to one of the fabric triangles around all three sides. Discard the other lining and fabric triangles or use them to make a second scarf.

2. Baste the lining and the fabric together around all three sides, machine stitch and trim following the directions for the self-lined scarf, Steps 9-12, making sure to have a 6-inch opening for pulling the scarf right side out.

3. Turn the scarf right side out and finish according to the directions for the self-lined scarf, Steps 13-14.

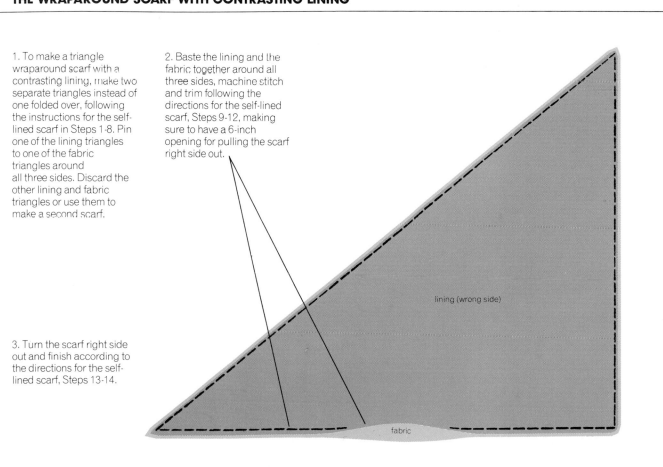

lining (wrong side)

fabric

A complete outfit made from circles

It is easy enough to visualize a circle as the basis of the beret at left—but the pullover and pants? Yet they too have a circular origin, and all three garments can be made with the simple instructions on the following pages. There are no patterns to follow, and few seams to stitch, so you should be able to finish your outfit in about two days.

Among the wide variety of possible choices of fabric are terry cloth, lamé, satin, wool, fake fur (for the hat), and, of course, knits. Silk is not advisable for the pullover or the hat. You will need a wide piece of fabric —at least 54 inches—to provide enough length for the pants. If the fabric you choose comes only in 45-inch widths, buy an extra half yard and seam two pieces together to create the necessary width. You will also need 30 inches of 48-inch-wide rib-knit sweater fabric for the collar, cuffs and waistband.

Before starting to work, clear off a large, flat surface—a good expanse of floor is fine—and assemble three simple tools: a compass and pencil, a thumbtack and a ball of unstretchable string. If your sewing machine does not have a marked throat plate or a seam guide (page 33), put a piece of cellophane tape on the throat plate 1/2 inch from the needle; this improvised seam guide will serve for most of the seams.

THE CIRCLE PULLOVER

A TAKING BODY MEASUREMENTS

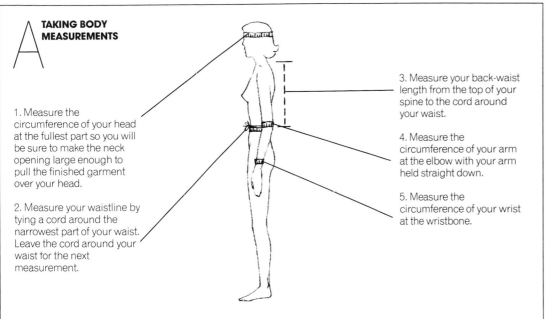

1. Measure the circumference of your head at the fullest part so you will be sure to make the neck opening large enough to pull the finished garment over your head.

2. Measure your waistline by tying a cord around the narrowest part of your waist. Leave the cord around your waist for the next measurement.

3. Measure your back-waist length from the top of your spine to the cord around your waist.

4. Measure the circumference of your arm at the elbow with your arm held straight down.

5. Measure the circumference of your wrist at the wristbone.

B MAKING THE CIRCLE

6. To make the circle pullover, you will need fabric as wide and as long as twice the back-waist length taken in Step 2, plus 2 inches on both the width and the length for seam allowances.

7. Fold the fabric lengthwise, wrong side out.

8. Then fold over one end crosswise to a distance equal to your back-waist length plus 1 inch.

9. To keep the fabric from slipping, pin the four thicknesses of fabric together at 4-inch intervals along the selvage edge and the raw edge.

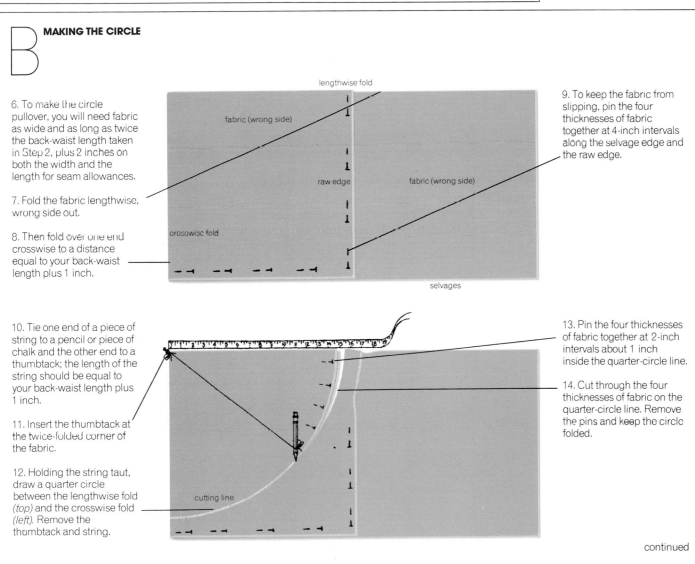

lengthwise fold

fabric (wrong side)

raw edge

fabric (wrong side)

crosswise fold

selvages

10. Tie one end of a piece of string to a pencil or piece of chalk and the other end to a thumbtack; the length of the string should be equal to your back-waist length plus 1 inch.

11. Insert the thumbtack at the twice-folded corner of the fabric.

12. Holding the string taut, draw a quarter circle between the lengthwise fold (top) and the crosswise fold (left). Remove the thumbtack and string.

cutting line

13. Pin the four thicknesses of fabric together at 2-inch intervals about 1 inch inside the quarter-circle line.

14. Cut through the four thicknesses of fabric on the quarter-circle line. Remove the pins and keep the circle folded.

continued

MARKING THE CIRCLE

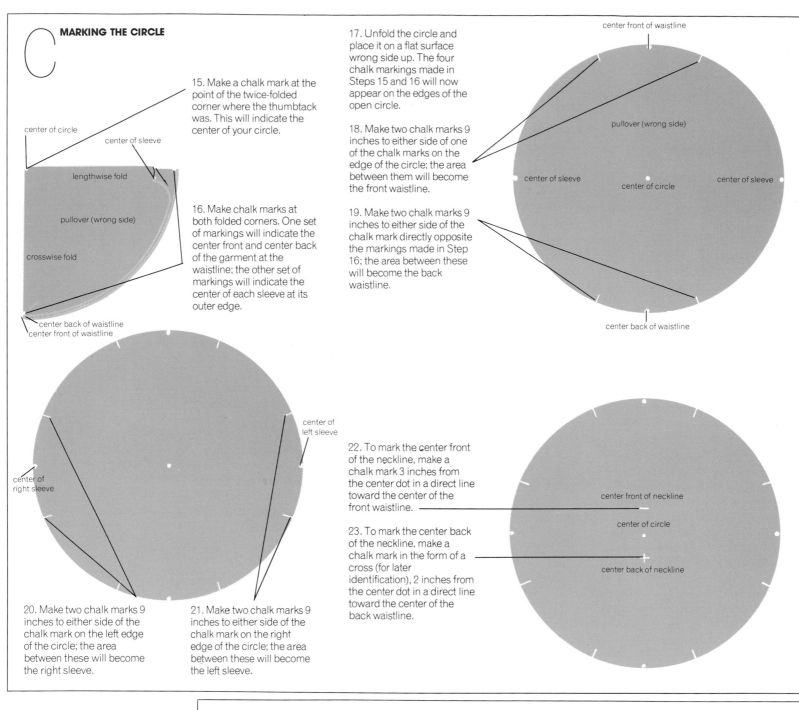

15. Make a chalk mark at the point of the twice-folded corner where the thumbtack was. This will indicate the center of your circle.

center of circle

center of sleeve

lengthwise fold

pullover (wrong side)

crosswise fold

center back of waistline
center front of waistline

16. Make chalk marks at both folded corners. One set of markings will indicate the center front and center back of the garment at the waistline; the other set of markings will indicate the center of each sleeve at its outer edge.

17. Unfold the circle and place it on a flat surface wrong side up. The four chalk markings made in Steps 15 and 16 will now appear on the edges of the open circle.

18. Make two chalk marks 9 inches to either side of one of the chalk marks on the edge of the circle; the area between them will become the front waistline.

19. Make two chalk marks 9 inches to either side of the chalk mark directly opposite the markings made in Step 16; the area between these will become the back waistline.

center front of waistline

pullover (wrong side)

center of sleeve   center of circle   center of sleeve

center back of waistline

center of left sleeve

center of right sleeve

20. Make two chalk marks 9 inches to either side of the chalk mark on the left edge of the circle; the area between these will become the right sleeve.

21. Make two chalk marks 9 inches to either side of the chalk mark on the right edge of the circle; the area between these will become the left sleeve.

22. To mark the center front of the neckline, make a chalk mark 3 inches from the center dot in a direct line toward the center of the front waistline.

23. To mark the center back of the neckline, make a chalk mark in the form of a cross (for later identification), 2 inches from the center dot in a direct line toward the center of the back waistline.

center front of neckline

center of circle

center back of neckline

D **MAKING THE NECKLINE OPENING**

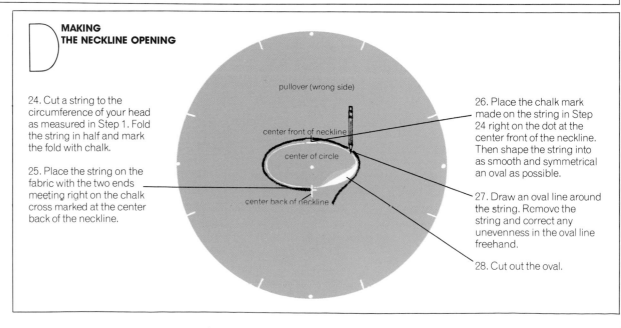

24. Cut a string to the circumference of your head as measured in Step 1. Fold the string in half and mark the fold with chalk.

25. Place the string on the fabric with the two ends meeting right on the chalk cross marked at the center back of the neckline.

pullover (wrong side)

center front of neckline

center of circle

center back of neckline

26. Place the chalk mark made on the string in Step 24 right on the dot at the center front of the neckline. Then shape the string into as smooth and symmetrical an oval as possible.

27. Draw an oval line around the string. Remove the string and correct any unevenness in the oval line freehand.

28. Cut out the oval.

E PREPARING THE SLEEVE AND WAISTLINE EDGES

29. Set your sewing machine at 6 stitches to the inch and run two lines of machine basting, one 1/4 inch, and the other 1/2 inch, from the outer edge of the circle; run these parallel basting lines between the markings that indicate the front waistline, the back waistline, the left sleeve and the right sleeve. Leave 4 inches of loose thread at both ends of each line of basting.

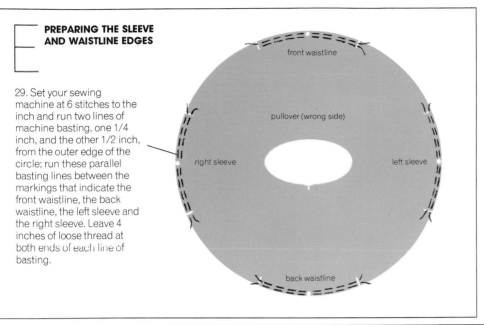

F STITCHING THE UNDERARM SEAMS

30. Fold the circle in half with the neck opening at the top.

31. Pin the front and the back of the pullover together at 2-inch intervals along the sides between the sleeve and waistline edges. Baste and remove the pins.

32. Reset your sewing machine to the normal 12 stitches to the inch and machine stitch the sides 1/2 inch from the edge. Remove the bastings.

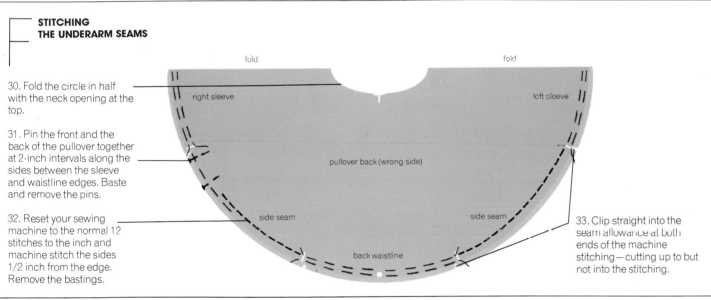

33. Clip straight into the seam allowance at both ends of the machine stitching—cutting up to but not into the stitching.

G GATHERING THE WAISTLINE AND SLEEVE EDGES

34. Insert a pin at each end of the machine-basted sections.

35. Wind the loose threads above and around the pin at one end, in a figure 8.

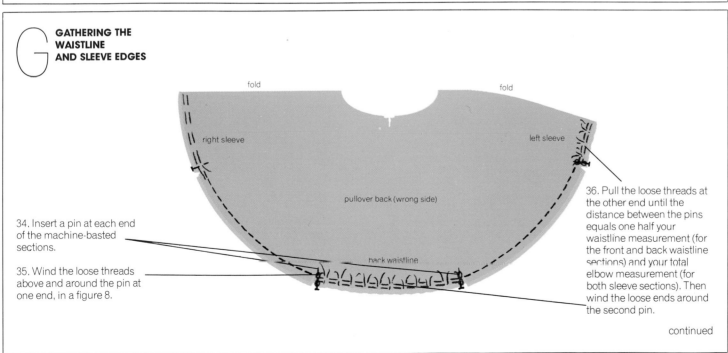

36. Pull the loose threads at the other end until the distance between the pins equals one half your waistline measurement (for the front and back waistline sections) and your total elbow measurement (for both sleeve sections). Then wind the loose ends around the second pin.

continued

H CUTTING OUT THE COLLAR, WAISTBAND AND CUFFS

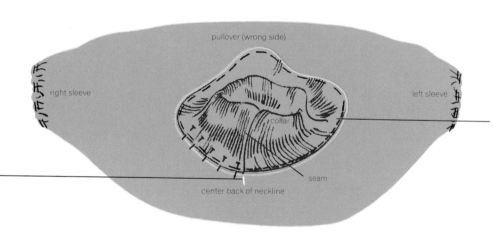

collar

waistband

cuff cuff

37. To make the collar, waistband and cuffs, you will need 30 inches of a single thickness of 48-inch-wide rib-knit sweater fabric (if the rib-knit fabric comes in tubular form, simply cut open one side of the tube).

38. Cut the rib-knit fabric in half lengthwise.

39. Cut the 15-inch-wide strips for your waistband, collar and cuffs. Make the waistband strip 1 inch longer than your waistline; the collar strip 1 inch longer than your head measurement and the cuff strips 1 inch longer than your wrist measurement.

SEWING THE WAISTBAND, COLLAR AND CUFFS

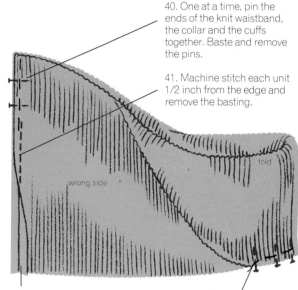

wrong side

fold

40. One at a time, pin the ends of the knit waistband, the collar and the cuffs together. Baste and remove the pins.

41. Machine stitch each unit 1/2 inch from the edge and remove the basting.

42. Press the seams of each unit open.

43. Fold over each unit; pin and baste the cut edge.

J ATTACHING THE WAISTBAND, COLLAR AND CUFFS

44. Turn the garment wrong side out and insert the waistband, collar and cuffs, one at a time, into the garment.

45. Pin the waistband, collar and cuffs to the garment. Align the collar seam with the chalk cross on the garment marking the center back of the neckline. Align the waistband seam with one of the side seams. Align the cuff seam with the side seam. Baste 3/8 inch from the edge. Remove the pins.

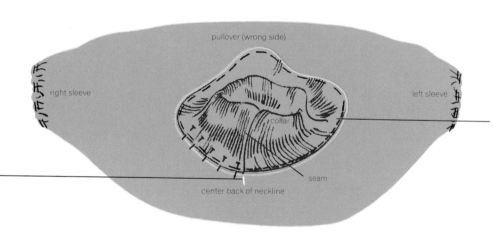

pullover (wrong side)

right sleeve

left sleeve

collar

seam

center back of neckline

46. Set your machine at 10 stitches to the inch and machine stitch around the neckline, waistline and sleeve edges 1/2 inch from the edge. Finish the circles by letting your stitching overlap 1/2 inch.

47. Remove the pins inserted in Step 34 to hold the bastings at the waistline and sleeve edges. Remove the bastings.

K FINISHING THE CIRCLE PULLOVER

48. Turn the garment right side out. Do not press.

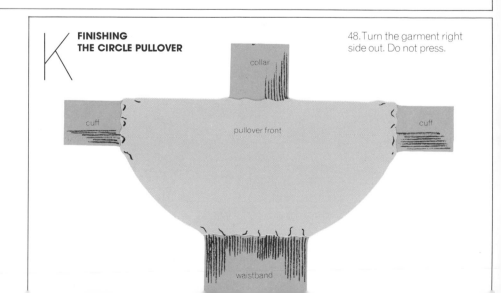

collar

cuff

pullover front

cuff

waistband

THE CIRCLE BERET

A MEASURING THE CIRCLES

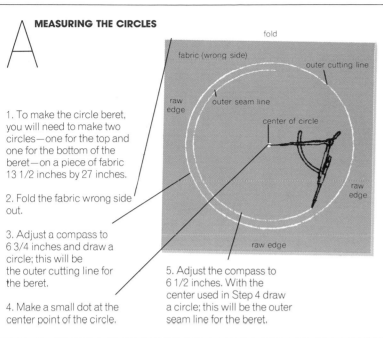

fold

fabric (wrong side)

outer cutting line

raw edge

outer seam line

center of circle

raw edge

raw edge

1. To make the circle beret, you will need to make two circles—one for the top and one for the bottom of the beret—on a piece of fabric 13 1/2 inches by 27 inches.

2. Fold the fabric wrong side out.

3. Adjust a compass to 6 3/4 inches and draw a circle; this will be the outer cutting line for the beret.

4. Make a small dot at the center point of the circle.

5. Adjust the compass to 6 1/2 inches. With the center used in Step 4 draw a circle; this will be the outer seam line for the beret.

B CUTTING OUT THE CIRCLES

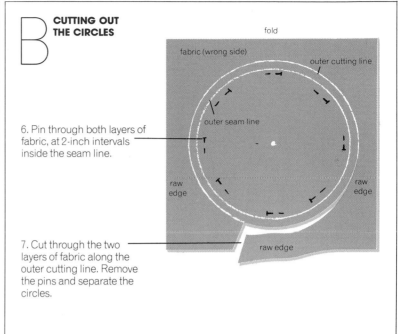

fold

fabric (wrong side)

outer cutting line

outer seam line

raw edge

raw edge

raw edge

6. Pin through both layers of fabric, at 2-inch intervals inside the seam line.

7. Cut through the two layers of fabric along the outer cutting line. Remove the pins and separate the circles.

C MAKING THE HEAD OPENING

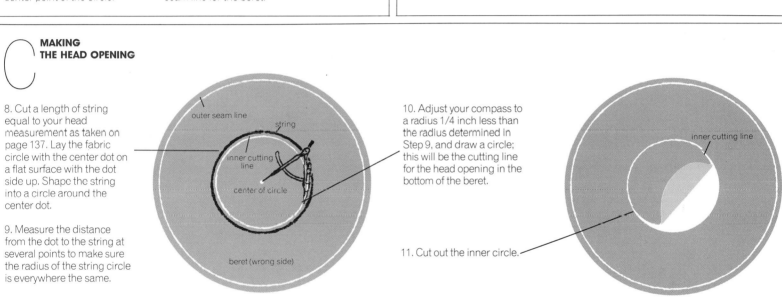

outer seam line

string

inner cutting line

center of circle

beret (wrong side)

inner cutting line

8. Cut a length of string equal to your head measurement as taken on page 137. Lay the fabric circle with the center dot on a flat surface with the dot side up. Shape the string into a circle around the center dot.

9. Measure the distance from the dot to the string at several points to make sure the radius of the string circle is everywhere the same.

10. Adjust your compass to a radius 1/4 inch less than the radius determined in Step 9, and draw a circle; this will be the cutting line for the head opening in the bottom of the beret.

11. Cut out the inner circle.

D JOINING THE CIRCLES

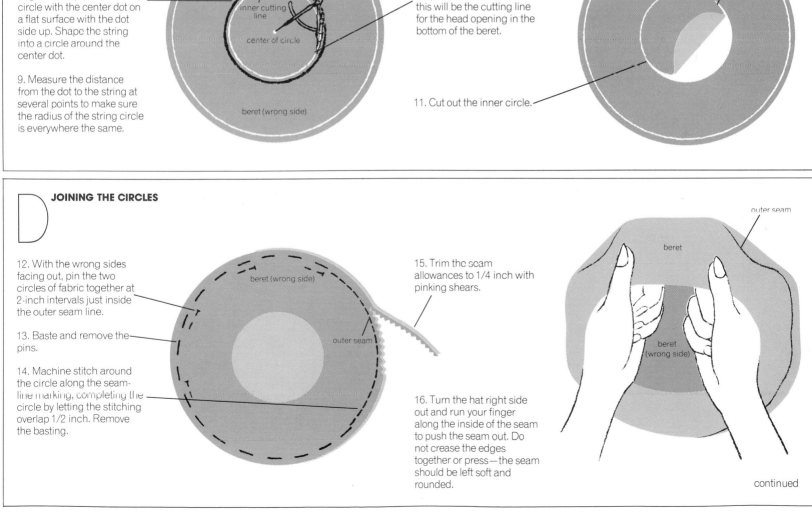

beret (wrong side)

outer seam

beret

outer seam

beret (wrong side)

12. With the wrong sides facing out, pin the two circles of fabric together at 2-inch intervals just inside the outer seam line.

13. Baste and remove the pins.

14. Machine stitch around the circle along the seam-line marking, completing the circle by letting the stitching overlap 1/2 inch. Remove the basting.

15. Trim the seam allowances to 1/4 inch with pinking shears.

16. Turn the hat right side out and run your finger along the inside of the seam to push the seam out. Do not crease the edges together or press—the seam should be left soft and rounded.

continued

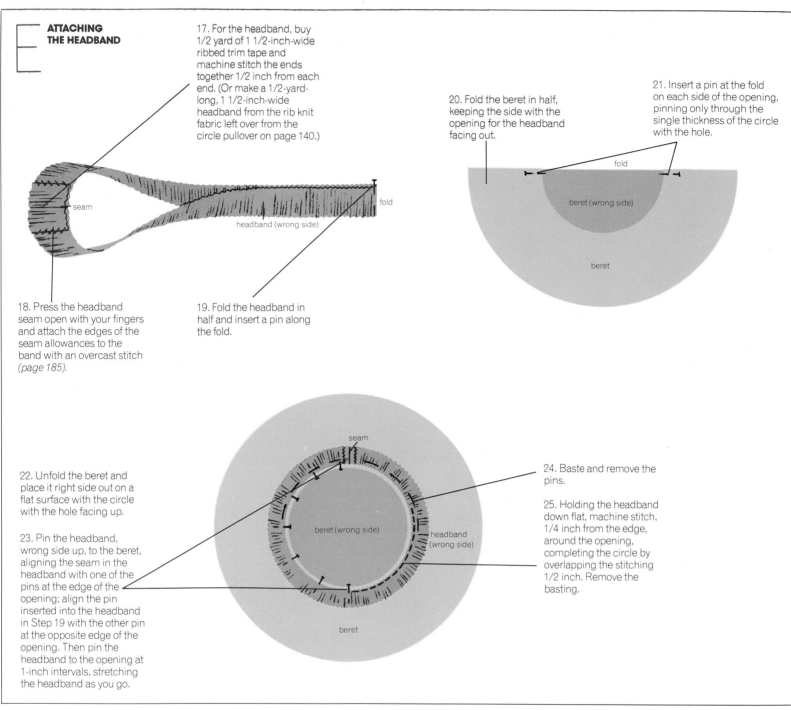

ATTACHING THE HEADBAND

17. For the headband, buy 1/2 yard of 1 1/2-inch-wide ribbed trim tape and machine stitch the ends together 1/2 inch from each end. (Or make a 1/2-yard-long, 1 1/2-inch-wide headband from the rib knit fabric left over from the circle pullover on page 140.)

seam

headband (wrong side)

fold

18. Press the headband seam open with your fingers and attach the edges of the seam allowances to the band with an overcast stitch (page 185).

19. Fold the headband in half and insert a pin along the fold.

20. Fold the beret in half, keeping the side with the opening for the headband facing out.

21. Insert a pin at the fold on each side of the opening, pinning only through the single thickness of the circle with the hole.

fold

beret (wrong side)

beret

seam

beret (wrong side)

headband (wrong side)

beret

22. Unfold the beret and place it right side out on a flat surface with the circle with the hole facing up.

23. Pin the headband, wrong side up, to the beret, aligning the seam in the headband with one of the pins at the edge of the opening; align the pin inserted into the headband in Step 19 with the other pin at the opposite edge of the opening. Then pin the headband to the opening at 1-inch intervals, stretching the headband as you go.

24. Baste and remove the pins.

25. Holding the headband down flat, machine stitch, 1/4 inch from the edge, around the opening, completing the circle by overlapping the stitching 1/2 inch. Remove the basting.

FINISHING THE BERET

26. When you have finished stitching the headband to the beret it will automatically fold inward because it was stretched when it was attached to the beret in Box E. Do not press.

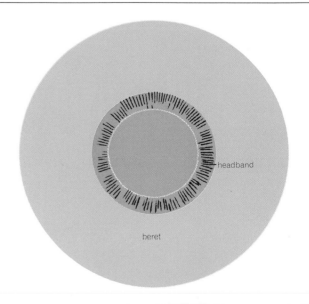

headband

beret

THE CIRCLE PANTS

TAKING BODY MEASUREMENTS

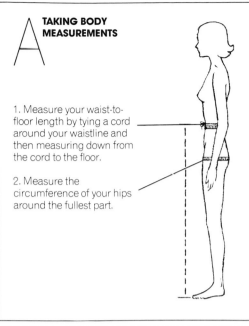

1. Measure your waist-to-floor length by tying a cord around your waistline and then measuring down from the cord to the floor.

2. Measure the circumference of your hips around the fullest part.

B PREPARING THE FABRIC

3. To make the circle pants, you will need to make two semicircles—one for each leg—using fabric at least 54 inches wide cut to a length equal to four times your waist-to-floor measurement plus 12 inches.

4. Spread the fabric out on a flat surface, wrong side down. Then fold over one end crosswise to a distance equal to your waist-to-floor measurement plus 7 inches.

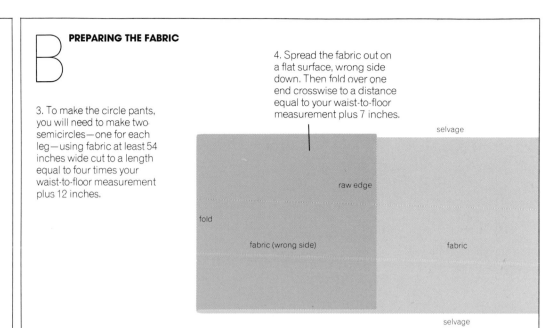

C MARKING THE WAISTLINE EDGE OF ONE PANTS LEG

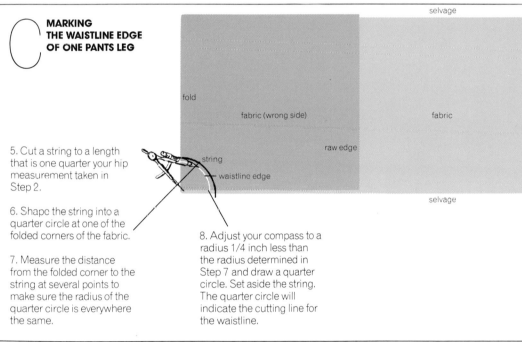

5. Cut a string to a length that is one quarter your hip measurement taken in Step 2.

6. Shape the string into a quarter circle at one of the folded corners of the fabric.

7. Measure the distance from the folded corner to the string at several points to make sure the radius of the quarter circle is everywhere the same.

8. Adjust your compass to a radius 1/4 inch less than the radius determined in Step 7 and draw a quarter circle. Set aside the string. The quarter circle will indicate the cutting line for the waistline.

D MARKING THE BOTTOM EDGE OF ONE PANTS LEG

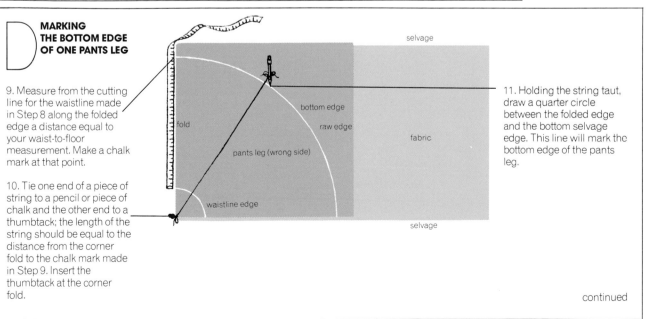

9. Measure from the cutting line for the waistline made in Step 8 along the folded edge a distance equal to your waist-to-floor measurement. Make a chalk mark at that point.

10. Tie one end of a piece of string to a pencil or piece of chalk and the other end to a thumbtack; the length of the string should be equal to the distance from the corner fold to the chalk mark made in Step 9. Insert the thumbtack at the corner fold.

11. Holding the string taut, draw a quarter circle between the folded edge and the bottom selvage edge. This line will mark the bottom edge of the pants leg.

continued

CUTTING OUT ONE PANTS LEG

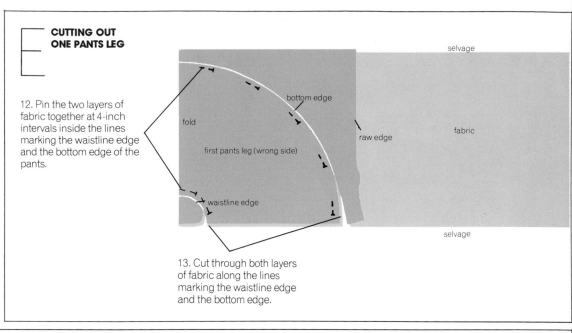

12. Pin the two layers of fabric together at 4-inch intervals inside the lines marking the waistline edge and the bottom edge of the pants.

13. Cut through both layers of fabric along the lines marking the waistline edge and the bottom edge.

CUTTING OUT THE SECOND PANTS LEG

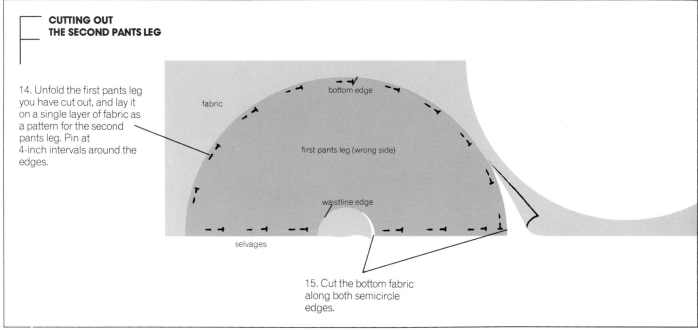

14. Unfold the first pants leg you have cut out, and lay it on a single layer of fabric as a pattern for the second pants leg. Pin at 4-inch intervals around the edges.

15. Cut the bottom fabric along both semicircle edges.

G SEAMING THE SEPARATE PANTS LEGS

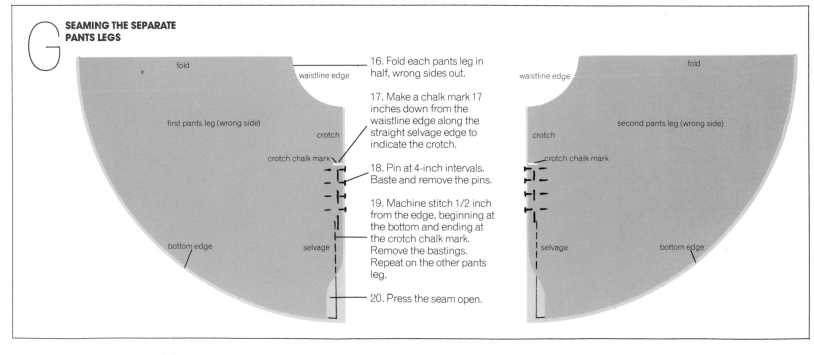

16. Fold each pants leg in half, wrong sides out.

17. Make a chalk mark 17 inches down from the waistline edge along the straight selvage edge to indicate the crotch.

18. Pin at 4-inch intervals. Baste and remove the pins.

19. Machine stitch 1/2 inch from the edge, beginning at the bottom and ending at the crotch chalk mark. Remove the bastings. Repeat on the other pants leg.

20. Press the seam open.

JOINING THE PANTS LEGS

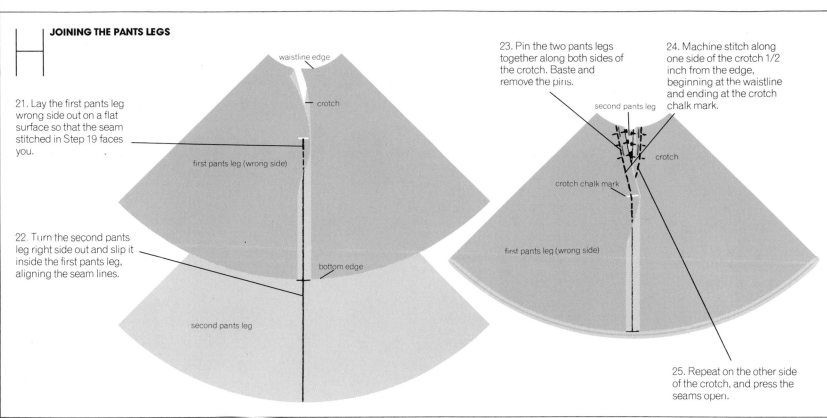

21. Lay the first pants leg wrong side out on a flat surface so that the seam stitched in Step 19 faces you.

22. Turn the second pants leg right side out and slip it inside the first pants leg, aligning the seam lines.

waistline edge

crotch

first pants leg (wrong side)

bottom edge

second pants leg

23. Pin the two pants legs together along both sides of the crotch. Baste and remove the pins.

24. Machine stitch along one side of the crotch 1/2 inch from the edge, beginning at the waistline and ending at the crotch chalk mark.

second pants leg

crotch

crotch chalk mark

first pants leg (wrong side)

25. Repeat on the other side of the crotch, and press the seams open.

COMPLETING THE PANTS

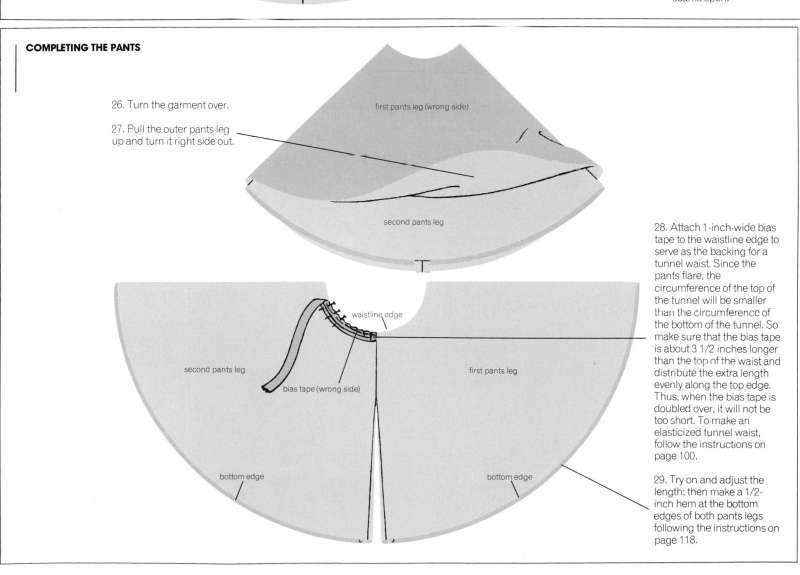

26. Turn the garment over.

27. Pull the outer pants leg up and turn it right side out.

first pants leg (wrong side)

second pants leg

waistline edge

second pants leg

bias tape (wrong side)

first pants leg

bottom edge

bottom edge

28. Attach 1-inch-wide bias tape to the waistline edge to serve as the backing for a tunnel waist. Since the pants flare, the circumference of the top of the tunnel will be smaller than the circumference of the bottom of the tunnel. So make sure that the bias tape is about 3 1/2 inches longer than the top of the waist and distribute the extra length evenly along the top edge. Thus, when the bias tape is doubled over, it will not be too short. To make an elasticized tunnel waist, follow the instructions on page 100.

29. Try on and adjust the length; then make a 1/2-inch hem at the bottom edges of both pants legs following the instructions on page 118.

A swirl of pleats from rectangles

The blouse and skirt at right, aswirl with pleats, were made from nothing more than simple rectangles. The blouse consists of one large rectangle for the top and sleeves, edged with four smaller pleated rectangles. The skirt is one long rectangle, pleated and seamed at the center back. All the pieces are cut so that the fabric selvages can serve as hems.

To make the blouse in a solid fabric or nondirectional print, use fabric at least 36 inches wide. To determine the length of the fabric, add 1 yard to the shoulder-upper arm measurement taken in Step 1 (opposite page) plus whichever is larger: six times the shoulder-upper arm measurement or 12 times the shoulder-to-bust measurement taken in Step 2. For a border print, as shown here, you will need about 75 per cent more. The skirt—in a solid or a border print—calls for fabric 1 inch wider than the desired length of the skirt and three times as long as your hip measurement, plus 12 inches. You will also need 1 1/2-inch-wide grosgrain ribbon for a waistband. Use a 75 per cent or, preferably, 100 per cent polyester crepe. Send the sections that require pleating to a commercial pleater.

THE BLOUSE

continued

A TAKING BODY MEASUREMENTS

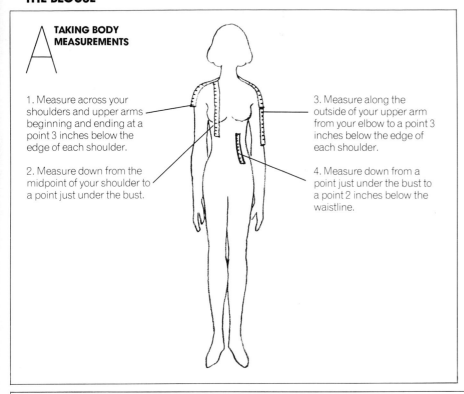

1. Measure across your shoulders and upper arms beginning and ending at a point 3 inches below the edge of each shoulder.

2. Measure down from the midpoint of your shoulder to a point just under the bust.

3. Measure along the outside of your upper arm from your elbow to a point 3 inches below the edge of each shoulder.

4. Measure down from a point just under the bust to a point 2 inches below the waistline.

B MAKING A PATTERN FOR THE BLOUSE

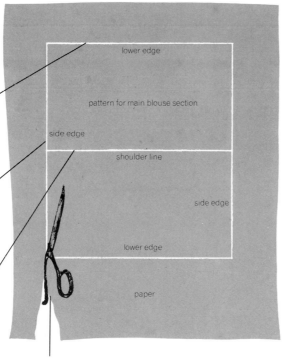

5. Lay a large sheet of paper, about 3 by 3 feet, on a flat surface.

6. Determine the width of the rectangle, and thus the width of the lower edges of the blouse, by adding 1 1/4 inches for seam allowances to the shoulder-upper arm measurement made in Step 1.

7. Determine the length of the rectangle, which will form the side edges of the main blouse section, by doubling the shoulder-to-bust measurement made in Step 2 and adding 1 1/4 inches for seam allowances.

8. To indicate the shoulder line, which will divide the rectangle equally into front and back sections, rule a line across the rectangle parallel to the two lines that indicate the lower edges.

9. Cut out the paper rectangle along the marked lines.

lower edge

pattern for main blouse section

side edge

shoulder line

side edge

lower edge

paper

10. Determine the length of the rectangle that will become the neckline facing by subtracting 7 1/4 inches from the shoulder-upper arm measurement made in Step 1.

11. Make the sides of this rectangle 5 inches long.

facing pattern

shoulder line

paper

12. To indicate the shoulder line, rule a line across the rectangle midway between and parallel to the two longer edges of the rectangle.

13. Cut out the facing pattern along the marked lines.

CUTTING OUT
THE BLOUSE

14. Lay the fabric wrong side up on a flat surface. Pin the pattern pieces for the main blouse section and the neckline facing to the fabric and cut them out.

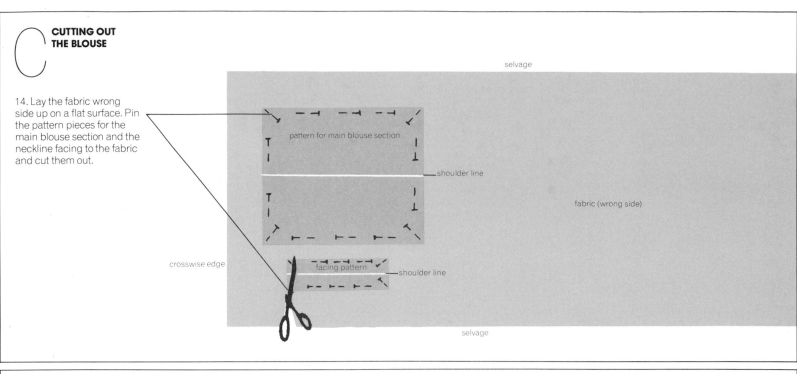

selvage

pattern for main blouse section

shoulder line

fabric (wrong side)

crosswise edge

facing pattern
shoulder line

selvage

D

CUTTING OUT
THE PLEATED SECTIONS

15. Lay the fabric wrong side up on a large flat surface and straighten one crosswise edge as shown on page 133, Box A, Steps 2-3.

16. To determine the length of fabric you will need to have pleated for the lower front and back sections of the blouse, measure both lower edges of the paper pattern made in Steps 5-9, multiply this number by three and add 12 inches to allow for adjustments.

17. Beginning at the straightened crosswise edge of the fabric, measure this length along one of the selvage edges and mark with a pin.

18. To determine the depth of the fabric to be pleated for the lower front and back sections of the blouse, take the bust-to-waist measurement made in Step 4 and add 1 inch for a seam allowance. Mark this measurement on the straightened crosswise edge of the fabric and draw a chalk line parallel to the selvage edge.

19. Complete the rectangle by making a chalk line, perpendicular to the selvage edge, connecting the pin mark made in Step 17 to the chalk line made in Step 18. Cut out the strip of fabric.

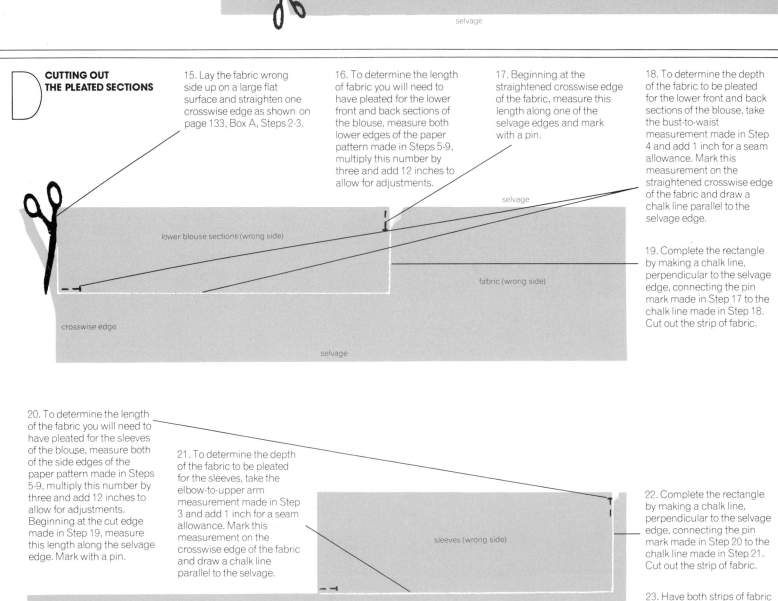

selvage

lower blouse sections (wrong side)

fabric (wrong side)

crosswise edge

selvage

20. To determine the length of the fabric you will need to have pleated for the sleeves of the blouse, measure both of the side edges of the paper pattern made in Steps 5-9, multiply this number by three and add 12 inches to allow for adjustments. Beginning at the cut edge made in Step 19, measure this length along the selvage edge. Mark with a pin.

21. To determine the depth of the fabric to be pleated for the sleeves, take the elbow-to-upper arm measurement made in Step 3 and add 1 inch for a seam allowance. Mark this measurement on the crosswise edge of the fabric and draw a chalk line parallel to the selvage.

sleeves (wrong side)

22. Complete the rectangle by making a chalk line, perpendicular to the selvage edge, connecting the pin mark made in Step 20 to the chalk line made in Step 21. Cut out the strip of fabric.

23. Have both strips of fabric commercially pleated in 1-inch knife pleats.

MARKING THE MAIN BLOUSE SECTION

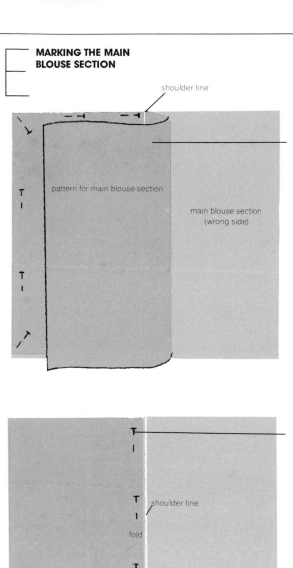

24. Remove the pins holding the pattern to the fabric on one side of the pattern marking for the shoulder line. Fold the pattern in half.

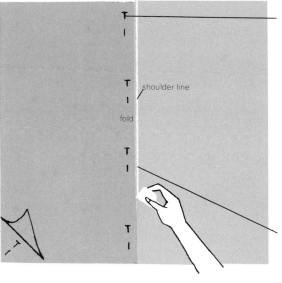

25. Crease the pattern along the shoulder line marking and pin at 4-inch intervals.

26. Mark the shoulder line on the fabric with chalk, using the folded edge of the paper pattern as a guide.

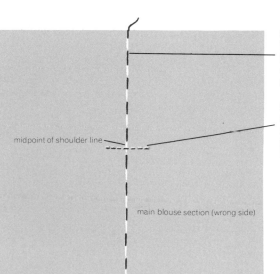
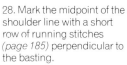

27. Remove the pattern from the fabric and run a line of basting stitches along the chalk line marking the shoulder.

28. Mark the midpoint of the shoulder line with a short row of running stitches *(page 185)* perpendicular to the basting.

MARKING THE FACING

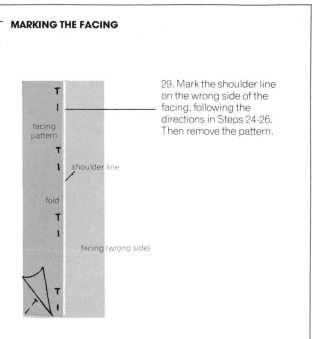

29. Mark the shoulder line on the wrong side of the facing, following the directions in Steps 24-26. Then remove the pattern.

30. To indicate the ends of the neckline opening, mark a point 2 inches from each end of the shoulder line.

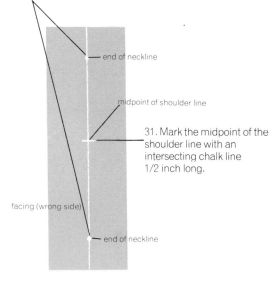

31. Mark the midpoint of the shoulder line with an intersecting chalk line 1/2 inch long.

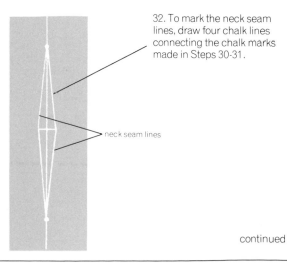

32. To mark the neck seam lines, draw four chalk lines connecting the chalk marks made in Steps 30-31.

continued

G ATTACHING THE FACING

33. Lay the main blouse section wrong side down and place the facing on it, wrong side up.

34. Pin the facing to the main blouse section along the shoulder-line markings, inserting the first pin at the midpoint markings.

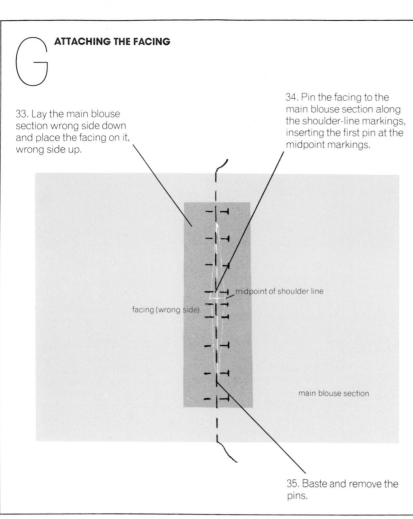

midpoint of shoulder line

facing (wrong side)

main blouse section

35. Baste and remove the pins.

36. Set your machine at 20 stitches to the inch, insert the needle 1 inch from one end of the neckline and stitch to the point. Pivot and take 2 stitches across the point, pivot again and stitch down along the other seam line for 1 inch.

37. Reset the stitch length to the normal 12 stitches to the inch and continue to stitch along the seam line to a point 1 inch from the other neckline point.

38. To finish the seam, repeat Steps 36 and 37 around the second point and the opposite neckline seam.

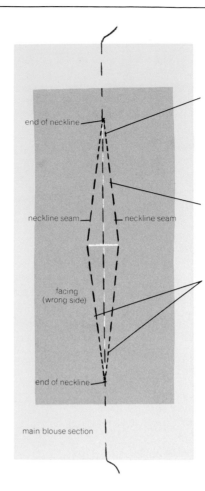

end of neckline

neckline seam

neckline seam

facing (wrong side)

end of neckline

main blouse section

H FINISHING THE FACING

39. Cut open the neckline along the basted shoulder line marking, cutting up to the points, but not into the stitches. Remove the bastings.

40. To finish the raw outer edge of the facing, trim it with pinking shears, rounding off the corners.

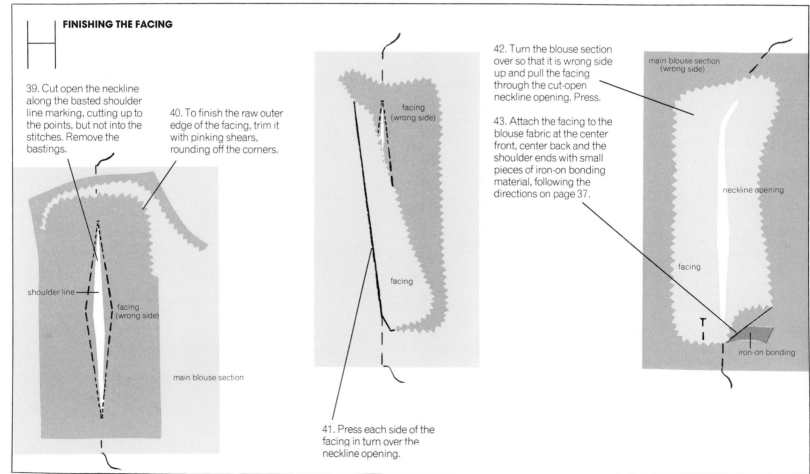

shoulder line

facing (wrong side)

main blouse section

facing (wrong side)

facing

41. Press each side of the facing in turn over the neckline opening.

42. Turn the blouse section over so that it is wrong side up and pull the facing through the cut-open neckline opening. Press.

43. Attach the facing to the blouse fabric at the center front, center back and the shoulder ends with small pieces of iron-on bonding material, following the directions on page 37.

main blouse section (wrong side)

neckline opening

facing

iron-on bonding

44. Place the long pleated fabric strip that will form the lower front and back edges of the blouse wrong side down on a flat surface. Fold the pleats and pin them together along the long cut edge. Leave the pleats unpinned along the selvage edge, which will serve as the hem.

45. To hold the pleats in place, baste 3/8 inch from the long cut edge. Remove the pins. Machine stitch 1/2 inch from the edge and remove the basting.

46. Repeat Steps 44 and 45 to fold, pin and stitch the pleats of the long pleated fabric strip that will form the sleeves.

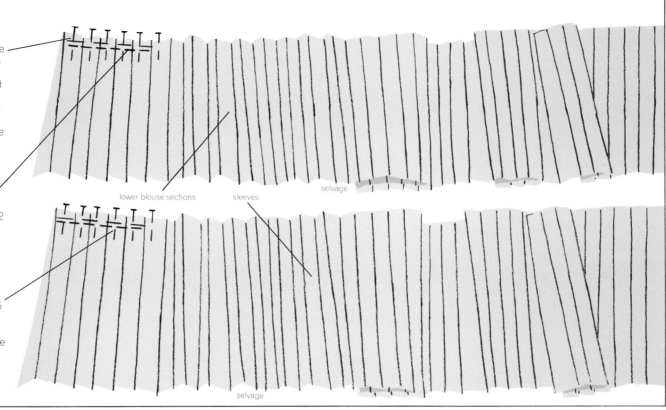

lower blouse sections   sleeves

selvage

selvage

ATTACHING THE
PLEATED LOWER EDGES

lower blouse section (wrong side)

47. Lay the main blouse section on a flat surface wrong side down. Place the long pleated strip for the lower edges of the blouse on it, wrong side up, aligning the stitched edge of the pleated section with one lower edge of the blouse.

48. Align the fold of the first 2-inch pleat segment with the left side edge of the main blouse section and trim away any excess pleating along that fold.

49. Pin the pleated section to one edge of the main blouse section.

50. Cut the pleated section off so that it is even with the right side edge of the blouse rectangle; trim away any excess layers from the last pleat so that the last inch of pleating adjacent to the right side edge of the blouse rectangle will be only one layer thick. Set aside the remaining pleating to be used on the opposite edge of the fabric (Step 53).

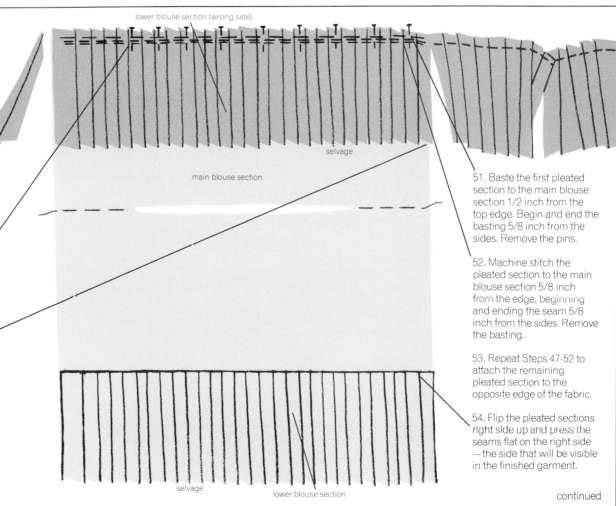

selvage

main blouse section

lower blouse section

51. Baste the first pleated section to the main blouse section 1/2 inch from the top edge. Begin and end the basting 5/8 inch from the sides. Remove the pins.

52. Machine stitch the pleated section to the main blouse section 5/8 inch from the edge, beginning and ending the seam 5/8 inch from the sides. Remove the basting.

53. Repeat Steps 47-52 to attach the remaining pleated section to the opposite edge of the fabric.

54. Flip the pleated sections right side up and press the seams flat on the right side —the side that will be visible in the finished garment.

continued

ATTACHING THE PLEATED SLEEVES

55. To attach the pleated sleeves to the side edges of the main blouse section, repeat Steps 47-54, with one exception: extend the pleated sections 5/8 inch beyond the edges rather than trimming them off flush with the edges.

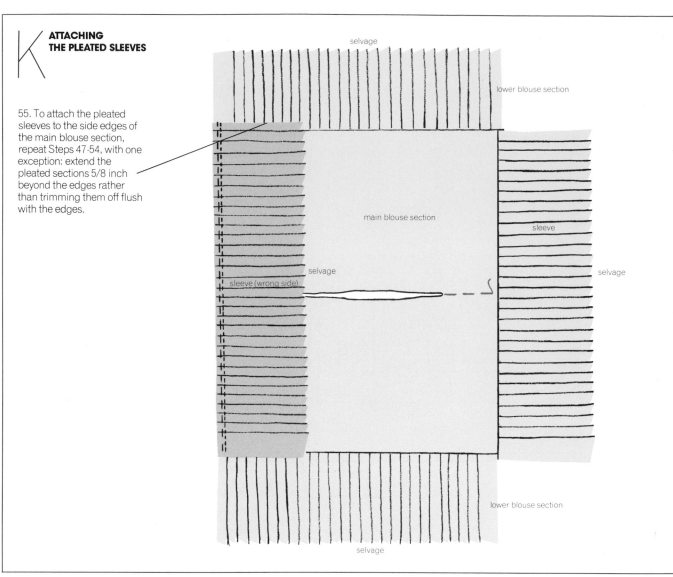

FINISHING THE BLOUSE

56. Turn the blouse wrong side out and finish the side seams and the underarm sleeve seams following the directions for the kimono sleeve, Boxes A-C, pages 95-96, stitching the seams 5/8 inch from the edge of the fabric.

57. Press the side seams and the underarm sleeve seams open. Remove all bastings.

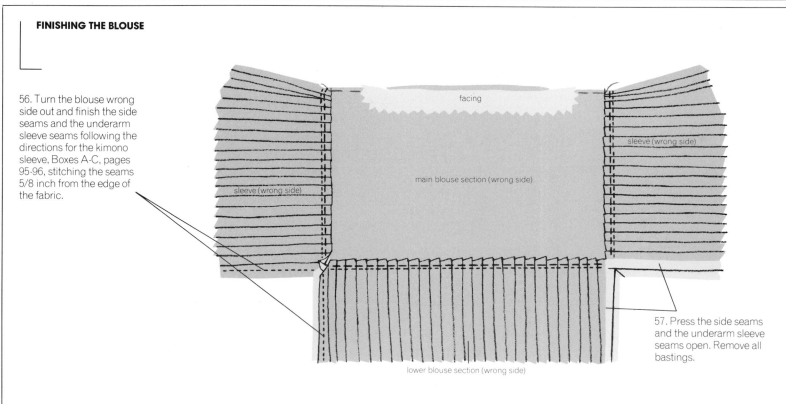

THE SKIRT

A TAKING BODY MEASUREMENTS

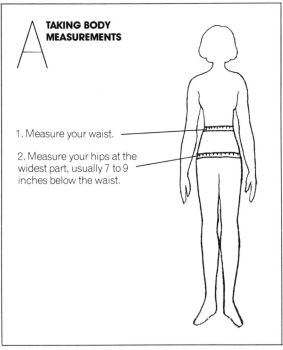

1. Measure your waist.

2. Measure your hips at the widest part, usually 7 to 9 inches below the waist.

B CUTTING THE FABRIC

3. Place the fabric wrong side up on a flat surface.

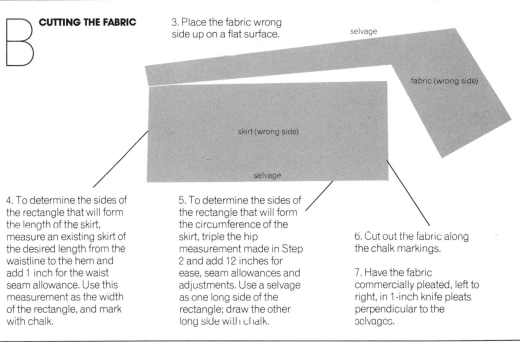

selvage

fabric (wrong side)

skirt (wrong side)

selvage

4. To determine the sides of the rectangle that will form the length of the skirt, measure an existing skirt of the desired length from the waistline to the hem and add 1 inch for the waist seam allowance. Use this measurement as the width of the rectangle, and mark with chalk.

5. To determine the sides of the rectangle that will form the circumference of the skirt, triple the hip measurement made in Step 2 and add 12 inches for ease, seam allowances and adjustments. Use a selvage as one long side of the rectangle; draw the other long side with chalk.

6. Cut out the fabric along the chalk markings.

7. Have the fabric commercially pleated, left to right, in 1-inch knife pleats perpendicular to the selvages.

C PREPARING THE PLEATED FABRIC

8. Place the pleated fabric wrong side down with the long cut edge, which will form the waistline, at the top and the selvage edge, which will serve as the hem, at the bottom.

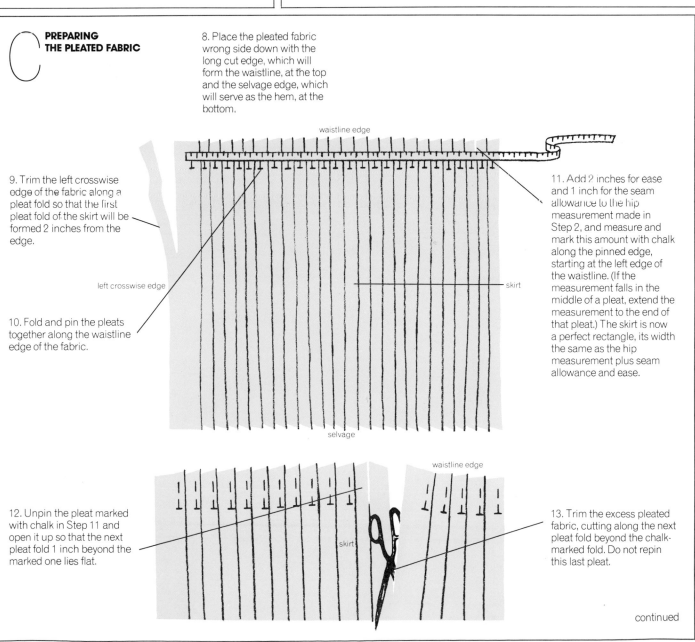

waistline edge

9. Trim the left crosswise edge of the fabric along a pleat fold so that the first pleat fold of the skirt will be formed 2 inches from the edge.

left crosswise edge

10. Fold and pin the pleats together along the waistline edge of the fabric.

skirt

11. Add 2 inches for ease and 1 inch for the seam allowance to the hip measurement made in Step 2, and measure and mark this amount with chalk along the pinned edge, starting at the left edge of the waistline. (If the measurement falls in the middle of a pleat, extend the measurement to the end of that pleat.) The skirt is now a perfect rectangle, its width the same as the hip measurement plus seam allowance and ease.

selvage

waistline edge

12. Unpin the pleat marked with chalk in Step 11 and open it up so that the next pleat fold 1 inch beyond the marked one lies flat.

skirt

13. Trim the excess pleated fabric, cutting along the next pleat fold beyond the chalk-marked fold. Do not repin this last pleat.

continued

D ADJUSTING THE WAISTLINE

14. To determine the amount of adjustment that will be required to reduce the hip width of the skirt to the narrower width at the waist, add 1 inch for ease to the waistline measurement made in Step 1, and subtract this figure from the hip measurement made in Step 2. The difference will be the amount of adjustment required. The amount will have to be distributed equally among all the pleats without taking in any pleat by more than 1/4 inch, or the skirt will not hang properly.

15. To take in the pleats, place the fabric wrong side down and measure out from each pleat fold the amount of adjustment required. Mark this point lightly with chalk close to the waistline edge.

16. Unpin each pleat, bring the folded edge of the pleat up to the chalk mark and repin the pleat.

17. Leave the last pleat fold at the right crosswise edge unpinned.

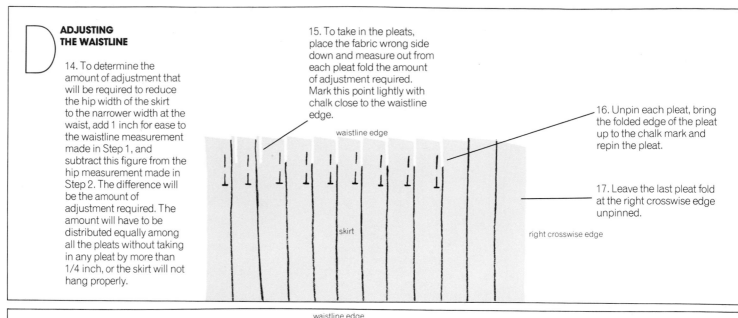

waistline edge

skirt

right crosswise edge

E STITCHING THE WAISTLINE

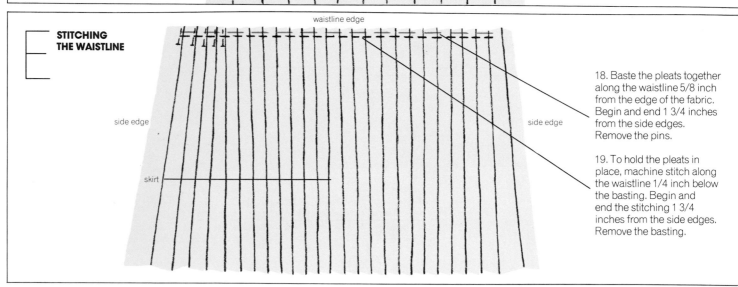

waistline edge

side edge

side edge

skirt

18. Baste the pleats together along the waistline 5/8 inch from the edge of the fabric. Begin and end 1 3/4 inches from the side edges. Remove the pins.

19. To hold the pleats in place, machine stitch along the waistline 1/4 inch below the basting. Begin and end the stitching 1 3/4 inches from the side edges. Remove the basting.

F MAKING THE CENTER BACK SEAM

20. With the wrong sides of the fabric facing out, match the side edges and pin them together 1 inch from the edge of the fabric. Pin from the hem toward the waist.

21. To indicate the length of the closure, measure and mark a point 8 inches down from the waistline edge.

22. Baste the center back seam 3/4 inch from the edge of the fabric, stitching from the hem to the mark indicating the bottom of the closure. Remove the pins.

23. Machine stitch 1 inch from the edge to the mark indicating the bottom of the closure. Remove the basting.

24. Press both seam allowances toward the left back.

25. Baste the left back seam allowance to the waistline edge.

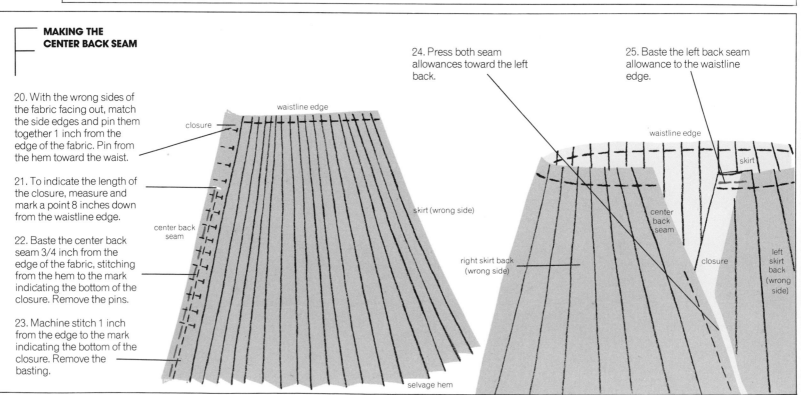

waistline edge

closure

center back seam

skirt (wrong side)

selvage hem

waistline edge

skirt

center back seam

right skirt back (wrong side)

closure

left skirt back (wrong side)

G | ATTACHING THE WAISTBAND

26. Turn the skirt right side out.

27. To make a waistband, cut a piece of 1 1/2-inch-wide grosgrain ribbon 3 1/2 inches longer than the measurement of the waistline of the skirt.

28. Pin the waistband to the right side of the skirt—the side that will be visible when the garment is completed—so that the lower edge of the ribbon overlaps the line of machine stitching securing the pleats by 1/8 inch. Extend the ends of the ribbon 1 3/4 inches beyond each of the open edges of the center back closure.

29. Baste the waistband to the skirt 1/2 inch from the lower edge. Remove the pins.

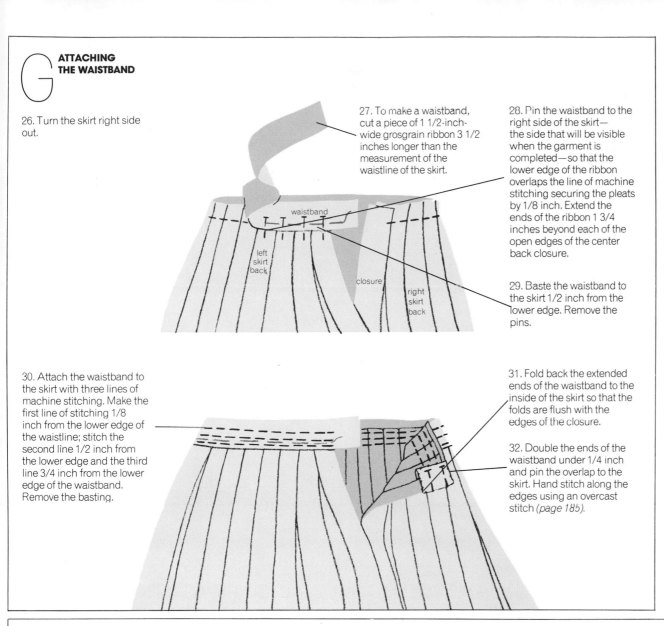

30. Attach the waistband to the skirt with three lines of machine stitching. Make the first line of stitching 1/8 inch from the lower edge of the waistline; stitch the second line 1/2 inch from the lower edge and the third line 3/4 inch from the lower edge of the waistband. Remove the basting.

31. Fold back the extended ends of the waistband to the inside of the skirt so that the folds are flush with the edges of the closure.

32. Double the ends of the waistband under 1/4 inch and pin the overlap to the skirt. Hand stitch along the edges using an overcast stitch (page 185).

H | FINISHING THE SKIRT

33. Place two hooks on the waistband, one near the top and the other near the bottom. Place the next hook just below the waistband and additional hooks at 1 1/2-inch intervals along the rest of the left closure.

34. Using a double strand of knotted thread, stitch around each metal ring, catching only the inside fabric layer.

35. Continue by sliding the needle under the hook and take a few stitches over the hook, under the bend. End with a fastening stitch (page 185) through the inside layer of fabric.

36. Place the overlap so that the bend of the hook falls at the point on the right closure where the straight eye is to be positioned. Sew each eye in place on the right closure by stitching around the two metal rings.

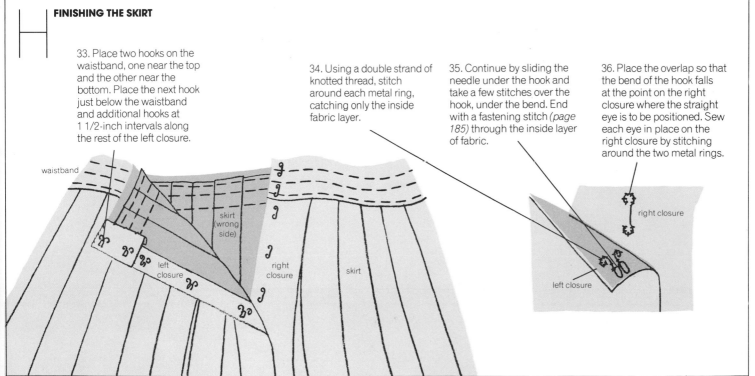

6
GIANT STRIDES WITH YARN AND NEEDLE

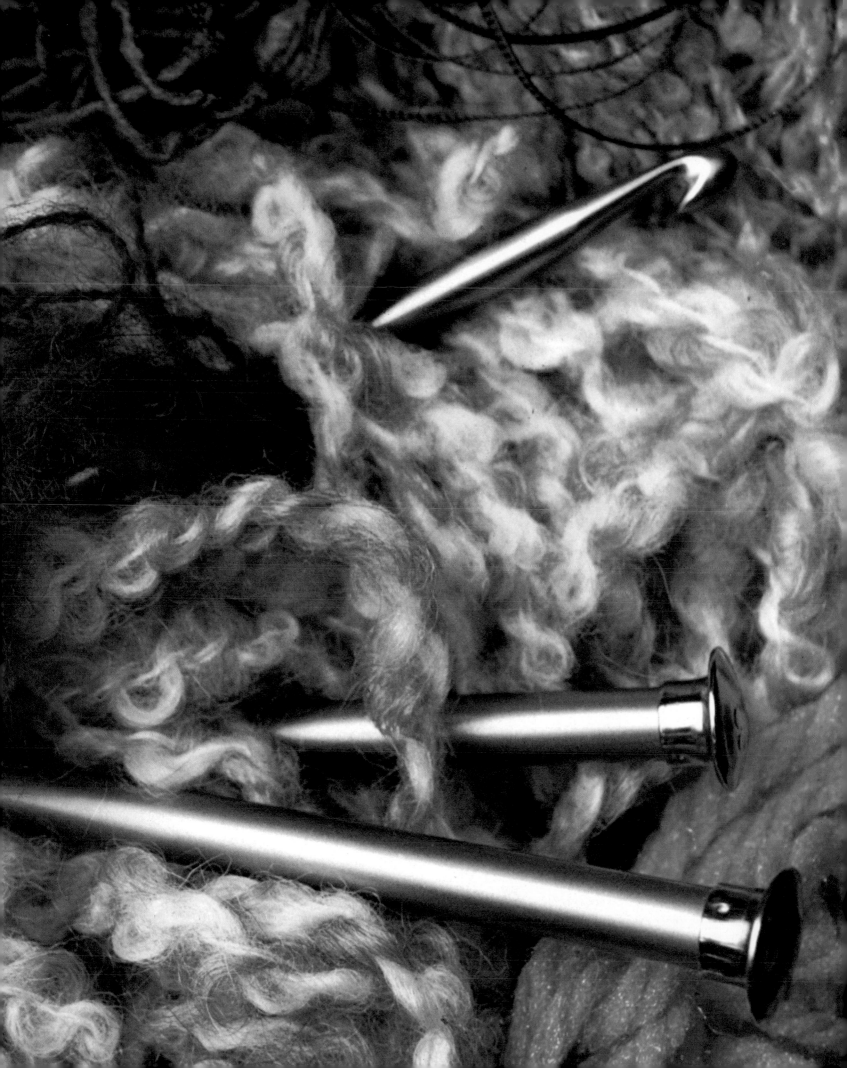

Knitting or crocheting projects are in one sense like journeys: their purpose is to get somewhere, to achieve an object that is beautiful or useful or amusing—and in some way a worthy record of the craftsman's time and effort. But like almost all 20th Century travelers, the knitter or crocheter—or, for that matter, the home sewer—is often unwilling or unable to spend inordinate amounts of time trying to reach

GIANT STITCHES FOR FASTER NEEDLEWORK

the destination. A little diversion along the way is called for—perhaps not the equivalent of a first-run movie or an eight-channel stereo headset, but some occasional pleasant scenery or a bit of interesting conversation. That is precisely what the "shortcuts to elegance" described in this section can offer. Without sacrificing beauty or utility—indeed, often contributing a splendid, striking and unique effect—they help to make the journey briefer or pleasanter.

Large knitting needles and crochet hooks lengthen the traveler's stride, so that more distance can be covered with each step. Pattern stitches offer the opportunity for variety; like lively talk or amusing incident, they agreeably alter the steady rhythm of stockinette or chain stitch.

And just as fine weather, an open road and a beautiful landscape can translate a routine trip into an excursion, novelty yarns—luxuriously soft mohair, glittering metallic thread—please both the hand and the eye with a sensuous satisfaction that can be an end in itself.

Above all, large needles and hooks are laborsaving devices. The fishermen who probably were mankind's first knitters must have stumbled onto this trick early, when they discovered that if they used a thicker bone or root or branch for their work, they could complete a fishnet much faster because far fewer stitches were needed. Today's novice needleworker should go ahead and test the equation.

Let us say that you propose to knit a coverlet for a doll's bed that measures 6 by 10 inches. All you have available is a pair of slender No. 3 needles, one of the smallest in the standard range of sizes. By the time you have completed a piece 6 inches wide by 10 inches long, you may well have knitted some 4,800 stitches—100 rows of 48 stitches each. If, however, you did the same work with No. 15 needles, among the largest in the conventional range, you could finish the 6-by-10 coverlet by using only 900 individual stitches—50 rows of 18 stitches each.

The sensation of striding across space with a giant's steps is clearly exhilarating and can inspire a great deal of zany ingenuity. In theory at least, a knitting needle can be fashioned from any rodlike object that is firm, smooth-surfaced (to avoid fraying the yarn), has a knob at one end and is capable of being whittled, filed or otherwise shaped to a point at the other end. One tourist in France came upon a shepherd who was knitting with old umbrella ribs. In the same make-do spirit, a large-needle knitting enthusiast named Dave Fougner, who raises horses in California, has whipped up a bunkhouse hammock of manila rope using "needles" that were made from pool cues. Designer Jeanne Damon, in attempting to establish contact with a class of emotionally disturbed children, finally was able to capture their interest by teaching them to knit —with whittled-down broom handles. And it was the enthusiastic response of those youngsters to their new craft that prompted her to create and promote the "Jumbo" No. 50 knitting needles, 1 1/4 inches in diameter, that can now be purchased in most needlework shops.

Bigger-needles-for-fewer-stitches is a formula that generally has a corollary: thicker yarn. The large needles or the chunky crochet hook will create looser, airier stitches. Such a lacy lattice effect can be charming for a purely decorative piece. But the more utilitarian pieces must be governed by their purpose. The fisherman's net must have a small enough gauge to keep the captive fish from slipping through. And a coverlet can have no claim to warmth when it is more hole than fiber. One way to close up those interstices, knitters have learned, is to use a thicker yarn. And a common device for thickening the yarn is simply to knit with two, three or four strands of yarn together.

That technique, then, opens up a whole new world of dazzling variety. The colors and textures on pages 170 and 171 demonstrate the trick of combining yarns, thus tempting the artist that is lurking in all of us. Why not blend two strands of mauve yarn with one of lavender? Or perhaps use a black, a gray and a white together, to produce a pepper-and-salt tweed effect? Soon you will find yourself dabbling in color with all the zest and adventurousness of an Impressionist painter. Experiments with texture will follow: instead of the customary worsted yarns, you might use a cloud-soft mohair or a lively crimped bouclé; instead of yarn itself, try a glossy ribbon, a rough twine or a glistening lamé cord.

But beware: the richer and more luxuriant the special effects you want to achieve with the use of novelty yarns, the simpler and more basic the stitch should be. Conversely, if you make sure that you keep the colors and textures of the yarn simple, you are then free to introduce a variety of pattern stitches.

All knitting produces a pattern, of course, even the simplest. Your first efforts with knitting needles will produce a rough-surfaced fabric of scalloping lines in horizontal rows. You may refer to it by the modest term of "plain knitting," or the more professional-sounding "garter stitch."

When you advance a step by learning to purl (page 186), you can vary the routine by knitting one row and purling the next, and your work will take on an entirely different character: alternate rows result in a vertical pattern, with chainlike rows of flat, smooth texture, in the well-known stockinette pattern. Then you can vary the approach again, by alternating each stitch—knit one, purl one, knit one, purl one, in even-numbered rows—to produce the familiar rib pattern. And if you work the rib pattern stitch in odd-numbered rows rather than in even ones (rows of 43 or 45 stitches, for instance, instead of 44) you will quickly discover that the ribs have disappeared and have been replaced by a new pebbly-textured pattern, called moss or seed.

Many elaborate pattern stitches are popular for use with big knitting needles and thick yarns because the patterns take on a whole new dimension when they are attempted on a large scale. And they add enormously to your options. By introducing a filigree pattern stitch into the simple gown shown on page 173, for example, the designer has created an attractive and distinctive border for the dress.

In large patterns or small, knitting and crocheting have a wondrous dual capacity: while tying the yarn into intricate knots, they loosen the knots buried inside the knitter. One London psychologist has prescribed knitting as "about the best tranquilizer you can find"—a not altogether accidental discovery that large numbers of men as well as women have made on their own as they concentrate on their new interest. At a deeper level, the continuous manipulation of needle, stitch and yarn in ever-new combinations stimulates creative expression. Craftsmen suddenly turn into inspired artists—and meanwhile artists find that they can redefine their former attitudes toward art with the expressive medium of yarn.

Frank Lincoln Viner, like many of his contemporaries, started his artistic career as a painter but he has since branched out into the use of more unorthodox materials, concepts and forms. After teaching himself to crochet several years ago, he began to create not only "body sculpture"—one-of-a-kind capes, ponchos, bags and hats—but also a private phantasmagoria of unique objects, including the almost free-floating creature that is woven from terra cotta yarn and illustrated below.

Although Viner maintains that the resemblance is pure coincidence, his suspended creature made of yarn reminds some people of Charlotte, the appealing spider heroine of E. B. White's classic tale, *Charlotte's Web.* In fact, Charlotte could easily qualify as the patron saint of all those who practice the crafts of yarn and thread. It was Charlotte who, in a supreme synthesis of skill and love, saved the life of her friend, Wilbur the pig, by weaving a series of laudatory manifestos into her web over his pen—SOME PIG! TERRIFIC!—and making Wilbur thenceforth a local celebrity. There's the moral: in the hands of the Charlottes of this world, technical prowess could even be transformed into a life-sustaining art.

Frank Lincoln Viner's crochet *Sculpture,* from the artist's 1970 one-man show, indulged his fascination with crochet as a medium to explore the transformation of limp forms into stable constructions. Viner explained that his work was inspired by sea life. But whether this piece is viewed as a fronded sea anemone or as a spider (which it looks like to many observers), it powerfully suggests the vitality and mystery of living creatures.

Vertical Twist

V Design

Diagonal Texture

162

Vertical Column

A colorful range of knit patterns

Like New England leaves in autumn, these swatches of knitting patterns illustrate the range of design options open even to a knitting newcomer. None of the four patterns is difficult; each highlights the simplest styles. The Vertical Twist can give a man's sweater the look of cable stitch with half the effort. Both the V design and the Diagonal Texture pattern have eye-catching surfaces that rescue simple designs—a scarf, a bolero jacket. The chaste regularity of the Vertical Column makes it an ideal vehicle for multicolored yarns. Instructions for knitting these patterns are on pages 166-167.

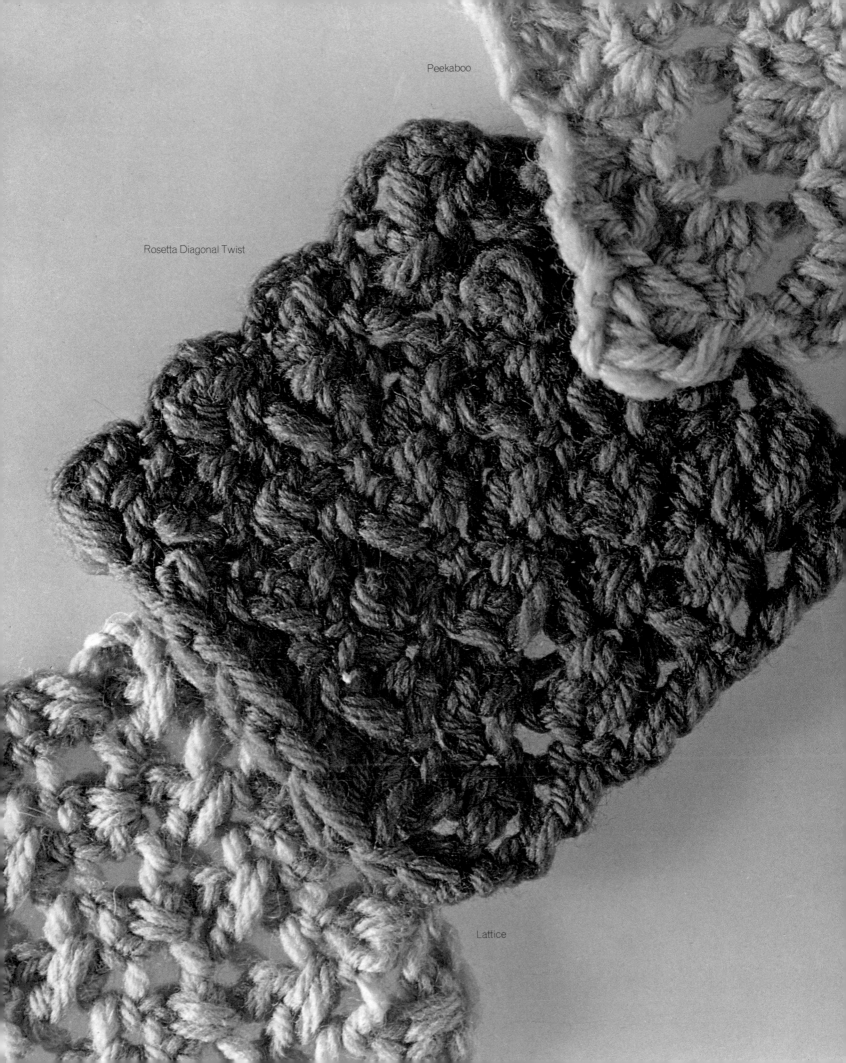

Peekaboo

Rosetta Diagonal Twist

Lattice

Lovely latticework in crochet

Triple Crochet

A comparison of these crocheted squares with the knitted swatches on the preceding pages is an instant lesson in how the two techniques differ. Knitting tends to produce a close-woven "fabric," crocheting an openwork "lace." The Peekaboo pattern, with its horizontal openwork rows, makes an effective contrast banding to insert in plainer textures. Rosetta Diagonal Twist has an intriguing three-dimensional surface that peps up a plain style like an A-line sheath; the pattern forms a scallop edge, creating an interesting hemline or sleeve bottom. Classic, versatile triple crochet can be worked quickly and is recommended when a simple, straight look is desired—on a long tunic, for example. The airiness of the lattice pattern adapts well to accessories like vests or caps. Instructions for crocheting these patterns are on pages 167-169.

Instructions for knit and crochet patterns

The instructions on these and the following two pages are for knitting and crocheting the patterns that are pictured on pages 162-165 and are used in making the garments shown on pages 172-173. The knitted swatches were made with Size 13 needles and knitting worsted yarn. The crocheted swatches were made with a Size 15 wooden crochet hook and knitting worsted yarn.

By using different sizes of needles or hooks and different types of yarn, you can create almost limitless variations on the patterns as shown on pages 170-171. Directions for the basic knitting and crocheting stitches not shown in the drawings on these pages can be found in the Appendix.

KNITTED PATTERNS

V DESIGN

Cast on the required number of stitches, making sure the number is a multiple of four. *Row 1:* Knit 3 stitches, slip 1 stitch *(drawing 1, below)*. Repeat these 4 stitches across the row, ending with slip 1. *Row 2:* Slip 1 stitch, keeping the yarn between you and the work *(drawing 2)*; purl 3 stitches. Repeat these 4 stitches across the row, ending with purl 3. *Row 3:* Repeat row 1. *Row 4:* Make a row of knit stitches, beginning with the yarn between you and the work and under the right needle *(drawing 3)*. *Row 5:* Knit 1 stitch, slip 1 stitch, knit 2 stitches. Repeat these 4 stitches across the row, ending with knit 2. *Row 6:* Purl 2 stitches, slip 1 stitch, purl 1 stitch. Repeat these 4 stitches across the row, ending with purl 1. *Row 7:* Repeat row 5. *Row 8:* Repeat row 4. Repeat rows 1-8 for the pattern.

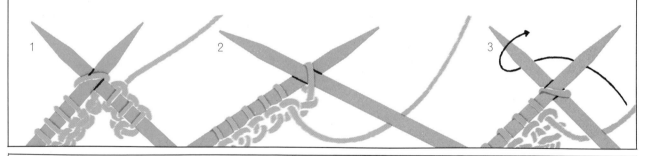

VERTICAL TWIST

Cast on the required number of stitches, making sure the number is a multiple of four. *Row 1:* Knit the second stitch on the needle—skipping over the first *(drawing 1, below)* —but do not slip it off the needle. Now knit the first stitch on the needle *(drawing 2)*. Slide both stitches off the needle at once. Purl the next 2 stitches. Repeat these 4 stitches across the row, ending with purl 2. *Row 2:* Make a row of purl stitches. Repeat rows 1 and 2 for the pattern.

DIAGONAL TEXTURE

Cast on the required number of stitches, making sure they are a multiple of two. *Row 1:* Slip a stitch onto the right needle, inserting the needle from back to front as if purling. Knit 1 stitch and loop the yarn over the right needle *(drawing 1, below)*. Pass the slipped stitch over the knit stitch and the yarn that has been looped over the needle *(drawing 2)*; two stitches now remain on the right needle and a diagonal stitch has been formed *(drawing 3)*. Repeat across the row, ending with the pass-over stitch. *Row 2:* Make a row of purl stitches. *Row 3:* Knit 1 stitch. Slip 1 stitch as if to purl, knit 1 stitch, loop the yarn over the right needle. Pass the slipped stitch over the knit stitch and the yarn that has been looped over the needle. Repeat these stitches across the row, beginning with the slip stitch and ending with knit 1. *Row 4:* Repeat row 2. Repeat rows 1-4 for the pattern.

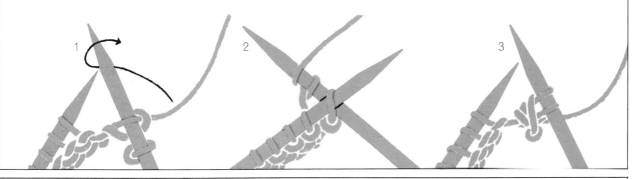

VERTICAL COLUMN

Cast on the required number of stitches, making sure that they are a multiple of two. *Row 1:* Knit 1 stitch, slip 1 stitch, inserting the needle from back to front as if to purl. Repeat these 2 stitches across the row, ending with a slip stitch. *Row 2:* Make a row of purl stitches. Repeat rows 1 and 2 for the pattern.

CROCHETED PATTERNS

LATTICE

Make a foundation chain with an even number of stitches. *Row 1:* Chain 2 stitches. Make a double crochet stitch in the fourth chain stitch from the hook *(drawing 1, below)*, then go back and make a double crochet stitch in the third chain stitch from the hook *(drawing 2)*. Skip 1 chain stitch, make a double crochet stitch in the next chain stitch, then go back and make a double crochet stitch in the skipped chain stitch as shown *(drawing 3)*. Repeat this sequence —skip 1 stitch, double crochet in the next, then double crochet in the skipped stitch—across the row. Chain 2 and turn. *Row 2:* Skip 1 double crochet stitch, make a double crochet in the next stitch, inserting the hook through both loops of the stitch. Then go back and make a double crochet in the skipped stitch, inserting the hook through both loops of the stitch. Repeat this sequence across the row. Chain 2 and turn. Repeat row 2 for the pattern.

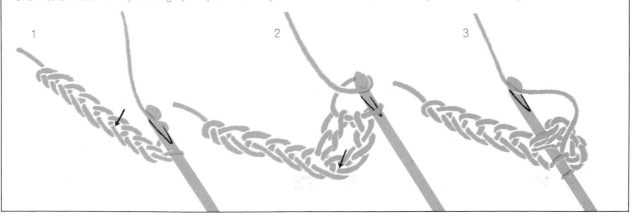

TRIPLE CROCHET

Make a foundation chain consisting of any desired number of stitches. *Row 1:* Chain 3 stitches. Bring the yarn over the hook from back to front twice and insert the hook into the fourth chain stitch from the hook *(drawing 1, below).* Bring the yarn over the hook again *(drawing 2)* and draw it through the loop closest to the tip *(drawing 3).* Bring the yarn over the hook again *(drawing 4)* and draw it through the 2 loops closest to the tip *(drawing 5).* Repeat the last step twice more *(drawings 6-9),* bringing the yarn over the hook and drawing it through the 2 loops closest to the tip until only 1 loop remains on the hook. These steps represent 1 triple crochet stitch. Complete the row with triple crochet stitches, chain 3 and turn. *Row 2:* Bring the yarn over the hook twice, then insert the hook through both loops of the next stitch. Bring the yarn over the hook again

and draw it through the 2 loops closest to the tip. Bring the yarn over the hook again and draw it through the 2 loops closest to the tip three more times. Make triple crochet stitches across the row. Chain 3 and turn. Repeat row 2 for the pattern.

To increase the number of stitches on a triple crochet row, make 2 triple crochet stitches in the same stitch. To decrease the number of stitches on a triple crochet row, begin by pulling the yarn through a stitch as if to make a single crochet stitch; then pull the yarn through the first loop on the hook, leaving 2 loops on the hook. Make a triple crochet stitch in the next stitch, pulling the yarn through the loops in the usual way, until there are 3 loops left on the hook; then pull the yarn through all 3 of the loops, leaving only 1 loop on the hook.

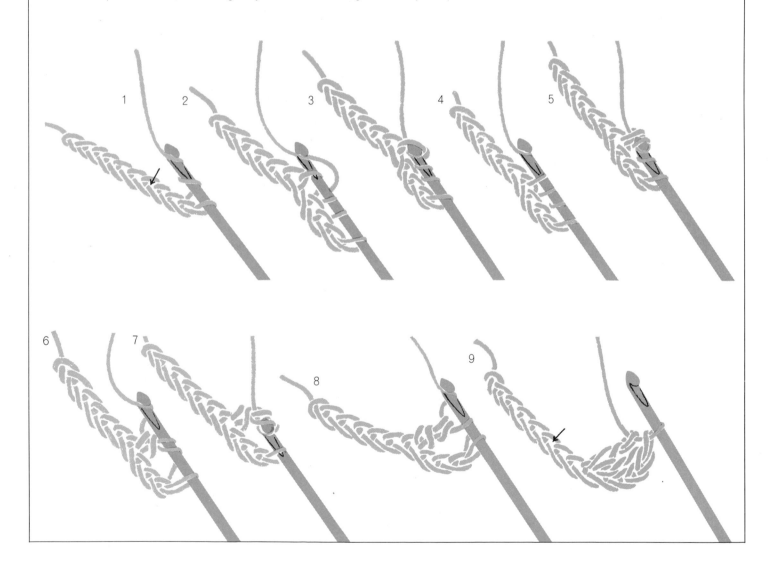

ROSETTA DIAGONAL TWIST

Make a foundation chain with an odd number of stitches. *Row 1:* Chain 1 stitch and make a single crochet stitch in the second chain from the hook. Make a triple crochet stitch *(drawings 1-9, at left)* in the next chain stitch, then a single crochet stitch in the following chain. Repeat the sequence in each stitch across the row, alternating a triple and single crochet stitch and ending the row with a single crochet. Chain 3 and turn. *Row 2:* Make a triple crochet stitch in the first single crochet stitch, inserting the hook through both loops of the stitch; then make a single crochet in the next triple crochet stitch. Repeat this sequence across the row, alternating triple and single crochet stitches. End with a triple crochet. Chain 1 and turn. *Row 3:* Make a single crochet stitch in the first triple crochet stitch, make a triple crochet in the next stitch, a single crochet, then repeat this sequence across the row, alternating single and triple crochet stitches. End with a single crochet. Chain 3 and turn. Repeat rows 2 and 3 for the pattern.

PEEKABOO

Make a foundation chain of the desired number of stitches, making sure the number is a multiple of three, plus one. *Row 1:* Chain 3 stitches. Make 2 double crochet stitches in the fourth chain from the hook, then skip the next 2 chain stitches. In the next chain, make a slip stitch by picking up the next stitch *(drawing 1, below)* and pulling the yarn through it as well as the loop on the hook *(drawing 2),* chain 3, and make 2 double crochet stitches in this same chain. Repeat this sequence across the row in every third chain —a slip stitch, chain 3 and 2 double crochets. End with a slip stitch in the last chain. Chain 3 and turn. *Row 2:* By- pass the chain stitches and make 2 double crochet stitches in the first slip stitch, inserting the hook through both loops of the stitch. Skip 2 double crochet stitches and in the next chain-3 space, make a slip stitch, chain 3 and make 2 double crochet stitches. Repeat this sequence across the row—skip the 2 double crochet stitches, slip stitch, chain 3 and 2 double crochet in each chain-3 space. End the row with a slip stitch in the turning chain space of the previous row. Chain 2 and turn. Repeat row 2 for the pattern. *Note:* Each sequence of slip stitch, chain 3 and 2 double crochet in a chain-3 space creates a "shell."

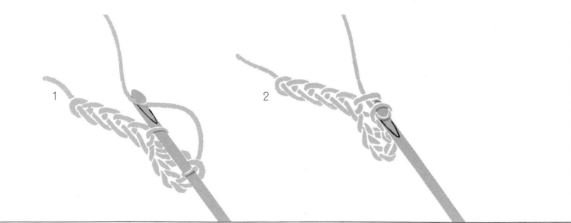

taffeta ribbon

mohair yarn

bulky yarn and mohair yarn

chenille yarn

bouclé yarn

Novel yarns for textural surprises

The birthday party air of these scattered samples—like scraps of fallen gift wrappings—shows the rewards of venturing beyond standard worsted yarns. All the squares here are in simple patterns—a knit rib or triple crochet—yet each has a unique look and feel because of its widely differing material. Bulky cotton chenille has an inviting velvet surface. Bouclé creates a crinkly texture; mohair is fuzzy. Metallic thread lends a glitter to plain yarn. Taffeta ribbon produces an attractive gloss. The bulky yarn, when it is mixed with mohair strands, knits into a veritable bird's nest of luxurious softness.

wool yarn and metallic thread

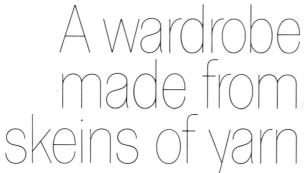

A wardrobe made from skeins of yarn

These eye-catching fashions with uncluttered lines exploit the timesaving advantages—as well as the versatility—of large needles and hooks. Each of these three styles can be knitted or crocheted easily. Yet each garment's austere design makes it a perfect medium for novel pattern stitches—which in each case are artfully placed for maximum effect.

The short sheath is enhanced by the intricate "V" pattern of its stitch. The three-piece suit is given added interest by a bold Vertical Twist pattern stitch, which is interrupted in the jacket with horizontal stockinette stripes in contrasting colors. The long-sleeved evening gown, with a matching floor-length coat, displays the benefits of this needlework at its best: a tasteful combination of only two pattern stitches lends Juno-esque elegance to a starkly simple design. Directions for both knitting and crocheting all three of these outfits begin on page 176.

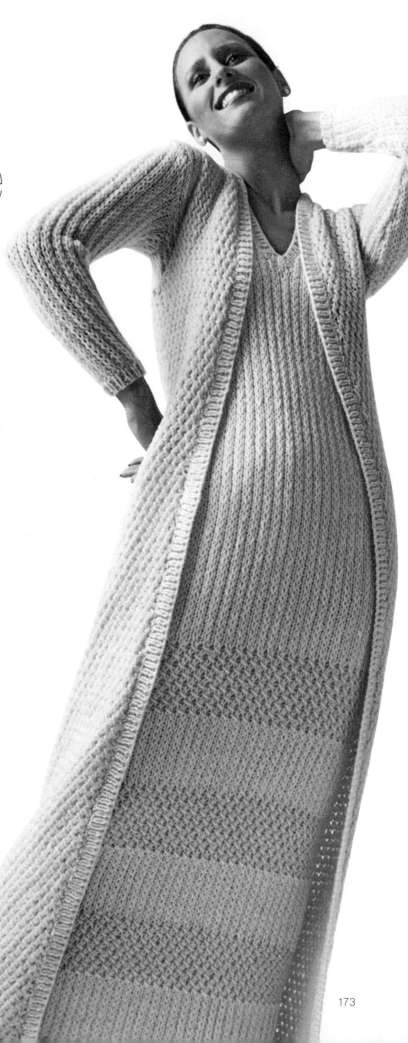

Soft mohair for matching accessories

Two yarns of furry mohair—one strand a variegated pink, white and brown, the other a solid maroon —are here combined to produce a subtle raspberry parfait effect. The head-hugging cap and its matching collar and cuffs can add a quick high-fashion lift to a solid-color dress, sweater or jacket.

All three accessories can be adapted readily. The cap can be made longer so that the edge turns twice, thus forming a wider frame for the face. The cuffs can be either short or long, and the collar can be extended into a long band to provide a border for the front opening of a coat. Worked in a simple rib pattern on a large crochet hook or knitting needles, the ensemble can be made swiftly whether it is crocheted, as shown here, or knitted. Directions for both of these methods appear on pages 182-183.

Instructions for the knit and crochet projects

The instructions for knitting or crocheting in this book describe each step fully in simple terms. Most books, magazines and patterns use a shorthand of standard abbreviations; the ones translated here are basic terms you will encounter in most of the other instructions for knitting or crocheting projects.

KNITTING ABBREVIATIONS

K—knit	**REP**—repeat
P—purl	**PAT**—pattern
ST—stitch	**SL**—slip stitch
YO—yarn over	**PSSO**—pass slipped stitch over

*—starting point for a repeated sequence of steps: when instructions tell you to "rep from *," read back in the instructions to find the point (*) where you must begin to repeat.

CROCHETING ABBREVIATIONS

SC—single crochet	**HDC**—half double crochet
CH—chain	**DC**—double crochet
HK—hook	**TRC**—triple crochet
ST—stitch	**SK**—skip
REP—repeat	**LP**—loop
PAT—pattern	**SP**—space

*—starting point for a repeated sequence of steps: when instructions tell you to "rep from *," read back in the instructions to find the point (*) where you must begin to repeat.

CHECKING THE GAUGE

All knit and crochet instructions are preceded by a stitch gauge, a specification of the number of stitches per inch (and often how many rows per inch) you must have if your project is to come out the proper size.

To check the gauge—to make sure your needle or hook and yarn provide the desired number of stitches per inch—knit or crochet a sample swatch before beginning your project. It should measure at least 4 by 4 inches and be made with the yarn and needles or hook recommended in the pattern. If two sizes of needles or hook are required—a smaller one for a ribbed edging and a larger one for the main part of the garment—the gauge is measured using the larger needles or hook.

Remove the swatch from the needles or hook without binding off. Lay it on a flat surface and count the stitches

per inch, measuring with a ruler, not a tape measure. If the gauge calls for more stitches per inch, change to smaller needles or a smaller hook. If the gauge calls for fewer stitches per inch use a larger hook or needles. This change of needle size will also adjust the row-per-inch gauge.

BLOCKING THE FINISHED WORK

To press, or "block," each garment, lay it on a flat surface, cover it with a damp cloth and press very lightly with a warm iron. Do not pin the garment to the pressing surface or let the iron rest too long in one area. To enlarge or reduce the size of the garment a little, dampen it lightly, then stretch it or push it together as you lay it out.

KNITTING THE DRESS, THE SUIT, AND THE LONG DRESS AND COAT

The following instructions are for knitting the dresses, coat and jacket pictured on pages 172-173; instructions for crocheting these garments can be found on pages 179-182. The directions are for size 10; changes for sizes 12, 14, 16 and 18 follow in parentheses in that order. The number of skeins of yarn needed are for size 10; the number of skeins needed for sizes 12, 14, 16 and 18 follow in parentheses in that order. All stitches and patterns used are described on pages 166-169 or in the Appendix.

THE SLEEVELESS STREET-LENGTH DRESS

You will need 4 (5,6,7,8) four-ounce skeins of knitting worsted. Use straight knitting needles Sizes 10 and 13, an aluminum crochet hook Size G, and a plastic crochet hook Size Q for the optional self-belt. Using the Size 13 needles, knit a sample swatch to check the gauge, which is 4 stitches per inch.

THE BACK: With Size 13 needles, cast on 76 (80,84,88,92) stitches. Work in the V pattern *(page 166)* for 3 1/2 inches, then—still maintaining the pattern—decrease 1 stitch at the beginning and end of the next row. Repeat this decrease every 3 1/2 inches 5 times more. Work now on 64 (68,72,76,80) stitches until the piece measures 31 inches.

THE ARMHOLES: Bind off 4 (4,5,5,6) stitches at the beginning of each of the next 2 rows, then decrease 1 stitch at the beginning and end of the next row. Repeat this decrease every other row 2 (3,3,4,4) times more. Work now on 50 (52,54,56,58) stitches until the piece measures 7 (7 1/4, 7 1/2, 7 3/4, 8) inches above the armhole shaping.

THE SHOULDERS: Bind off 5 (6,6,7,7) stitches at the beginning of each of the next 2 rows, then bind off 5 (5,6,6,7) stitches at the beginning of each of the next 2 rows. Bind off loosely the remaining 30 stitches for the back of the neck.

THE FRONT: Work the same as the back until the piece measures 28 inches, then shape the V-neck. Work across 32 (34,36,38,40) stitches, then join a second ball of yarn. Work across the remaining 32 (34,36,38,40) stitches. Working on both sides at once, work 1 row, then decrease 1 stitch at each neck edge. Repeat this decrease every 1/2 inch 14 times more. At the same time, when the piece measures the same as the back measured to the underarm edge, shape the armholes as you did on the back. When the piece measures the same as the back measured to the shoulders, shape the shoulders as you did on the back.

THE FINISHING TOUCHES: Sew the side and shoulder seams. For the optional self-belt, use a Size Q hook and 6 strands of yarn; chain 81, leaving 8 inches of yarn free at the start. Fasten off, leaving 8 inches of yarn free. Double over the free 8 inches at each end and knot them through the starting and finishing stitches. To make the braid trim for the neckband, use a Size Q hook and 6 strands of yarn; chain 34; fasten off. For each armhole, use 6 strands of yarn, chain 21; fasten off. Sew the neckband and arm-bands in place with an overcast stitch *(page 185)*. Block, following the instructions opposite.

THE THREE-PIECE SUIT

You will need 9 (10,12,13,15) four-ounce skeins of the main color *(pearl gray in the picture on pages 172-173)*, 1 skein each of colors A *(bittersweet)* and B *(eggshell)* for all sizes, and 1 (1,1,2,2) skein of color C *(taupe)*. Use straight knitting needles Sizes 10 and 13, an aluminum crochet hook Size G, and 1/2-inch-wide elastic measured to fit your waist. Using Size 13 needles, knit a sample swatch to check the gauge, which is 4 stitches per inch.

The skirt

With Size 13 needles and the main color yarn, cast on 76 (80,84,88,92) stitches. Work even in the Vertical Twist pattern *(page 166)* for 2 3/4 inches, then decrease 1 stitch at the beginning and end of the next row. Repeat this decrease every 2 3/4 inches 5 times more. Work on 64 (68,72, 76,80) stitches until the piece measures 17 inches, or 9 inches less than the desired finished length; end with a wrong-side row. Decrease 1 stitch at the beginning and end of the next row and repeat this decrease every 1 inch 7 times more. Work on 48 (52,56,60,64) stitches until the piece measures 25 inches, or 1 inch less than the desired finished length. Change to Size 10 needles and knit 1, purl 1 in a ribbing pattern for 1 inch. Bind off loosely in the ribbing pattern. Make a second piece the same as the first.

THE FINISHING TOUCHES: Sew the side seams. To make the casing for the waistband, work on the wrong side of the skirt. Join the main color yarn at the left top back edge and with a Size G crochet hook, work around to the left top front edge of the skirt by repeating the following: chain 3, skip 1 inch, work a slip stitch *(page 169)* at the bottom of the waistband, chain 3, skip 1 inch, work a slip stitch at the top of the waistband. Fasten off. Cut the elastic to fit your waist, draw it through the casing, and sew the short ends securely together. Using the crochet hook, work 2 rows of single crochet stitches around the bottom of the skirt. Block, following the instructions opposite.

The vest

THE BACK: With Size 13 needles and the main color yarn, cast on 64 (68,72,76,80) stitches. Work in the Vertical Twist pattern *(page 166)* until the piece measures 21 inches.

THE ARMHOLES: Bind off 4 (4,5,5,6) stitches at the beginning of each of the next 2 rows, then decrease 1 stitch at the beginning and end of the next row. Repeat this de-

crease every other row 3 times more. Work even on 48 (52, 54,58,60) stitches until the piece measures 7 (7 1/4, 7 1/2, 7 3/4, 8) inches above the armhole edge.

THE SHOULDERS: Bind off 8 (9,9,10,10) stitches at the beginning of each of the next 2 rows, then bind off 8 (8,9,9,10) stitches at the beginning of each of the next 2 rows. Bind off loosely the remaining 16 (18,18,20,20) stitches for the back of the neck.

THE FRONT: Work the same as the back until the piece measures 19 inches.

THE V-NECK: To shape the two sides of the V, work across 32 (34,36,38,40) stitches, join a second ball of yarn, and work across the remaining 32 (34,36,38,40) stitches. Working on both sides at once, work the next row. On the following row, decrease 1 stitch at each neck edge. Repeat this decrease every 1 inch 7 (8,8,9,9) times more. At the same time, when the piece measures the same as the back measured to the underarm edge, shape the armholes as you did on the back. When the piece measures the same as the back did to the shoulders, shape the shoulders as you did on the back.

THE FINISHING TOUCHES: Sew the left shoulder seam. To make the neckband, use Size 10 needles and the main color yarn. With the right side (the side that will be visible in the finished garment) facing you, pick up and knit 90 (94,98,102,106) stitches around the neck edge. Place a marker before and after the center stitch. Working in a knit 1, purl 1 ribbing pattern, decrease at the center front as follows: work 1 row in the ribbing pattern to within 2 stitches of the center marker, purl 2 together, knit 1, purl 2 together, continue in the ribbing pattern on the remaining stitches. For the next row, work in the ribbing pattern to within 2 stitches of the center marker, knit 2 together, purl 2, knit 2 together, and continue the ribbing across the row. Repeat these 2 rows twice more, then bind off loosely in the ribbing pattern. Sew the neckband opening, the right shoulder seam and side seams. With a crochet hook, work 2 rows of single crochet stitches around the bottom and armhole edges. Block, following the instructions opposite.

The jacket

THE BACK: With Size 13 needles and the main color yarn, cast on 68 (72,76,80,84) stitches. Work 5 rows in the Vertical Twist pattern *(page 166)*, switching to color A for row 6. Knit row 7 with color B, purl row 8 with color C, knit row 9 with color C and purl row 10 with the main color. Repeat these 10 rows for the striped pattern to be used throughout the jacket. Work until the piece measures 21 inches.

THE ARMHOLES: Bind off 6 (6,6,7,7) stitches at the beginning of each of the next 2 rows, then decrease 1 stitch at the beginning and end of the next row. Repeat this decrease every other row 2 (2,3,3,3) times more. Work even on 50 (54,56,58,62) stitches until the piece measures 7 1/2 (7 3/4, 8, 8 1/4, 8 1/2) inches above the armhole edge.

THE SHOULDERS: Bind off 8 (9,9,10,10) stitches at the beginning of each of the next 2 rows. Then bind off 8 (8,9,9,10) stitches at the beginning of each of the next 2 rows. Bind off loosely the remaining 18 (20,20,20,22) stitches for the back of the neck.

THE LEFT FRONT: With Size 13 needles and the main color yarn, cast on 32 (34,36,38,40) stitches. Work in the striped Vertical Twist pattern until the piece measures the same as the back measured to the underarm edge; end at the side edge.

THE ARMHOLE: Bind off 6 (6,6,7,7) stitches at the beginning of the next row, then decrease 1 stitch at the same edge every other row 3 (3,4,4,4) times. Work even on 23 (25,26,27,29) stitches until the piece measures 5 1/2 (5 3/4, 6, 6 1/4, 6 1/2) inches above the armhole edge; end at the front edge.

THE NECK: Bind off 4 (4,4,4,5) stitches at the beginning of the next row, then decrease 1 stitch at the same edge every other row 3 (4,4,4,4) times. Work even on 16 (17,18,19, 20) stitches until the piece measures the same as the back measured to the shoulder; end at the side edge.

THE SHOULDER: Shape the shoulder as you did on the back.

THE RIGHT FRONT: Work to correspond to the left front, reversing all shaping.

THE SLEEVES: With Size 13 needles and the main color yarn, cast on 36 (36,40,40,44) stitches. Work in the striped Vertical Twist for 2 inches. Maintaining the striped pattern, increase 1 stitch at the beginning and end of the next row and repeat this increase every 2 inches 5 (6,5,6,5) times more. Work on 48 (50,52,54,56) stitches until the piece measures 18 inches, or the desired length; end with the same part of the stripe as you did on the back and fronts.

THE SHOULDER CAP: Bind off 6 (6,6,7,7) stitches at the beginning of each of the next 2 rows. Decrease 1 stitch at the beginning and end of every other row until 10 stitches remain. Bind off 2 stitches at the beginning of each of the next 2 rows, then bind off the remaining stitches. Repeat for the second sleeve.

THE FINISHING TOUCHES: Sew the side, sleeve and shoulder seams. Sew in the sleeves. To make the ribbing for the jacket, use Size 10 needles and the main color yarn. With the right-hand side of the jacket facing you, pick up and knit 239 (243,243,247,247) stitches around the fronts and neck of the jacket. Work in a knit 1, purl 1 ribbing pattern for 6 rows, then bind off loosely in the ribbing pattern. With the main color yarn and the crochet hook, work 2 rows of single crochet stitches around the bottom and sleeve edges. Block, following the instructions on page 176.

THE LONG DRESS WITH SLEEVELESS COAT

You will need 6 (7,8,9,10) four-ounce skeins of knitting worsted for the dress, and 7 (8,9,10,11) for the coat. Use straight needles Sizes 10 and 13, a round needle Size 10, and an aluminum crochet hook Size G. Using the Size 13 needles, knit a sample swatch to check the gauge, which is 4 stitches per inch.

The dress

THE BACK: With Size 13 needles, cast on 78 (82,86,90,94) stitches. Work in the Diagonal Texture pattern (*page 167*) for 4 inches. Changing to the Vertical Column pattern (*page 167*), decrease 1 stitch at the beginning and end of the next row. Work in the Vertical Column pattern for 4 inches more, then change back to the Diagonal Texture pattern, decreasing 1 stitch at the beginning and end of the next row. Continue to alternate 4 inches of the two patterns and to decrease 1 stitch at the beginning and end of the row every 4 inches 5 times more. When the piece measures 28 inches and 64 (68,72,76,80) stitches remain, work in the Vertical Column pattern until the piece measures 50 inches, or the desired length to the underarm.

THE ARMHOLES: Working in the Vertical Column pattern for the remainder of the back, bind off 4 stitches at the beginning of each of the next 2 rows. Decrease 1 stitch at the beginning and end of the next row and repeat this decrease every other row 2 (3,3,4,4) times more. Work on 50 (52,56,58,62) stitches until the piece measures (7 1/4, 7 1/2, 7 3/4, 8) inches above the start of the armhole edge.

THE SHOULDERS: Bind off 8 (9,9,10,10) stitches at the beginning of each of the next 2 rows, then bind off 8 (8,9,9,10) stitches at the beginning of each of the next 2 rows. Bind off loosely the remaining 18 (18,20,20,22) stitches for the back of the neck.

THE FRONT: Work the same as the back until the piece measures 48 inches, or 2 inches less than the back measured to the underarm. To shape the two sides of the V-neck, work across 32 (34,36,38,40) stitches. Join a second ball of yarn and work across the remaining 32 (34,36,38,40) stitches. Working on both sides of the front at once, work 1 row. On the next row, decrease 1 stitch at each neck edge. Repeat this decrease every 3/4 inch 8 (8,9,9,10) times more and at the same time, when the piece measures the same as the back measured to the underarm, shape the armholes as you did on the back. When the piece measures the same as the back measured to the shoulders, shape the shoulders as you did on the back.

THE SLEEVES: With Size 10 straight needles, cast on 28 (28,30,30,32) stitches. Knit 1, purl 1 in a ribbing pattern for 4 rows. Change to Size 13 needles and working in the Vertical Column pattern to the completion of the sleeves, work for 1 inch. Increase 1 stitch at the beginning and end of the next row and repeat this increase every 1 1/2 inches 8 (9,9, 10,10) times more. Work now on 46 (48,50,52,54) stitches until the piece measures 18 inches, or the desired length to the underarm edge.

THE SLEEVE CAP: Bind off 4 stitches at the beginning of each of the next 2 rows, then decrease 1 stitch at the beginning and end of every other row for 4 (4 1/4, 4 1/2, 4 3/4, 5) inches. Bind off 2 stitches at the beginning of each of the next 6 rows, then bind off the remaining stitches.

THE FINISHING TOUCHES: Sew the left shoulder seam. For the neckband, use Size 10 straight needles. With the right side of the work facing you, pick up and knit 90 (94,98, 102,106) stitches around the neck edge. Place a marker before and after the center stitch. Working in a knit 1, purl 1 ribbing for 4 rows, decrease at the center front in the following way: On the first row, work in the ribbing pattern to within 2 stitches of the center marker, purl 2 together, knit 1, purl 2 together and continue the ribbing pattern across the row. On the second row, work in the ribbing pattern to within 2 stitches of the center marker, knit 2 together, purl

1, knit 2 together and continue in the ribbing pattern across the row. Repeat these 2 rows once more, then bind off loosely in the ribbing pattern. Sew the neckband opening the right shoulder seam, side and sleeve seams. Sew in the sleeves. Block, following the instructions on page 176.

The sleeveless coat

THE BACK: With Size 13 needles, cast on 90 (94,98,102, 106) stitches. Using the Diagonal Texture pattern *(page 167)* throughout, work for 4 inches. Decrease 1 stitch at the beginning and end of the next row; repeat this decrease every 4 inches 9 times more. Work now on 70 (74, 78,82,86) stitches until the back measures 46 inches, or 4 inches less than the dress measured to the underarm edge.

THE ARMHOLES: Bind off 6 stitches at the beginning of each of the next 2 rows, then decrease 1 stitch at the beginning and end of the next row. Repeat this decrease every other row 3 (4,4,5,5) times more. Work on 50 (52,56, 58,62) stitches until the piece measures 7 (7 1/4, 7 1/2, 7 3/4, 8) inches above the start of the armhole edge.

THE SHOULDERS: Bind off 8 (9,9,10,10) stitches at the beginning of each of the next 2 rows, then bind off 8 (8,9,9,10) stitches at the beginning of each of the next 2 rows. Bind off loosely the remaining 18 (18,20,20,22) stitches for the back of the neck.

THE LEFT FRONT: With Size 13 needles, cast on 42 (44,46, 48,50) stitches. Working in the Diagonal Texture pattern as on the back, work for 4 inches. On the following row, decrease 1 stitch at the side edge; repeat this decrease at the same edge every 4 inches 9 times more. Work on 32 (34, 36,38,40) stitches until the piece measures the same as the back measured to the underarm edge, ending at the side edge.

THE ARMHOLE: Bind off 6 stitches at the beginning of the next row, then decrease 1 stitch at the same edge every other row 3 (4,4,5,5) times more. Work on 23 (24,26, 27,29) stitches until the piece measures 5 (5 1/4, 5 1/2, 5 3/4, 6) inches above the start of the armhole edge, ending at the front edge.

THE NECK: Bind off 3 stitches at the beginning of the next row, then decrease 1 stitch at the same edge every other row 4 (4,5,5,6) times. Work on 16 (17,18,19,20) stitches until the piece measures the same as the back measured to the shoulder.

THE SHOULDER: Shape the shoulder as you did on the back and fasten off.

THE RIGHT FRONT: Work to correspond to the left front, reversing all the shaping.

THE FINISHING TOUCHES: Sew the side and shoulder seams. To make the ribbing for the fronts and neck, use Size 10 round needles and cast on 640 (644,648,652,656) stitches. Working back and forth across the needle, knit 1, purl 1 in a ribbing pattern for 4 rows, then bind off loosely in the ribbing pattern. Sew the ribbing in place, using an overcast stitch *(page 185)*. With the crochet hook, work 1 row of single crochet around the armholes. Block, following the instructions on page 176.

NOTE: This coat should be the same length as the dress worn under it. If the coat is short, additional length can be gained by working in a single crochet stitch along the bottom edge. Alternately, using Size 10 straight needles, and working on the right side of the garment, pick up the same number of stitches along the hem as were originally cast on. Then work them in a knit 1, purl 1 ribbing for as many rows as desired; bind off loosely in the ribbing pattern.

CROCHETING THE DRESS, THE SUIT, AND THE LONG DRESS AND COAT

The following instructions are for crocheting the dresses, jacket and coat pictured on pages 172-173. All the directions for the sleeveless dress are for small sizes (sizes 8-10); the changes in the number of stitches necessary for medium (sizes 12-14) and large (sizes 16-18) follow in parentheses, in that order. The directions for the other garments are for size 10; changes for sizes 12, 14, 16 and 18 follow in parentheses in that order. The number of skeins of yarn needed are for size 10; the number of skeins needed for sizes 12, 14, 16 and 18 follow in parentheses in that order. All stitches and patterns used are described on pages 166-169 or in the Appendix.

THE SLEEVELESS STREET-LENGTH DRESS

You will need 6 (8,10) four-ounce skeins of knitting worsted. Use aluminum crochet hooks Sizes H and J and a plastic crochet hook Size Q for the optional self-belt.

Crochet a sample swatch to check the gauge, which is 1 crocheted shell per inch on the Size J hook.

THE BACK: With a Size J hook, chain 61 (67,73). Work in the Peekaboo pattern *(page 169)* on 20 (22,24) shells for 8 inches. Then decrease 1 shell at the beginning of each of the next 2 rows by omitting the first set of double crochet stitches at the beginning of the row and starting the row with a shell in the next chain-3 space. Work in the Peekaboo pattern on 18 (20,22) shells until the piece measures 16 inches, then decrease 1 shell at the beginning of each of the next 2 rows. Work in the Peekaboo pattern on 16 (18, 20) shells until the piece measures 31 inches.

THE ARMHOLES: Decrease 1 shell at the beginning of each of the next 6 (6,8) rows. Work on 10 (12,12) shells until the piece measures approximately 7 (7 1/2, 8) inches above the start of the armhole edge.

THE SHOULDERS: Slip stitch *(page 169)* across 2 (3,3) shells at the beginning of the next row by making a slip stitch in each stitch and 2 slip stitches in each chain-3 space. Work in the Peekaboo pattern to within the last 2 (3,3) shells and fasten off.

THE FRONT: Work as you did the back until the piece measures 28 inches. To shape the V-neck: work in the Peekaboo pattern across 8 (9,10) shells, then chain and turn. Working on these stitches only, decrease 1 shell at the beginning of the next row and repeat this decrease every fourth row 2 times more. At the same time, when the piece measures the same as the back measured to the underarm edge, shape the armhole as you did the armhole on the back. When 2 (3,3) shells remain and the piece measures the same as the back measured to the shoulder, shape the shoulder as you did on the back and fasten off. Attach the yarn where the V-neck began and work the other side of the front to correspond, reversing all shaping.

THE FINISHING TOUCHES: Sew the side and shoulder seams. Crochet the braid trim for the neck and armholes and the optional self-belt, following the instructions on page 177. Block, following the instructions on page 176.

THE THREE-PIECE SUIT

You will need 7 (8,9,10,11) four-ounce skeins of the main color *(pearl gray in the picture on pages 172-173),* 1 skein each of color A *(bittersweet)* and B *(eggshell)* for all sizes, and 1 (1,1,2,2) skein of color C *(taupe).* Use aluminum crochet hooks Sizes H and J, and crochet a sample swatch to check the gauge, which is 3 stitches per inch on the Size J hook. You will also need 1/2-inch wide elastic to fit the waist of the skirt.

The skirt

With a Size J hook and the main color, chain 58 (62,64,68, 70). Work in the Lattice pattern *(page 167)* for 3 inches, then decrease 1 stitch at the beginning and end of the next row. Repeat this decrease every 3 inches 4 times more. Work on 48 (52,54,58,60) stitches until the piece measures 17 inches, or 9 inches less than the desired finished length. Now decrease 1 stitch at the beginning and end of the next row and repeat this decrease every 1 inch 5 times more. Work on 36 (40,42,46,48) stitches, until the piece measures 25 inches, or 1 inch less than the desired finished length. Change to a Size H hook and work in a single crochet pattern for 1 inch, then fasten off. Make a second piece the same as the first.

THE FINISHING TOUCHES: Sew the side seams. To make the casing for the waistband, work on the wrong side of the skirt. Join the main color yarn at the left top back edge of the skirt with a Size H crochet hook; work around to the left top front edge of the skirt by repeating the following: chain 3, skip 1 inch, work a slip stitch *(page 169)* at the bottom of the waistband, chain 3, skip 1 inch, and work a slip stitch at the top of the waistband. Fasten off. Cut the elastic to fit your waist, draw it through the casing and sew the short ends securely together. Using a Size J hook, work 2 rows of single crochet around the bottom edge of the skirt. Block, following the instructions on page 176.

The vest

THE BACK: With a Size J hook and the main color yarn, chain 48 (52,54,58,60). Work even in the Lattice pattern *(page 167)* until the piece measures 21 inches.

THE ARMHOLES: Slip stitch *(page 169)* across 3 (3,3,4,4) stitches, work to within the last 3 (3,3,4,4) stitches, then chain and turn. Work 1 row, then decrease 1 stitch at the beginning and end of the next row. Repeat this decrease every other row twice more. Work on 36 (40,42,44,46) stitches until the piece measures 7 (7 1/4, 7 1/2, 7 3/4, 8) inches above the start of the armhole edge.

THE SHOULDERS: Slip stitch across 6 (7,7,7,8) stitches, work to within the last 6 (7,7,7,8) stitches, chain and turn. On the next row, slip stitch across 6 (7,7,7,7) stitches, work to within the last 6 (7,7,7,7) stitches, then chain and turn.

Slip stitch across the remaining 12 (14,14,16,16) stitches for the back of the neck.

THE FRONT: Work the same as the back, in the Lattice pattern, until the piece measures 19 inches. To shape the V-neck, work across 24 (26,27,29,30) stitches, chain and turn. Working on these stitches only, decrease 1 stitch at the beginning of the next row. Repeat this decrease at the same edge every 3/4 inch 5 (6,6,7,7) times more. At the same time, when the piece measures the same as the back measured to the underarm edge, shape the armhole as you did on the back. Then, when the piece measures the same as the back measured to the shoulder, shape the shoulder as you did on the back. Fasten off and attach the yarn at the point where the V-neck shaping began. Work the other side of the vest front to correspond, reversing all shaping.

THE FINISHING TOUCHES: Sew the left shoulder seam. To make the neckband, use a Size H hook. With the right side of the vest facing you, work 1 row of single crochet stitches around the neck, picking up enough stitches so that your work lies flat. Place a marker before and after the center stitch. Work for 1 inch in the ribbed crochet pattern —making single crochet stitches through the back loops only—and decrease 1 stitch before the first and after the second marker on each row. Fasten off. Sew the neckband opening, the right shoulder seam and the side seams. With a Size J hook, work 2 rows of single crochet stitches around the bottom and armhole edges. Block, following the instructions on page 176.

The jacket

THE BACK: With the Size J hook and the main color yarn, chain 52 (54,58,60,64). For the stripe, work rows 1-3 in the Lattice pattern *(page 167)* with the main color yarn. Work row 4 in a single crochet pattern with color A, row 5 with color B, rows 6 and 7 with color C and row 8 with the main color yarn. Repeat rows 1-8, maintaining the Lattice pattern. Work until the piece measures 21 inches.

THE ARMHOLES: Slip stitch *(page 169)* across 3 stitches at the beginning of the next row, work the Lattice pattern across to within the last 3 stitches, then chain and turn. Work 1 row, then decrease 1 stitch at the beginning and end of the next row. Repeat this decrease every other row 2 (2,2,3,3) times more. Work on 40 (42,46,46,50) stitches until the piece measures 7 1/2 (7 3/4, 8 1/4, 8 1/4, 8 1/2) inches above the armhole edge.

THE SHOULDERS: Slip stitch across 6 (7,7,7,8) stitches, work to within the last 6 (7,7,7,8) stitches, chain and turn. On the next row, slip stitch across 6 (6,7,7,7) stitches, work to within the last 6 (6,7,7,7) stitches, chain and turn. Slip stitch across the remaining 16 (16,18,18,20) stitches and fasten off.

THE LEFT FRONT: With a Size J hook and the main color yarn, chain 24 (26,28,28,30). Work in the striped Lattice pattern until the piece measures the same as the back measured to the underarm edge; end at a side edge.

THE ARMHOLE: Slip stitch across 3 stitches at the beginning of the next row, then decrease 1 stitch at the same edge every other row 3 (3,3,4,4) times. Work on 18 (20,22,21,23) stitches until the piece measures 5 1/2

(5 3/4, 6, 6 1/4, 6 1/2) inches above the start of the armhole shaping, ending at the front edge.

THE NECK: Slip stitch across 3 (4,5,4,5) stitches at the beginning of the next row, then decrease 1 stitch at the same edge every other row 3 (3,3,3,3) times. Work now on 12 (13, 14,14,15) stitches until the piece measures the same as the back measured to the shoulder.

THE SHOULDER: Shape the shoulder as you did on the back.

THE RIGHT FRONT: Work to correspond to the left front, reversing all the shaping.

THE SLEEVES: With a Size J hook and the main color yarn, chain 28 (28,30,30,32). Work in the striped Lattice pattern for 2 1/2 inches, then—still maintaining the pattern—increase 1 stitch at the beginning and end of the next row. Repeat this increase every 2 1/2 inches 4 (4,4,4,5) times more. Work now on 38 (38,40,42,44) stitches until the piece measures 18 inches, or the desired length. End with the same part of the striped pattern as on the back and fronts.

THE SHOULDER CAP: Slip stitch across 3 stitches at the beginning of the next row, work to within the last 3 stitches, chain and turn. Work 1 row, then decrease 1 stitch at the beginning and end of every other row for 4 (4 1/4, 4 1/2, 4 3/4, 5) inches. On the next row, slip stitch across 3 stitches, work to within the last 3 stitches, chain and turn. Slip stitch across the entire next row and fasten off. Repeat for the second sleeve.

THE FINISHING TOUCHES: Sew the side, sleeve and shoulder seams, then sew in the sleeves. With the Size H hook and the main color yarn, work 1 row of single crochet stitches around the fronts and neck of the garment with the right-hand side of the jacket facing you. Pick up enough stitches so that the work lies flat. Work the ribbed crochet pattern—making single crochet stitches through the back loops only of each stitch—for 1 inch, then fasten off. With the Size J hook and the main color yarn, work 2 rows of single crochet around the bottom and sleeve edges. Block, following the instructions on page 176.

THE LONG DRESS WITH SLEEVELESS COAT
You will need 7 (8,9,10,11) four-ounce skeins of knitting worsted for the dress and 5 (6,7,8,9) skeins for the coat. Use aluminum crochet hooks in Sizes H and J. Crochet a sample swatch to check the gauge, which is 5 stitches per 2 inches on a Size J hook for the Rosetta Diagonal Twist pattern and 4 stitches per inch on the Size H hook for the triple crochet pattern.

The dress
THE BACK. With a Size J hook, chain 50 (52,54,56,58). Work in the Rosetta Diagonal Twist pattern (page 169) for 4 inches, ending on a right-side row. Chain 1 and turn. With a Size H crochet hook, work across the next row in a single crochet stitch, increasing the stitches at evenly spaced intervals until they number 78 (82,86,90,94). Make a row of triple crochet stitches (page 168), decreasing 1 stitch at the beginning and end of the row. Work in the triple crochet pattern for 4 inches, ending with a right-side row. Chain 1 and turn. With a Size J hook, work across the

next row with single crochet, decreasing the stitches at evenly spaced intervals until they number 48 (50,52,54,56). Work in the Rosetta Diagonal Twist for 4 inches, ending on a right-side row, and decreasing 1 stitch at the beginning and end of the first row of the new pattern.

Continue to work in this manner, alternating 4 inches of the Rosetta Diagonal Twist pattern and 4 inches of the triple crochet pattern, ending each 4-inch stripe with a right-side row, changing the hook size for the last single crochet row, and increasing or decreasing on that row in the manner established; there should always be 2 stitches less for the pattern about to be used than the number of stitches on which the last stripe of that particular pattern was worked. Continue also to decrease 1 stitch at the beginning and end of the first row of each new stripe.

Complete 7 stripes, ending with a right-side row of the Rosetta Diagonal Twist pattern; the piece should measure approximately 28 inches. Change to a Size H hook and work the last single crochet row on 64 (68,72,76,80) stitches. Work in the triple crochet pattern until the back is 50 inches, or the desired length to the underarm.

THE ARMHOLES: Slip stitch (page 169) across 4 stitches at the beginning of the next row, then triple crochet to within the last 4 stitches. Chain 3 and turn. Triple crochet across the next row, then decrease 1 stitch at the beginning and end of the following row. Continuing in the triple crochet pattern, repeat this decrease every other row 2 (3,3,4,4) more times. Work now on 50 (52,56,58,62) stitches until the piece measures 7 (7 1/4, 7 1/2, 7 3/4, 8) inches above the start of the armhole edge.

THE SHOULDERS: Slip stitch across 8 (9,9,10,10) stitches, then triple crochet across the row to within the last 8 (8, 9, 10,10) stitches, chain and turn. On the next row, slip stitch across 8 (8,9,9,10) stitches, triple crochet to within the last 8 (8,9,9,10) stitches, chain and turn. Slip stitch across the remaining 18 (18,20,20,22) stitches and fasten off.

THE FRONT: Work the same as the back until the piece measures 48 inches, or 2 inches less than the back measured to the underarm edge. To shape the V-neck, work across 32 (34,36,38,40) stitches in the triple crochet pattern, chain and turn. Decrease 1 stitch at the beginning of the next row. Repeat this decrease at the same edge every 3/4 inch 8 (8,9,9,10) times more. At the same time, when the piece measures the same as the back measured to the underarm edge, shape the armhole as you did on the back. When the piece measures the same as the back measured to the shoulder, shape the shoulder as you did on the back. Fasten off. Work the other side of the front to correspond, reversing all shaping.

THE SLEEVES: With a Size H hook, chain 28 (28,30,30,32) stitches. Work in the triple crochet pattern for 2 inches, then increase 1 stitch at the beginning and end of the next row. Repeat this increase every 1 1/2 inches 8 (9,9,10, 10) times more. Work on 46 (48,50,52,54) stitches until the piece measures 18 inches, or the desired length to the underarm.

THE SLEEVE CAP: Slip stitch across 4 stitches at the beginning of the next row, then triple crochet stitch to within the last 4 stitches, chain 3 and turn. Make a row of triple crochet stitches, then decrease 1 stitch at the beginning and end of every other row for 4 (4 1/4, 4 1/2, 4 3/4, 5) inches. On the next row, slip stitch across 3 stitches, triple crochet to within the last 3 stitches, chain and turn. Slip stitch across the next row and fasten off.

THE FINISHING TOUCHES: Sew the left shoulder seam. To make the neckband, use a Size H hook. With the right side of the dress—the side that will be visible in the finished garment—facing you, work 1 row of single crochet stitches around the neck edge, picking up enough stitches so that the neckline lies flat. Place a marker before and after the center stitch. Work for 1 inch in the ribbed crochet pattern—making single crochet stitches through the back loops only of the stitches—and decrease 1 stitch before the first and after the second marker on each row. Fasten off. Sew the neckband opening and the right shoulder seam. Sew the side and sleeve seams, then sew in the sleeves. Block, following the instructions on page 176.

The sleeveless coat

THE BACK: With a Size J hook, chain 56 (58,60,64,66). Using the Rosetta Diagonal Twist pattern (page 169) throughout, work for 4 inches. Decrease 1 stitch at the beginning and end of the next row, and repeat this decrease every 4 inches 7 times more, making sure to maintain the pattern. Work on 40 (42,44,48,50) stitches until the piece measures 46 inches, or 4 inches less than the desired length of the dress to the underarm.

THE ARMHOLES: Slip stitch (page 169) across 3 (2,2,3,3) stitches and work to within the last 3 (2,2,3,3) stitches. Chain and turn. Work 1 row, then decrease 1 stitch at the beginning and end of every other row twice. Work on 30 (34,36,38,40) stitches until the piece measures 7 (7 1/4, 7 1/2, 7 3/4, 8) inches above the start of the armhole edge, ending on a wrong-side row.

THE SHOULDERS: Slip stitch across 5 (6,6,6,7) stitches, work to within the last 5 (6,6,6,7) stitches, chain and turn. On the next row, slip stitch across 4 (5,5,6,6) stitches, work to within the last 4 (5,5,6,6) stitches, chain and turn. Slip stitch across the remaining 12 (12,14,14,14) stitches and fasten off.

THE LEFT FRONT: With a Size J hook, chain 30 (32,34,36, 38). Using the Rosetta Diagonal Twist pattern throughout, work for 4 inches, ending at the side edge. Decrease 1 stitch at the beginning of the next row and repeat this decrease every 4 inches 7 times more. Work on 22 (24,26,28, 30) stitches until the piece measures the same as the back measured to the underarm edge, ending at the side edge.

THE ARMHOLE: Slip stitch across 3 (2,2,3,3) stitches, chain and turn. Work 1 row, then decrease 1 stitch at the same edge every other row twice. Work on 17 (20,22,23,25) stitches until the piece measures 5 (5 1/4, 5 1/2, 5 3/4, 6) inches above the start of the armhole edge, ending at the front edge.

THE NECK: Slip stitch across 4 (5,6,6,6) stitches and work to the end of the row. Work the next row, then decrease 1 stitch at the neck edge. Repeat this decrease at the same edge every other row 2 (2,3,4,4) times more. Work on 10

(12,12,12,14) stitches until the piece measures the same as the back measured to the shoulder. Shape the shoulder as you did on the back, and fasten off.

THE RIGHT FRONT: Work to correspond to the left front, reversing all shaping.

THE FINISHING TOUCHES: Sew the side and shoulder seams. To make the ribbing for the fronts and neck, use a Size H hook. With the right side of the coat—the side that will be visible in the finished garment—facing you, work 1 row of single crochet stitches around the edges, picking up enough stitches so the neckline and fronts lie flat. Work in the ribbed crochet pattern—making single crochet stitches through the back loops only—for 1 inch, then fasten off. Work 1 row of single crochet around the armholes. Block, following the instructions on page 176.

NOTE: This coat should be the same length as the dress worn under it. If the coat is short, add length by working the ribbed crochet pattern around the bottom.

CROCHETING THE CAP, COLLAR AND CUFFS

The following instructions are for crocheting the accessories pictured on pages 174-175; knitting instructions for them can be found opposite. The crocheted cap, collar and cuffs fit all sizes, and all stitches used to make them are explained in the Appendix.

THE CAP

You will need 2 one-ounce skeins of yarn in solid color A and 2 one-ounce skeins of a variegated color B, to be used together as one heavier yarn. In the picture on pages 174-175, a strand of maroon mohair yarn is joined with a strand of pink variegated mohair yarn for the raspberry shade. Use a wood crochet hook, Size 15, and a tapestry needle for the back seam in the cap. Crochet a sample swatch to check the gauge, which is 7 stitches per 3 inches.

THE CUFF: Using 1 strand each of colors A and B joined together, chain 19 stitches. Single crochet across the row of chain stitches, chain 1 and turn. Begin a ribbed crochet pattern by making a single crochet in each stitch across the row but putting the hook through the back loop only of each stitch. Chain 1 and turn. Repeat this row until the piece measures 18 inches. Do not break off the yarn.

THE CROWN: Turn the work sideways so the ribs appear vertical. Pick up 36 evenly spaced stitches along one long edge, working a single crochet stitch in each loop you pick up. Crochet 1 row in the ribbed pattern stitch, chain 1 and turn. On the second row, begin decreasing. Crochet in the ribbed pattern for 4 stitches, then decrease by single crocheting 2 stitches together. Continue the pattern across the row, decreasing every fifth stitch. The row will now contain 30 stitches. Chain 1 and turn. For the third row, crochet the pattern across the row, chain 1 and turn. For the fourth row, crochet in the ribbed pattern for 3 stitches, then single crochet 2 stitches together. Repeat, decreasing every fourth stitch across the row. The row will now contain 24 stitches. Chain 1 and turn. For the fifth row, crochet the pattern across the row. On the sixth row, crochet in the ribbed pattern for 2 stitches and then crochet 2 stitches together. Repeat, decreasing every third stitch, across the row. The row will now contain 18 stitches. Chain 1 and turn. Continue to alternate rows in the ribbed pattern with rows in which you decrease every 2 stitches, until 6 stitches remain.

THE FINISHING TOUCHES: Fasten off by cutting the yarn, leaving a long double strand of at least 15 inches attached to the work. Thread the double yarn through a tapestry needle and weave the needle through the remaining 6 stitches; draw it tight. Sew up the back seam of the cap.

THE TURN-OVER COLLAR (TURTLENECK)

You will need 2 one-ounce skeins of yarn in a solid color A and 2 one-ounce skeins in a variegated color B, to be used together. Use a wood crochet hook in Size 15. Crochet a sample swatch to check the gauge, which is 7 stitches per 3 inches.

Using 1 strand each of colors A and B together, make a foundation chain of 22 stitches. Make a single crochet stitch in each stitch across the row, then chain 1 and turn. Begin a ribbed crochet pattern by making a single crochet in each stitch across the row but putting the hook through the back loop only of each stitch. Chain 1 and turn. Continue to make rows of the pattern stitch until the piece measures 24 inches. Fasten off by cutting the yarn 1 inch from the work and drawing both strands through the last loop of the last stitch; pull tight. Attach the collar to a garment with a slip stitch *(page 185)*, using cotton thread and a sewing needle.

THE CUFFS

You will need 1 one-ounce skein of yarn in a solid color A and 1 one-ounce skein in a variegated color B, to be used together. Use a wood crochet hook in Size 15. Crochet a sample swatch to check the gauge, which is 7 stitches per 3 inches.

Using 1 strand each of colors A and B together, make a foundation chain of 22 stitches. Turn and make a single crochet stitch in each stitch across the row. Chain 1 and turn. Begin the ribbed crochet pattern by making a single crochet in each stitch across the row by putting the hook through the back loop only of each stitch. Chain 1 and turn. Continue the rows of the pattern stitch until the piece measures 7 inches. Do not break off the yarn. Align the two long edges of the cuff, forming a cylinder, and join them by doing a row of slip stitches *(page 169)* through the stitches along both edges. Fasten off by cutting the yarn 1 inch from the work and drawing the strands through the last loops. Make a second cuff in the same way. Attach both cuffs to the sleeves with a slip stitch *(page 185)*, using cotton thread and a sewing needle.

KNITTING THE CAP, COLLAR AND CUFFS

The following instructions are for knitting the accessories pictured on pages 174-175. The knitted cap, collar and cuffs fit all sizes, and all stitches used to make them are explained in the Appendix.

THE CAP

You will need 2 one-ounce skeins of yarn in a solid color A and 2 one-ounce skeins in a variegated color B, to be used together. Use straight knitting needles, Size 11, and a tapestry needle for the back seam of the cap. Knit a sample swatch to check the gauge, which is 3 stitches per inch.

THE CUFF: Using 1 strand each of colors A and B together, cast on 52 stitches. Knit 2, purl 2 across the row to form a rib pattern. Continue the pattern on every row until the piece measures 8 inches.

THE CROWN: Increase 1 stitch at the beginning of the row, knit across, and increase 1 stitch at the end of the row. Knit the next row on 54 stitches. Purl the next 2 rows. On the next row, knit 7 stitches, knit 2 together. Continue to knit, decreasing every eighth stitch across the row. Knit across the next row on 48 stitches. On the next row, purl 6 stitches, purl 2 stitches together and continue to purl, decreasing every seventh stitch across the row.

Purl across the next row on 42 stitches. On the next row, knit 5 stitches, knit 2 together and continue to knit, decreasing every sixth stitch across the row. Knit across the next row on 36 stitches. Continue to purl 2 rows and knit 2 rows, decreasing 6 stitches in every other row until 6 stitches remain.

THE FINISHING TOUCHES: Bind off, leaving a strand of double yarn at least 15 inches long. Use a double yarn and a tapestry needle and weave the needle through the remaining 6 stitches; draw it tight. Sew the back seam.

THE TURN-OVER COLLAR (TURTLENECK)

You will need 2 one-ounce skeins of yarn in a solid color A and 2 one-ounce skeins in a variegated color B, to be used together. Use straight knitting needles in Size 11. Knit a sample swatch to check the gauge, which is 3 stitches per inch.

Using 1 strand each of colors A and B together, cast on 72 stitches. Knit 2, purl 2 across the row to form a rib pattern. Continue the pattern on every row until the work measures 9 inches. Bind off loosely in the ribbed pattern. Attach the collar to a garment with a slip stitch *(page 185)*, using cotton thread and a sewing needle.

THE CUFFS

You will need 1 one-ounce skein of yarn in a solid color A and 1 one-ounce skein in a variegated color B, to be used together. Use straight knitting needles in Size 11 and a tapestry needle for sewing seams. Knit a sample swatch to check the gauge, which is 3 stitches per inch.

Using 1 strand each of colors A and B together, cast on 20 stitches for each cuff. Knit 2, purl 2 across the row to form the rib pattern. Continue the pattern on every row until the work measures 9 inches. Bind off loosely in the ribbed pattern. Cut the yarn, leaving a strand of double yarn at least 15 inches long. Join the long sides of the cuff by threading the double strand through a tapestry needle and joining the edges. Make a second cuff in the same way. Attach the cuffs to the sleeves with a slip stitch *(page 185)*, using cotton thread and a sewing needle.

GLOSSARY

BARTACK: A hand-worked trim for reinforcing the ends of buttonholes and other points of strain.

BASTE: To stitch fabric pieces together temporarily, or to indicate pattern markings on both sides of the fabric. Basting stitches can be made either by hand or by machine, generally at 6 stitches to the inch, and are removed when permanent stitching is completed.

BIAS: A direction diagonal to the threads forming woven fabric—the warp and the weft, or "grains." The true bias is at a 45° angle to the grains.

BIAS TAPE: A folded strip of nylon, rayon or cotton, cut diagonally to the fabric threads—on the bias—so that it will stretch to cover curved and straight edges of a garment piece. Double-fold bias tape, 1/4 inch wide, is usually called bias binding and is only made of cotton. It is used to bind raw edges.

CLIP: A short cut into the fabric outside a seam to help it lie flat around curves and corners.

CLOSURE: The part of a garment on which fasteners—such as buttons or zippers—are placed to open and close the garment; also, the fasteners themselves.

DART: A stitched fabric fold, tapering to a point at one or both ends, that shapes fabric around curves.

DRESSMAKER'S CARBON: A marking paper, available in several colors and white, used to transfer construction lines from pattern to fabric.

EASE: The even distribution of fullness, without forming gathers or tucks, that enables one section of a garment to be smoothly joined to a slightly smaller section, such as in the seam attaching a sleeve to its armhole or in the hem of a flared skirt.

EDGE STITCH: Machine stitching that is made on the visible side of the garment, very close to the finished edges.

FACING: A piece of fabric, frequently the same as that used in the garment, that covers the raw fabric edge at openings such as necklines and armholes. It is first sewn to the visible side of the opening, then turned to the inside so that the seam between it and the garment is enclosed.

FASTENER: Any device that opens and closes a garment—button, hook and eye, snap or zipper.

GATHERING: Pulling material together by means of small basting stitches to create fullness, as in the bodice section joined to a shoulder yoke.

GRADING: Trimming each seam allowance within a multilayer seam—the fabric and facing—to a different width in order to reduce bulk and make the finished seam lie flat.

GRAIN: The direction of threads in woven fabrics. The warp—the threads running from one cut end of the material to the other—forms the lengthwise grain. The weft, or woof—the threads running across the lengthwise grain from one finished edge of the fabric to the other—forms the crosswise grain. Only if the two grains are at right angles to each other is the fabric aligned on the "true grain."

MACHINE BASTE: See BASTE.

MACHINE STITCH: To stitch permanent seams or finished edges by machine, generally at 12 stitches per inch. A line of machine stitching is usually reinforced with backstitching at both ends. Insert the needle 1/2 inch in from the beginning of the line, stitch in reverse to the outside edge and then stitch the line. At the end of the line, stitch in reverse 1/2 inch.

NOTCH: A V- or diamond-shaped marking made on the edge of a garment piece as an alignment guide. It is meant to be matched with a similar notch or group of notches on another piece when the two pieces are joined. Also a triangular cut into a curved seam to help it lie flat.

PRESSER FOOT: The part of a sewing machine that holds fabric steady at the point where it is being advanced and the needle is stitching it. The "all-purpose," or general purpose, foot has two prongs, or "toes," of equal length, and is used for most stitching. The "straight-stitch" foot has one long and one short toe, and can be used for straight stitching and stitching over fabrics of varying thicknesses. The conventional "zipper" foot has only one toe and is used to stitch zippers and tapes. A special foot is needed to sew invisible zippers.

REINFORCE: To strengthen an area that will be subjected to strain, such as a waistline with seam ribbon, an underarm seam with extra stitches, or a corner seam or a pocket with a small patch of fabric.

ROLL: To manipulate fabric between the fingers, usually along a seam line, in order to bring the line of seam stitching out to the edge or to turn the stitching to the invisible side.

SEAM ALLOWANCE: The extra width of fabric —usually 5/8 inch—that extends outside the seam line.

SEAM TAPE: A flat tape of finishing fabric—rayon or nylon with a woven edge or nylon or polyester stretch lace—usually 1/2 to 5/8 inch wide, that is sewn over a seam to reinforce it or is used to attach hems. Lace tape may also be used for ornamentation.

SELVAGE: The lengthwise finished edges on woven fabric.

SHANK: The link between the button and the fabric to which it is sewn. The shank can be made with thread or it can be part of the button, but it must be long enough to allow for the thickness of the overlapping fabric.

SLIDE FASTENER: See ZIPPER.

STAYSTITCH: A line of machine stitching sewn on or alongside the seam line of a garment piece before the seam is stitched. Stay stitching is used as a reinforcement to prevent curved edges from stretching, and as a guide for folding an edge accurately.

THROAT PLATE: A flat metal piece with a hole through which the needle passes as it stitches. A general-purpose throat plate has a wide hole that will accommodate sideways motion of the needle; many machines also have a second throat plate with a small hole, which prevents soft fabrics and knits from being pulled down into the machine and puckering during stitching. All throat plates have guide lines marked on both the left and the right sides to help you sew a straight seam.

TOPSTITCH: A line of machine or hand stitching on the visible side of the garment parallel to a seam.

TRACING WHEEL: A small wheel attached to a handle, used in conjunction with dressmaker's carbon to transfer markings from pattern pieces to fabric. Tracing wheels with serrated edges can be used for most fabrics; plain edges are used for knit fabrics to prevent the material from snagging.

TRIM: To cut away excess fabric in the seam allowance after the seam has been stitched. Also, a strip of fabric—such as braid or ribbon—used to decorate a garment.

UNDERSTITCH: A line of machine stitching sewn alongside the original seam that attaches the seam allowance to the facing and prevents the facing from rolling out.

YOKE: A garment part that crosses the shoulders and joins the front and back bodice, sometimes accented by gathering of the bodice.

ZIGZAG STITCH: A serrated line of machine stitching used as decoration or to prevent raveling of raw edges, particularly on knits.

ZIPPER, sometimes called slide fastener: A mechanical fastener consisting of two tapes on the edges of which are parallel lines of teeth or coils that can be interlocked by a sliding bracket, or slider.

HAND STITCHES

The diagrams below indicate how to make the elementary hand stitches referred to in this volume.

THE FASTENING STITCH

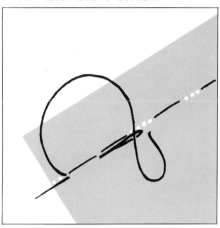

To end a row with a fastening stitch, insert the needle back 1/4 inch and bring it out at the point at which the thread last emerged. Make another stitch through these same points for extra firmness. To begin a row with a fastening stitch, leave a 4 inch loose end and make the initial stitch the same way as an ending stitch.

THE RUNNING STITCH

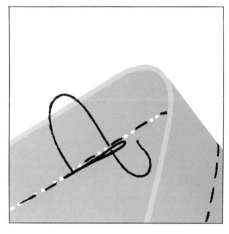

Insert the needle, with knotted thread, from the wrong side of the fabric and weave the needle in and out of the fabric several times in 1/8-inch, evenly spaced stitches. Pull the thread through. Continue across, making several stitches at a time, and end with a fastening stitch. When basting, make longer stitches, evenly spaced.

THE CATCH STITCH

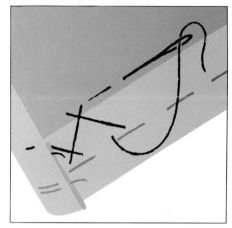

Working from left to right, anchor the first stitch with a knot inside the hem 1/4 inch down from the edge. Point the needle to the left and pick up one or two threads on the garment directly above the hem, then pull the thread through. Take a small stitch in the hem only (not in the garment), 1/4 inch down from the edge and 1/4 inch to the right of the previous stitch. End with a fastening stitch.

THE SLIP STITCH

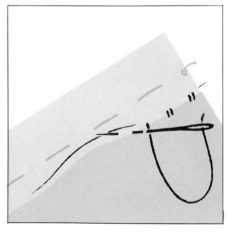

Fold under the hem edge and anchor the first stitch with a knot inside the fold. Point the needle to the left. Pick up one or two threads of the garment fabric close to the hem edge, directly below the first stitch, and slide the needle horizontally through the folded edge of the hem 1/8 inch to the left of the previous stitch. End with a fastening stitch.

THE HEMMING STITCH

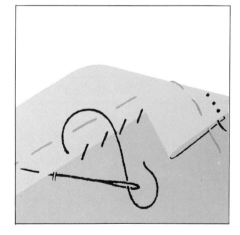

Anchor the first stitch with a knot inside the hem; then pointing the needle up and to the left, pick up one or two threads of the garment fabric close to the hem. Push the needle up through the hem 1/8 inch above the edge; pull the thread through. Continue picking up one or two threads and making 1/8-inch stitches in the hem at intervals of 1/4 inch. End with a fastening stitch.

THE OVERCAST STITCH

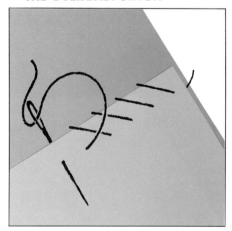

Draw the needle, with knotted thread, through from the wrong side of the fabric 1/8 to 1/4 inch down from the top edge. With the thread to the right, insert the needle under the fabric from the wrong side 1/8 to 1/4 inch to the left of the first stitch. Continue to make evenly spaced stitches over the fabric edge and end with a fastening stitch.

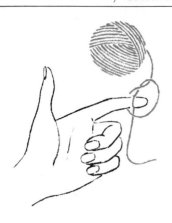

1. Form a slipknot in the yarn, leaving a free end long enough for the number of stitches to be cast on (allow about 1 inch per stitch).

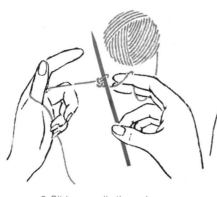

2. Slide a needle through the slipknot and hold the needle in your right hand. Loop the yarn attached to the ball over your right index finger and loop the free end of the yarn around your left thumb.

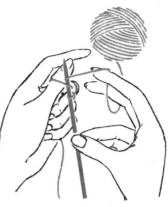

3. Insert the tip of the needle through the loop on your left thumb and bring the yarn attached to the ball under and over the needle from left to right.

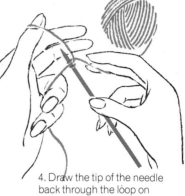

4. Draw the tip of the needle back through the loop on your thumb, then slip the loop off your thumb. Pull the short end of the yarn down to tighten the loop, which is now a stitch. Repeat Steps 2-4 for the required number of stitches.

THE KNIT STITCH

1. Insert the right needle in the front of the stitch closest to the tip of the left needle, as shown. Bring the yarn under and over the right needle.

2. Pull the right needle back through the stitch, bringing with it the loop of yarn. Slide this loop—which is now a stitch—off the left needle and onto the right. Repeat Steps 1 and 2 for each knit stitch.

THE PURL STITCH

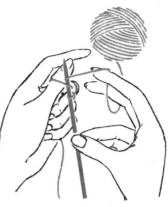

1. Insert the right needle into the stitch closest to the tip of the left needle, as shown. Bring the yarn around and under the right needle.

2. Push the needle back through the stitch, bringing with it the loop of yarn —which is now a stitch. Transfer this new stitch to the right needle, letting it slip off the left needle as you do so. Repeat Steps 1 and 2 for each purl stitch.

INCREASING STITCHES

1. On a knit row, insert the right needle through the back of a stitch. Knit the stitch, but do not drop it off the left needle.

2. Knit the same stitch in the ordinary way, and transfer the two stitches to the right needle.

1. On a purl row, insert the right needle from right to left through the horizontal loop at the bottom of a stitch. Make a purl stitch but do not let it slide off the left needle.

2. Now insert the right needle into the vertical loop above the horizontal one. Purl the stitch in the ordinary way, and slide both loops onto the right needle.

DECREASING STITCHES

1. Insert the right needle into two stitches instead of one, either from front to back as shown, for a knit stitch, or from back to front as for a purl stitch. Proceed as though you were knitting or purling one stitch at a time.

BINDING OFF STITCHES

1. Knit (or purl) two stitches. Then insert the left needle through the front of the second stitch from the tip of the right needle.

2. With the left needle, lift the second stitch on the right needle over the first stitch and let it drop.

CROCHETING/ **THE CHAIN STITCH**   **THE SINGLE CROCHET STITCH**

1. Form a loose slipknot around the crochet hook, about 1 inch from the end of the yarn. Grasp the yarn attached to the ball with the tip of the hook and pull the yarn through the slipknot with the tip of the hook, as shown.

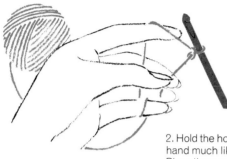

2. Hold the hook in your right hand much like a pencil. Place the yarn from the ball around the left little finger, then up and over the left index finger. Grasp the free end of the yarn between the thumb and middle finger of the left hand.

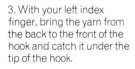

3. With your left index finger, bring the yarn from the back to the front of the hook and catch it under the tip of the hook.

4. Pull the tip of the hook through the loop on the hook, bringing the yarn with it to create the first chain stitch in the foundation chain. Repeat Steps 1-4 to form a chain of the desired length.

1. To single crochet the first row after a foundation chain, insert the hook through the second chain stitch from the hook (arrow)—do not count the loop on the hook.

2. With two loops now on the hook, bring the yarn over the hook from back to front and catch it under the tip as shown. Then draw the yarn caught under the tip through the loop closest to the tip.

3. Bring the yarn over the hook again and draw it through both of the loops that were on the hook; there is now only a single loop on the hook. Insert the crochet hook into the next chain stitch and repeat Steps 1 and 2. At the end of each row, chain one stitch if the next row is to be worked in single crochet, two stitches for a double crochet pattern, and three stitches for a triple crochet pattern.

4. Turn the work to crochet back across the previous row. Insert the hook through both loops of the second stitch from the edge, as shown, and all subsequent stitches on this and all rows after the foundation chain.

THE DOUBLE CROCHET STITCH

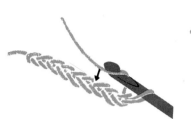

1. To double crochet the first row of stitches after a foundation chain, count back to the third chain stitch from the hook *(arrow)*—do not count the loop on the hook. Swing the yarn over the hook from back to front, then insert the hook through this third chain stitch.

2. Bring the yarn over the hook again and draw it through the loop closest to the tip. Bring the yarn over the hook again and draw it through the two loops closest to the tip.

3. Bring the yarn over the tip again and draw it through the remaining two loops on the hook. At the end of each row, chain one stitch if the next row is to be worked in single crochet, two stitches for double crochet and three stitches for triple crochet.

4. Turn the work to crochet back across the previous row. Bring the yarn over the hook and insert the hook through both loops of the second stitch from the edge *(arrow)* on this and all rows after the first.

INCREASING STITCHES

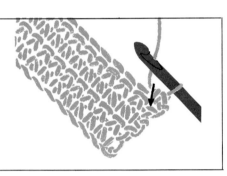

To increase stitches, work one stitch—either a single, double or triple crochet, as called for in the instructions —then insert the crochet hook back into the same loop or loops *(arrow)* and repeat the stitch.

DECREASING STITCHES, SINGLE CROCHET

1. To decrease in a row of single crochet stitches, insert the hook into both loops of a stitch. Bring the yarn over the hook and draw it through the two loops closest to the tip; this leaves two loops on the hook.

2. Insert the hook through both loops of the next stitch. Bring the yarn over the hook and draw it through the two loops closest to the tip. Bring the yarn over the hook again and draw it through the three remaining loops on the hook.

DECREASING STITCHES, DOUBLE CROCHET

1. To decrease in a row of double crochet stitches, bring the yarn over the hook and insert it through both loops of a stitch. Bring the yarn over the hook again, as shown, and draw it through the two loops closest to the tip. Then bring the yarn over the hook again and insert it through both loops of the next stitch.

2. Again bring the yarn over the hook and draw it through the two loops closest to the tip, as shown; there are now five loops on the hook. Bring the yarn over the hook again and draw it through the two loops now closest to the tip. Repeat the process until there are three loops remaining on the hook. Then pull the yarn through the three remaining loops.

CREDITS

Sources for the illustrations in this book are shown below. Credits from left to right are separated by semicolons, from top to bottom by dashes.

Cover—Design by Jean Srebnick and Ty Hargrove. 6,7—Dan Budnik. 11—Tasso Vendikos except right drawing by Nicholas Fasciano. 14 through 19—Dan Budnik. 20,21—Ken Kay. 24,25—Courtesy Newspaper Collection, The New York Public Library, Astor, Lenox and Tilden Foundations. 26 through 37—Ken Kay. 38,39—Pete Turner. 43—Bert Bach. 44 through 55—Pete Turner. 59—Drawings by Steven Cervantes except center by Nicholas Fasciano. 60 —Drawings by John Sagan—Drawings by John Sagan except bottom by Jane Poliotti. 61—Drawings by John Sagan—Drawings by Raymond Skibinski; Drawings by Jane Poliotti. 62—Pete Turner. 63 through 67 —Drawings by John Sagan. 68—Pete Turner. 69 through 79—Drawings by Raymond Skibinski. 80—Pete Turner. 81 through 87 —Drawings by Raymond Skibinski. 88 —Pete Turner. 89 through 97—Drawings by John Sagan. 98—Pete Turner. 99 through 105—Drawings by John Sagan. 106—Pete Turner. 107 through 113—Drawings by Raymond Skibinski. 114—Pete Turner. 115 through 119—Drawings by John Sagan. 120,121—Tasso Vendikos. 124—Michael Avedon, TIME-LIFE Picture Agency, © 1972 Time Incorporated. 125—Peter Knapp; Bert Stern. 126,127—John F. Wagaman courtesy Pasadena Museum of Modern Art—Private Collection. 128—Tasso Vendikos. 129 through 135—Drawings by John Sagan. 136—Tasso Vendikos. 137 through 145—Drawings by John Sagan. 146—Tasso Vendikos. 147 through 155 —Drawings by Ted Kliros. 156,157—Tasso Vendikos. 161—Peter Moore. 162 through 165—Ken Kay. Knitting and crochet by Annette Feldman. 166 through 169—Drawings by John Sagan. 170,171—Ken Kay. Knitting and crochet by Annette Feldman. 172 through 175—Tasso Vendikos. Knitting and crochet by Annette Feldman. 185 through 188—Drawings by John Sagan.

ACKNOWLEDGMENTS

For their help in the preparation of this book the editors would like to thank the following individuals: Hazel Arnett; Helen Barer; Karen Booth; Stephen Burrows; Audrey Foote; Susan Gordon; Violet Mock; Betty Silverman; Marion Steinmann; Arden Sweeny, Celanese Fibers Marketing Co.

The editors would also like to thank the following companies: Avagolf Knits; Bloomingdale's; Boris Kroll Fabrics, Inc.; Bratman Bros., Inc.; Central Shippee, Inc.; Darlington Fabrics Corp.; Mr. Dino, division of USI, Inc.; Held Fabrics, Inc.; Henri Bendel, Inc.; I. Miller Shoes; Jane Irwill Industries; Lord & Taylor; Paron Fabrics; Raymond Migili Pleating Co.; Scalamandré; The Singer Company; Staron-Lafitte; Stroheim and Romann; Vanity Fabrics, Inc.; Weller Fabrics.

Accessories (crocheted or knitted), *174-175;* instructions for, 182-183
Acetate, 42
Acrilan, 43
Acrylic(s), 43; other names for, 43
Adjustment(s) to patterns, 60-61
Antron, 42
Arnel triacetate, 42

Balenciaga, 10; one-seam coat introduced by, 10, *11*
Bateau neckline, 57, 68, *76-78;* fabrics suitable for, *charts* 50-53; how to make, 76-78
Bedsheet(s), 40, 41; advantages of, 41; for circle outfit, 41
Belt: as shortcut, *59;* tie, 98, *102-103*
Beret, circle, *136;* how to make, *141-142*
Binding off (knitting), *186*
Blended fabric(s), *44-45, charts* 50-53
Blocking (crocheting and knitting), 176
Blouse, from rectangles, *146-152;* fabric for, 146; how to make, *147-152. See also* Pullover
Bodice, gathered, with yoke. *See* Yoke shoulder(s)
Bonding material, 34, *37*
Bouclé yarn, 160, *170-171*
Bulky yarn, *170,* 171
Burrows, Stephen, 13; designs and techniques by, *18, 19*
Button shank gauge, *37*
Buttonhole(s), in-seam, 106; how to make, *109-110*
Buttonhole(s), machine: attachment for, *20, 30-31;* how to make, *30-31*
Buttonhole loops, 106; how to make, *111-113;* tubing turner for, 34, *36*

Cantrece, 42
Cap (crocheted or knitted), 174, *175;* instructions for, 182-183
Cap sleeve, 57-58, *88;* fabrics for, *chart* 50-51, 88; how to make, *89-92*
Cape(s), *6-7,* 9, *16-17,* 161; fabrics for, *16-17,* 41, *chart* 52-53
Carbon, dressmaker's, 29
Care of fabrics. *See* Fabric(s)
Casing, 58, *98-102*
Casting on (knitting), *186*
Catch stitch (hand sewing), *185*
Chain stitch (crochet), *187*
Chalk, tailor's, 26, *charts* 50-53; how to use, *27-28*
Chanel, Gabrielle "Coco," 13, 123

Chenille yarn, *170,* 171
Circle(s), 11, 122, 123, 125. *See also* Circle outfit
Circle outfit, *136;* beret, *136, 141-142;* fabrics for, 41, 136; how to make, *137-145;* pants, 41, *136, 143-145;* pullover, 41, *136, 137-140*
Cleaning. *See* Fabric(s)
Closure(s), 58-59, *106-113;* buttonhole loops, 106, *111-113;* buttonholes, in-seam, 106, *109-110;* for double-faced fabrics, *chart* 52-53; invisible zipper, 106, *107-109*
Coat(s): evening, 13, 41; one-seam, by Balenciaga, 10, *11*
Coat and evening gown (crocheted or knitted), *173;* instructions for, 178-179, 181-182
Collar(s), 11, *59*
Collar (crocheted or knitted), 174, *175;* instructions for, 183
Cording (casing), *19, 102-103*
Courrèges, André, 124; design by, *125*
Crepe, *chart* 52-53, 67; characteristics of, *chart* 52-53; fiber content of, *chart* 52-53; polyester, *48, 67,* 146; prepleated, *48,* 146; styles for, *chart* 52-53, 146
Creslan, 43
Crochet pattern(s), *164-165, 167-169;* instructions for, 166, *167-169;* lattice, *165, 167;* peekaboo, *164,* 165, *169;* rib, *174-175;* rosetta diagonal twist, *164,* 165, *169;* for simple styles, 173; swatches of, *164-165;* triple, *164-165, 168, 170-171;* variations in, with hook size and type of yarn, 166. *See also* Crochet stitch(es); Crocheting
Crochet stitch(es), instructions for, *169, 187-188. See also* Crochet pattern(s)
Crocheting, 156-174; abbreviations for, 176; accessories, *174-175;* as art form, *160-161;* blocking, 176; gauge, 176; "lace" produced by, 165; with large hook, 12, 159, 160; with novelty yarns, 159, 160, *170-171, 174-175;* pattern stitches, 159, 160, *164-165, 167-169,* 173; sculpture of, *161;* with several strands of yarn, 160, *174-175;* shortcuts in, 158-160, 173; styles in, *172-173, 174-175;* with thicker yarn, 12, 160. *See also* Crochet pattern(s); Crochet stitch(es)
Cuffs (crocheted or knitted), *174-*

175; instructions for, 183
Cutting: heavy fabric, *26;* without snagging, 26

Dacron, 42
Decreasing (crochet), 187
Decreasing (knitting), 186
Design(s), fabric, 46-47
Design(s), fashion: geometric, 11, *128, 136,* 146; machine stitching as part of, 12
Detail(s) in fashions, 9, 13
Diagonal texture pattern (knitting), *162-163;* instructions for, *167*
Diagonal twist pattern, rosetta (crocheting), *164,* 165; instructions for, *169*
Dolman sleeve, 10, 88; fabrics suitable for, *charts* 50-53; how to make, *93-94*
Double crochet, 187
Double hem, how to make, *118*
Double-faced fabric, *16-17, 48-49, chart* 52-53; cape and skirt of, *16-17;* care of, *chart* 52-53; fiber content of, *chart* 52-53; hems for, 114, *119;* patterns for, *chart* 52-53; practical tips for, *chart* 52-53; for reversible garments, 12; seams for, *62, 63-64;* sewing accessories for, *chart* 52-53; shopping suggestions for, *chart* 52-53; styles suitable for, *chart* 52-53; uses of, 12, 48, *chart* 52-53
Drawstring(s), how to make, 98, *101, 102*
Drawstring tunnel(s), 58; how to make, *101-102;* uses of, 58, 98
Dress(es): with built-in shortcuts, 56-58; of bulky fabrics, *16, 17;* with elasticized waist, 56, *98,* 100; with preshirred fabric, *14-15, chart* 52-53; from upholstery fabric, 16, *17,* 41
Dress(es) (crocheted or knitted), 43, *172, 173;* instructions for, 176, 178, 179-180
Dressmaker's carbon, 29
Dry cleaning. *See* Fabric(s)

Edging(s). *See* Hem(s)
Elasticized fabric, *14*
Elasticized waistline(s), 98, *99-101;* double-, *98,* 100; fabrics suitable for, *charts* 50-53; how to make, *99-101;* single-, *99-100;* of skirt, *101*
Even-feed foot, 30, *33, chart* 50-51, 128
Evening costume(s), *18-19,* 41; by Stephen Burrows, *18-19*

175; instructions for, 183
Cutting: heavy fabric, *26;* without snagging, 26

Evening gown and coat (crocheted or knitted), *173;* instructions for, 178-179, 181-182

Fabric(s), *38-49, charts* 50-53; acetate, 42; Acrilan, 43; acrylic, 43; Antron, 42; Arnel triacetate, 42; bedsheets, drip-dry, 40-41; blended, 42, 44-45; Cantrece, 42; care of, 50, *charts* 50-53; changing styles in, 9; characteristics of, 41-43, 50, *charts* 50-53; choosing, 41, 50, 56; for circle outfit, 41, 136; clinging, 41; construction of, *43;* cotton, 43, 48, *49,* 62; crepe, *48, chart* 52-53, 67, 146; Creslan, 43; Dacron, 42; double-faced, 12, *16-17,* 41, *48-49, chart* 52-53, 62, *63, 114, 119;* elasticized, 11, *14-15,* 41, 48, 49, *chart* 52-53; even-feed foot for, 30, *33;* felt, 40-41, 42, *43, 48,* 50, *chart* 52-53, 62, 64, 67; fiber content of, 50, *charts* 50-53; flannel, 62; Fortrel, 42; fur, fake, 136; fuzzy, even-feed foot for, 30, *33;* for gathering, 80; for geometric shapes, 16, 41; Helanca, 43; jersey, 41, 67, 114, 128; knit, 10, 41, *43, 44-45,* 50, *chart* 50-51, 62, *66,* 67, 114, 128, 136; knit, tubular, 11, 14, *15,* 41, *43, 44-45;* Kodel, 42; lamé, 136; for lettuce hem, 58; Lycra, 14, *15,* 43, 67; of natural fibers, 42-43; Nomex, 42; nylon, 42; origins of, 42-43; Orlon, 43; pleated, 41, *48;* polyester, 42, *48,* 67, 146; practical tips for, *charts* 50-53; preelasticized, 11, *14-15,* 41, 48, *49, chart* 52-53; preembroidered, 41; prepleated, 41, *48;* prequilted, 41; preshirred, 11, *14-15;* 41, 48, *49, chart* 52-53; Qiana, 42; quilted, 41; rayon, 42; for rectangle outfit, 146; scissors for, special, *20-21, 26;* selecting, 50; sewing accessories for, 50, *charts* 50-53; shirred, 11, *14-15,* 41, 48, *49, chart* 52-53; silk, 9; slipcover, 50, *chart* 50-51; slippery, 30, 33; spandex, 43, *44-45,* 67; step-saver, *chart* 52-53; stretch, 43, *44-45,* 67; of synthetic fibers, 10-11, 12, 42-43, *44-45; tapa,* 42; terry, stretch, *45,* 67; terry cloth, 136; transferring pattern markings to, 28-29, 60, *61;* Trevira, 42; for triangle dress, 128; upholstery, 16, *17,* 40, 41, *46-47,* 50, *chart*

50-51, 62, 67; uses of, 50, *charts* 50-53; variety of, 40-43; wool, 16-*17, 43, 44,* 45, *48-49,* 136; woven, *43;* Zefran II, 43
Facing(s), neckline, 68, *69-77*
Fastener(s). *See* Closure(s)
Fastening stitch (hand sewing), *185*
Felt, *48,* 50, *chart* 52-53; care of, *chart* 52-53; characteristics of, 48, 50, *chart* 52-53; construction of, 42, *43,* 48; fiber content of, *chart* 52-53; origin of, 42; practical tips for, *chart* 52-53; seams for, 62, *64,* 67; sewing accessories for, *chart* 52-53; shopping suggestions for, *chart* 52-53; uses of, *chart* 52-53; wool, magnified, *43*
Filigree pattern (crocheting or knitting), 160
Fortrel, 42
Fougner, Dave, 159

Garter stitch pattern (knitting), 160; instructions for, 160
Gathered bodice, with yoke. *See* Yoke shoulder(s)
Gathering, 80, *84-85,* 86
Gauge (crocheting and knitting), 176
Geometric forms, sewing with, 11, *16-17,* 120, *128-155;* fabrics for, *16-17,* 41
Gown(s), based on triangle, *128-132;* with preshirred bodice, *14-15;* of tubular knit, 14, *15*
Gown, evening, and coat (crocheted or knitted), *173;* instructions for, 178-179, 181-182

Halston, 11
Helanca, 43
Hem(s), *114-119;* with bonding strip, *37;* double finish, 114, *118;* on double-faced fabrics, 114, 119; lace-edged, 58, 114, *117-118;* lettuce, 13, *18, chart* 50-51, 58, *114, 115;* shortcut fabrics for, 114; zigzag, 58, 114, *116-117*
Hem gauge, 26, *28*
Hemming stitch (hand sewing), *185*
Hook-and-eye shoulder, 59, *80;* how to make, *81-83*
Hook(s), crochet. *See* Crocheting

In-seam buttonhole(s), 106, *109-110;* how to make, *109-110*
Increasing (crochet), *187*

Increasing (knitting), *186*
Inventions, sewing, 22-24, *24-25*
Invisible zipper, 59, *106;* how to attach, *107-109;* special foot for, 30, *32,* 106
Invisible zipper foot, 30, *32*
Iron-on bonding material, 34, *37*

Jacket(s), 163, *172-173*
Jersey, 41, *chart* 50-51, 67, 114, 128
Jumper(s), 41

Kimono sleeve, T-shaped, 57, 58, 88; fabrics suitable for, *charts* 50-53; how to make, *95-97*
Kloss, John, 12-13
Knit fabric(s), 41, *43, 44-45,* 50, *chart* 50-51; care of, *chart* 50-51; characteristics of, 10, 11, 41, 43, *chart* 50-51; for circular outfit, 136; hems for, 114, *118;* jersey, 41, *chart* 50-51, 67, 114, 128; patterns for, *chart* 50-51, 128; plain, *chart* 50-51; practical tips for, *chart* 50-51, 128; purl, *chart* 50-51; rib, *chart* 50-51; scissors for, *20-21,* 26; seams for, 62, *66,* 67; sewing accessories for, *chart* 50-51; shopping suggestions for, *chart* 50-51; with stretch yarns, 43, *45;* terry, stretch, *45,* 67; for triangle dress, 128; tubular, 11, 14, *15,* 41, *43, 44-45;* uses of, *chart* 50-51; zigzag hem for, 114
Knit stitch, instructions for, *186*
Knitting, *156-174;* abbreviations for, 176; blocking, 176; fabric produced by, 165; gauge, 176; with large needles, 12, 159-160; needles, 160; with novelty yarns, 159, 160, *170-171,* 174; pattern stitches, 159, 160-161, *162-163, 166-167,* 173; with several strands of yarn, 160, 174; shortcuts in, 158-160, 173; styles in, *172-173,* 174; with thicker yarn, 12, 160. *See also* Knitting pattern(s); Knitting stitch(es)
Knitting pattern(s), 159, 160-161, *162-163, 166-167;* diagonal texture, *162-163, 167;* filigree, 160; garter stitch, 160; instructions for, *166-167;* moss, 160; plain knitting, 160; rib, 160, *170-171,* 174; seed, 160; for simple styles, 173; stockinette, 160, *172-173;* swatches of, *162-163;* V design, *162,* 163, *166, 172,* 173; variations in, with

needle size, and type of yarn, 166; vertical column, *163, 167;* vertical twist, *162,* 163, *166, 172-173. See also* Knitting; Knitting stitch(es)
Knitting stitch(es), instructions for, *186. See also* Knitting; Knitting pattern(s)
Kodel, 42

Labor-saving devices, 56-59
Lace-edged hem, 114; how to make, *117-118*
Lamé cord, 160
Lapped seam. *See* Seam(s)
Lattice pattern (crochet), *165;* instructions for, *167*
Lettuce hem, *18,* 58; fabrics suitable for, *chart* 50-51, 114; how to make, *115*
Loop(s), buttonhole, 106; how to make, *111-113*
Loop turner, *36,* 106, 112
Lycra, 14, *15,* 43, 67

Marker, metal, 26, *29;* how to use, *29*
Measurement(s): adjusting pattern to, *60-61*
Metallic yarn, 159, *171*
Mohair yarn, 159, 160, *170-171, 174-175*
Moss pattern (knitting), 160; instructions for, 160

Neckline(s), *68-79;* bateau, 57, 76-78; collarless, 11, 57, *68-79;* fabrics suitable for, *charts* 50-53; facings, 68, *69-77;* square, *68, 69-71;* standing, 57, *78-79;* V-, closed-front, *72-73;* V-, open-front, 74-75
Needle(s): knitting, 160; sewing, *charts* 50-53
Nomex, 42
Nylon, 42, 43

Orlon, 43
Overcast stitch (hand sewing), 185

Pants, circle, 41, *136;* how to make, *143-145*
Pattern(s), crochet. *See* Crochet pattern(s)
Pattern(s), fabric, *46-47*
Pattern(s), knitting. *See* Knitting pattern(s)
Pattern(s), sewing, 12, *56-59;* adapting shortcut techniques

to, 58-59; adjusting, to size, *60-61;* with built-in shortcuts, 56; easy-to-make, 57; with few pieces, 56, *59;* selecting, 57-58, 59; for specific fabrics, *charts* 50-53; transferring markings from, 29, *charts* 50-53, 60, *61*
Pattern markings, transferring, 29, *charts* 50-53, 60, *61;* with metal marker, *29;* with tailor's chalk, *28;* with tracing wheel, 60, *61*
Peekaboo pattern (crochet), *164,* 165; instructions for, *169*
Pins, *chart* 50-51
Plain knitting. *See* Garter stitch
Pleating, 12, *chart* 52-53, *146*
Polyester: characteristics of, 42; crepe, *48,* 67, *146;* other names for, 42; prepleating, *48*
Preelasticized fabric(s). *See* Fabric(s)
Preembroidered fabric(s). *See* Fabric(s)
Prepleated fabric(s). *See* Fabric(s)
Prequilted fabric(s). *See* Fabric(s)
Preshirred fabric(s). *See* Fabric(s)
Preshrinking, *charts* 50-53
Pullover, circle, 41, *136;* how to make, *137-140*
Purl knit fabric, *chart* 50-51
Purl stitch (knitting), 160, *186;* instructions for, *186*

Qiana, 42

Rabanne, Paco, 124; disk dress designed by, *124*
Rayon, 42
Rectangle(s): blouse and skirt from, *146-155;* designs from, 11, dress made from, 16, *17;* for ruffles, 125; skirt from, 125
Reversible seam(s). *See* Seam(s)
Rhodes, Zandra, 13
Rib knit fabric, *chart* 50-51
Rib pattern (knitting), 160, *170-171;* instructions for, 160
Ribbon, for knit or crochet, 160, *171*
Rosetta diagonal twist pattern (crochet), *164,* 165; instructions for, *169*
Ruffin, Clovis, 13
Running stitch (hand sewing), *185*

Sant' Angelo, Giorgio di, 11
Scarf, triangle, *128;* how to make, *133-135*
Scissors: buttonhole, 30; electric, *26;* dressmaker's shears, *chart* 50-51; for heavy fabrics, *26;* for

knits, *20-21, 26, chart* 50-51
Sculpture, crocheted, *161*
Seam(s), 62-67; binding, *65, 66;* for double-faced fabric, 41, 62, *63;* with extra seam allowance, 62, *65;* for felt, 62, *64;* finishing, *chart* 50-51, 62, *65, 66;* grading, 62, *67;* for heavy fabrics, 62, *65;* for knits, 62, *66;* lapped, *64;* plain, 62, *63;* ravel-proofing, 62, *65;* reversible, 62, *63;* stabilized, 62, *66;* stretchable, 62, *66;* trimming, 62, *67;* for upholstery fabrics, *chart* 50-51, 62, *65;* variations of, 62; zigzag, 13
Seam gauge, *21*
Seam guide, 30, *33,* 128, 136
Seed pattern (knitting), 160; instructions for, 160
Sewing accessories, *charts* 50-53
Sewing aids, *34-37;* bonding material, iron-on, 34, *37;* button shank gauge, *37;* tape, adhesive, for sewing, *34-35;* tubing turner, 34, *36*
Sewing gauge, 26, *27*
Sewing machine, attachments for, *30-31;* buttonhole, *20, 30-31;* even-feed foot, 30, *33;* invisible-zipper foot, 30, *32;* seam guide, 30, *33;* versatility of, 30
Shank gauge, button, *37*
Shears: dressmaker's, *chart* 50-51; for knits, *chart* 50-51. *See also* Scissors
Sheath (knitted or crocheted), *172;* instructions for, 176, 179-180
Sheet(s). *See* Bedsheet(s)
Shoulder, hook-and-eye, 80; how to make, *81-83*
Shoulder(s), yoke. *See* Yoke shoulder(s)
Single crochet, *187*
Skirt(s): casing for, 98, *100-101;* circular, *chart* 52-53; of double-faced fabric, *16-17;* with elasticized waist, *100-101;* fabrics for, *16-17, chart* 52-53, 146; felt, *chart* 52-53; from rectangle, *146, 154-155*
Skirt marker, 24, 26, *28*

Sleeve(s), *59, 88-97;* cap, 57-58, *88, 89-92;* dolman, 10, 88, *93-94;* with drawstring tunnel at wrist, 58; kimono, T-shaped, 56, 57, 58, 88, *95-97;* for specific fabrics, *charts* 50-53
Slip stitch (crochet), *169*
Slip stitch (hand sewing), *185*
Slipcover fabric(s). *See* Upholstery fabric(s)
Spandex, 43, *44-45,* 67
Sportswear, 41, 43
Square neckline, *68;* fabrics suitable for, *charts* 50-53; how to make, *69-71*
Standing neckline, 57; fabrics suitable for, *charts* 50-53; how to make, *78-79*
Stella, Frank, 123, 126; paintings by, *126-127*
Stern, Bert, 125
Stitch(es), crochet. *See* Crochet stitch(es)
Stitch(es), hand sewing, instructions for, *185*
Stitch(es), knitting. *See* Knitting stitch(es)
Stockinette pattern (knitting), 160, *172-173;* instructions for, 160
Storing. *See* Fabric(s)
Stretch fabric(s), 43, *44-45*
Stretch lace, 114, *117*
Stretchable seam(s). *See* Seam(s)
Suit, three-piece (crocheted or knitted), *172-173;* instructions for, 177, 180-181
Sweaters, 10, 43
Synthetic fiber(s), 42-43; characteristics of, 12; fabrics knit from, *44-45;* scissors for, *20-21, 26*

Tailor tacks, *charts* 50-53
Tailor's chalk, 26, *27;* how to use, *27-28, charts* 50-53
Tapa, 42
Tape: adhesive on both sides, *34-35;* adhesive on one side, 34, *35;* iron-on, 12; zipper, 20, *21*
Terry, stretch, *45*
Thread, *charts* 50-53
Throat plate: marked, 128, 136;

small-hole, *chart* 50-51
Tie belt, attached, 98, *102-103;* how to make, *102-103*
Tie-end waistband: how to make, *104-105;* key to successful, 98
Tracing wheel: limitations of, 60; transferring pattern markings with, 26, *28-29,* 60, *61*
Trevira, 42
Triacetate, Arnel, 42
Triangle(s): designs from, 11, *16,* 122, 125; gown and scarf based on, *128-135*
Triple crochet, *164-165, 170-171;* instructions for, *168*
T-sleeve. *See* Kimono sleeve, T-shaped
Tubing turner, 34, *36*
Tubular knit. *See* Knit fabric(s)
Tunnel. *See* Casing
Twine, 160
Twist, vertical, pattern (knitting), *162, 163, 172-173;* instructions for, *166*

Understitching, 68
Upholstery fabric(s), *17, 46-47, chart* 50-51; care of, *chart* 50-51; characteristics of, 41, 46, *chart* 50-51; dress of, 16, *17;* for dress designs, 40; fiber contents of, *chart* 50-51; patterns of, *46-47;* practical tips for, *chart* 50-51; seams for, *chart* 50-51, 62, *65;* sewing accessories for, *chart* 50-51; shopping suggestions for, *chart* 50-51; uses of, *17,* 40-41, *chart* 50-51; width of, 46

V-design pattern (knitting), *162, 163, 172,* 173; instructions for, *166*
Vertical column pattern (knitting), *163;* instructions for, *167*
Vertical twist pattern (knitting), *162, 163, 166, 172-173;* instructions for, *166*
Viner, Frank Lincoln, 161; crochet sculpture by, *161*
V-neckline: closed front, how to

make, *72-73;* fabrics suitable for, *charts* 50-53; open front, how to make, *74-75*

Waistline(s), 98-105; with casing, 58, *98, 99-100, 101, 102;* double-elasticized, *98, 100;* drawstring, 58, 98, *101-102;* elasticized, *chart* 52-53, 56, 58, *98, 99-101;* of pants, with casing, 98; single-elasticized, *99-100;* of skirts, with casing, 98, *101;* with tie belt, attached, 98, *102-103;* tie-end waistband, 98, *104-105;* with tunnel, 58, 98, 99
Washing. *See* Fabric(s)
Wool, *16-17, 43,* 136; double-faced, *16-17;* fabrics, *43;* felt, *43;* tubular knit, *43, 44,* 45; woven, *43*
Woven fabric, *43*

Yarn(s), 12, 166, *170-171;* bouclé, 160, *170-171;* chenille, *170,* 171; combinations of, 160, *170-171;* lamé cord, 160; for larger needles and hooks, 160; metallic, 159, *171;* mohair, 159, 160, *170-171, 174-175;* multicolored, 163; multiple strands of, 160; novelty, 159, 160; ribbon, 160, *171;* twine, 160; worsted, 160, 166
Yoke shoulder(s), with gathered bodice, 80, *84-87;* fabrics for, *chart* 52-53; one-piece, how to make, 80, *84-86;* two-piece, how to make, 80, *86-87*

Zefran II, 43
Zigzag hem, 58, 114; how to make, *116-117*
Zipper(s), *charts* 50-53. *See also* Zipper, invisible
Zipper, invisible, 59, *106;* how to attach, *107-109;* special foot for, 30, *32,* 106
Zipper tape, 20, *21*